Mykola Golovin

Web Recommendations for E-Commerce Websites

Mykola Golovin

Web Recommendations for E-Commerce Websites

Online Optimization and Data Integration for successful Web Recommendations

Südwestdeutscher Verlag für Hochschulschriften

Impressum / Imprint
Bibliografische Information der Deutschen Nationalbibliothek: Die Deutsche Nationalbibliothek verzeichnet diese Publikation in der Deutschen Nationalbibliografie; detaillierte bibliografische Daten sind im Internet über http://dnb.d-nb.de abrufbar.
Alle in diesem Buch genannten Marken und Produktnamen unterliegen warenzeichen-, marken- oder patentrechtlichem Schutz bzw. sind Warenzeichen oder eingetragene Warenzeichen der jeweiligen Inhaber. Die Wiedergabe von Marken, Produktnamen, Gebrauchsnamen, Handelsnamen, Warenbezeichnungen u.s.w. in diesem Werk berechtigt auch ohne besondere Kennzeichnung nicht zu der Annahme, dass solche Namen im Sinne der Warenzeichen- und Markenschutzgesetzgebung als frei zu betrachten wären und daher von jedermann benutzt werden dürften.

Bibliographic information published by the Deutsche Nationalbibliothek: The Deutsche Nationalbibliothek lists this publication in the Deutsche Nationalbibliografie; detailed bibliographic data are available in the Internet at http://dnb.d-nb.de.
Any brand names and product names mentioned in this book are subject to trademark, brand or patent protection and are trademarks or registered trademarks of their respective holders. The use of brand names, product names, common names, trade names, product descriptions etc. even without a particular marking in this work is in no way to be construed to mean that such names may be regarded as unrestricted in respect of trademark and brand protection legislation and could thus be used by anyone.

Verlag / Publisher:
Südwestdeutscher Verlag für Hochschulschriften
ist ein Imprint der / is a trademark of
OmniScriptum GmbH & Co. KG
Heinrich-Böcking-Str. 6-8, 66121 Saarbrücken, Deutschland / Germany
Email: info@svh-verlag.de

Herstellung: siehe letzte Seite /
Printed at: see last page
ISBN: 978-3-8381-1580-1

Zugl. / Approved by: Leipzig, University of Leipzig, Dissertation Dr.-Ing., 2010

Copyright © 2010 OmniScriptum GmbH & Co. KG
Alle Rechte vorbehalten. / All rights reserved. Saarbrücken 2010

TABLE OF CONTENTS

PART I. INTRODUCTION 1

PART II. ADAPTIVE WEB RECOMMENDATIONS 5

1. Introduction 6

2. The Generic Recommendation System Architecture 9
2.1 Overview 9
2.2 Recommendation Selection Using Ontology Graphs 12
2.3 Generating Recommendation Rules 15

3. Feedback-based Optimization 18
3.1 Modeling the Problem of Optimizing Web Recommendations as Markov Decision Process and Applying Reinforcement Learning 18
3.2 "Drift of Interest" 22
3.3 Exploration versus Exploitation 24
3.4 Feedback Values 28
3.5 Optimization Algorithms 30

4. Implementation of the Real-life Prototypes and the Simulated Environment 32
4.1 Real-life Prototype Implementations 32
4.2 Adaptation of The Generic Architecture to The Prototypes 33
    4.2.1 Web Usage Data: Crawler Detection, Data Cleaning 33
    4.2.2 Ontology Graphs and Ontology Generators in Prototypes 36
    4.2.3 Recommendation Rule Generators in the Prototypes. 37
    4.2.4 Capturing Online Feedback in Prototypes 38
4.3 Simulated Environment Overview 39
4.4 Database Structure 41
    4.4.1 Recommendation Database 41
    4.4.2 Web Data Warehouse 42

5. Experiments on Real-Life Prototypes 46
5.1 Prerequisites and Effects of the Optimized Recommendations 46
5.2 Optimization Algorithms 47
5.3 User Groups 49
5.4 Comparison of Recommendation Generator-Based Optimization and Recommendation-Based Optimization 50

6. Experiments in the Simulated Environment 54

6.1 Evaluation of different recommendation selection algorithms 55
    6.1.1 Basic Recommendation Selection Algorithms..55
    6.1.2 Reward-only Algorithm with ε-greedy Balancing Technique without Aging
        (REWARD_ONLY)..57
    6.1.3 Reward-only Algorithms with ε-greedy Balancing Technique and Aging
        (REWARD_DEC)..60
    6.1.4 Reward-penalty algorithm (REWARD_PEN) 62
    6.1.5 Learning Behavior in Time for Different Algorithms..65
    6.1.6 Influence of the Number of Recommendations on the Acceptance Rate 66
    6.1.7 Simulation-based Comparison of the Recommendation Algorithms.................67
    6.1.8 Comparison of the Results Obtained from the Real-life Website and the
        Simulation 68
    6.1.9 Ontology-based Recommendation Selection Policies 69
6.2 Optimizing The Retrieval of Information From The Ontology Graphs...................71
6.3 Summary: Prototypes and Experiments 73

7. Related Work..74
7.1 Surveys 76
7.2 Hybrid Recommendation Systems 82
7.3 Methods of Evaluation of Recommendation Systems 85
7.4 Web Data Warehousing and Web Usage Mining 89
7.5 Markov Decision Process and Reinforcement Learning..93
7.6 Recommendation Systems Employing Ontologies 99

8. Summary..102

PART III. WEB RECOMMENDATIONS IN THE INTEGRATED DATA ENVIRONMENT 103

9. Introduction 104

10. Architecture of EC-Fuice 106
10.1 Overview of the EC-Fuice Architecture..106
10.2 Data Integration in EC-Fuice 109
    10.2.1 iFuice...110
    10.2.2 COMA and COMA++ 119
    10.2.3 Integration of Web Data using iFuice and COMA++.....................................126

11. Integrating Data: Experiments and Results 132
11.1 Integrating Product Data 134
11.2 Integrating Ontologies...141
    11.2.1 Manual Ontology Mappings 143
    11.2.2 Ontology Mappings Created Using COMA++ 145

11.2.3 Instance-based and Combined Mappings 148
11.2.4 Problems Discovered in the Process of Ontology Matching and Possibilities for Improvement 152
11.2.5 Evolution of data, ontologies and mappings 156
11.3 Integrating Data: Summary 158

12. EC-Fuice Implementation 160
12.1 Database Structure 160
  12.1.1 iFuice Database 160
  12.1.2 Web Portal Operational Database 162
  12.1.3 EC-Fuice Data Warehouse 163
12.2 EC-Fuice Web Portal Interface 166
  12.2.1 Overview of the Web Interface 166
12.3 Web Recommendations 169
  12.3.1 Types of recommendations 169
  12.3.2 Recommendations used in EC-Fuice web portal 173

13. Related Work and Discussion 177
13.1 Related Work in the Field of Data Integration 177
13.2 Related Work in the Field of Ontology Matching 185

14. Summary 192

PART IV. SUMMARY 193

REFERENCES 197

APPENDIX 1. SCREENSHOTS OF WEB RECOMMENDATIONS .. 211

APPENDIX 2. EXAMPLES OF RECOMMENDATION OPTIMIZATION 212

APPENDIX 3. EC-FUICE DATA PREPARATION SCRIPT 215

ABSTRACT

In recent years we see the continuing growth of the Internet. Not only is the number of internet users and websites increasing, but also the amount of information on the individual websites. Many websites are concerned with presenting their often very semantically versatile information in a concise and efficient way. This is especially true for large E-Commerce websites with large amount of product information. A frequently used technique to improve the presentation of data and navigation in these data is web recommendations. Web recommendations are hyperlinks, often augmented with short descriptive text and/or picture, which are shown on the website in addition to the usual content in order to lead users to potentially interesting information. The motivation for the use of web recommendations comes from both internet users and website owners. Internet users want to see interesting information; the website owners want their information to reach users quickly and to the full extent. Owners of commercial websites also employ web recommendations in order to sell additional products or services to the users and thus increase the sales turnover of their websites.

Many algorithms have been developed in order to generate such potentially interesting web recommendations automatically. These approaches are based on different intuitions about what might be interesting for the given user in a given situation. In this dissertation we study these approaches and show that each of them has its own specific drawbacks. To overcome these drawbacks, we present a combined adaptive algorithm, which gathers potential recommendations from different recommendation algorithms, presents them to users and refines them based on whether the users accept them or not. We employ ontology graphs as a convenient way of storing highly diverse information about the website which is required to make a decision on which recommendations should be presented. We have implemented and evaluated our architecture on two real-world websites, one of which is commercial and another non-commercial. In this dissertation we further present a comparative analysis of our approach and several other recommendation approaches using these real-world evaluations and show, that our algorithm is more successful in attracting user interest in form of additional clicks and purchases.

Based on the gained experience, we extend our approach to the case, when the data presented on a website are integrated from several data sources. This is a common case for large E-Commerce websites. In this setting we recognize an additional problem – the problem of data integration: we need to integrate both product data and additional semantic information, which we also represent as ontology graphs. We give special attention to the matching of the ontology graphs, since this problem needs to be solved for in order to present web recommendations. The integrated setting also gives us the possibility to explore some new types of recommendations. As a proof of concept, we have implemented an integrated E-Commerce web portal, which gathers data from several internet shops, represents them in integrated form and helps the web users to navigate through these data by presenting web recommendations.

ACKNOWLEDGEMENTS

I am deeply grateful to my doctoral supervisor Prof. Dr. Erhard Rahm for all the help and advices he was giving me while I was working on my PhD thesis, for the time spent on making countless comments and corrections which helped me improve the content, language and presentation style of my scientific work. Also I would like to thank him for the patience with which he was keeping me on the right track and tolerating my excursions into some rather distant areas of interest.

This thesis would not be possible without the financial support from the postgraduate program (Graduiertenkolleg) "Wissensrepräsentation" at the University of Leipzig, which is sponsored by the DFG (Deutsche Forschungsgemeinschaft - German Research Foundation). Hence, I want to thank Prof. Dr. Erhard Rahm and Prof. Dr. Gerhard Brewka, the speaker of the Graduiertenkolleg, for my acceptance into the program and the financial support provided to me.

I am deeply grateful to all the colleagues and friends at the Database Group of the Department of Computer Science, University of Leipzig for the very pleasant working environment and many friendly advices. In particularly I would like to thank Dr. Andreas Thor and David Aumüller for all the help, cooperation and support which I received from them. I would also like to express my gratitude to all the colleagues at the Graduiertenkolleg for creating the fruitful atmosphere of discussion and cooperation.

Parts of this thesis were completed during my work at Koch Media GmbH, Munich. I would like to thank the Director of IT Dr. Juri Vaisman and the management of the company for the understanding and support which I received from them during the work on this thesis. I am particularly thankful to my colleagues at Koch Media Dr. Miroslav Stimac and Thomas Gröber who spent their time on proofreading my thesis and encouraged me during the final stages of the work.

I would like to express my deepest appreciation and love to my wife Natasha for her support and for all the love and attention I was surrounded with during the work on this thesis. And finally, I convey my sonly love and gratitude to my parents Nadezhda and Vladimir for motivation and love which helped to finish this thesis.

PART I. INTRODUCTION

Summary

In recent years the Internet has continued its rapid growth. This growth involves not only the increase in the number of internet users and websites, but also in the increase of the amount of information on the individual websites. Many modern middle-sized to large websites become concerned with presenting their often semantically very versatile information in a concise and efficient way. One of the techniques which are often used to improve the presentation of the data and navigation in these data is the technique called "web recommendations". Web recommendations are hyperlinks, often augmented with short descriptive text and/or picture, which are shown on the website in addition to the original content with the intention to lead the user to interesting information. The motivation for use of web recommendations comes both from internet users and from website owners. Internet users want to see interesting information; the website owners want their information to reach the user quickly. The owners of commercial websites also employ web recommendations in order to sell additional products or services to the users and thus increase the sales turnover of their websites. Probably the best-known example of such usage is the website http://www.amazon.com, which heavily relies on web recommendations in order to present its products to the users. Another example which shows the importance of web recommendations is the website www.netflix.com, owned by one of the largest US-based online movie rental companies Netflix. In 2006, Netflix started a contest which offers a prize of one million US dollars to the developers of a recommendation system which could outperform Netflix's own recommendation system Cinematch by 10% in terms of prediction accuracy[1].

A significant number of algorithms has been developed in order to generate potentially interesting web recommendations automatically. These approaches are based on different intuitions about what might be interesting for the given user in a given situation. The main drawback of such approaches is the fact that the intuitions may or may not be relevant in some particular situation and that we are often unable to precisely judge how good one or another intuition is before the recommendation is presented to the user. To overcome this drawback, in Part II of the thesis we present a combined adaptive approach, which gathers potential recommendations from the existing recommendation algorithms, presents them to users and refines them based on whether the users accept them or not. The combined adaptive approach allows us to optimize the selection of interesting recommendations in the long run. We have investigated different algorithms for the

---

[1] For additional information please see http://www.netflixprize.com/. Unfortunately, the system presented in this thesis is not suitable for use with data available from Netflix, since these data do not contain user feedback, which is required by our system as described in Part II of this thesis.

optimization of the recommendations in a simulated environment. Furthermore, we have implemented and evaluated our recommendation architecture on two real-world websites, one of which is commercial and another non-commercial. We employ ontology graphs as a convenient way of storing highly diverse information about the website which is required to make a decision on which recommendations should be presented. In this thesis we present a comparative analysis of our approach and several other recommendation approaches using real-world evaluations. We show that our algorithm is more successful in attracting user interest in form of additional clicks and purchases.

Based on the gained experience, we extend our approach to the case when the data presented on the website are integrated from several data sources. This is a common case for modern large e-commerce websites. We handle this situation in Part III of this thesis. In this setting we recognize an additional problem – the problem of data integration: we need to integrate product data and additional semantic information, which we also represent as ontology graphs. Here, another beneficial function of web recommendations comes to light. Web recommendations can be used to help integrate the different data sources in one interactive website. We pay special attention to the matching of the ontology graphs, since this problem needs to be solved in order to present web recommendations. The integrated setting also gives us the possibility to explore some new types of recommendations. As a proof of concept, we have implemented an integrated e-commerce web portal which gathers data from several internet shops, represents them in an integrated form and helps the user to navigate through these data by presenting web recommendations.

Part II. Adaptive Web Recommendations

1. INTRODUCTION

In recent years web recommendations have become a technology familiar to most internet users. The usage of web recommendations has become particularly widespread on the e-commerce websites, such as internet shops. One well known example of use of a recommendation system is the online store Amazon.com. Such e-commerce websites use web recommendations to increase usability, customer satisfaction and commercial profit. The schema of interaction between the user, the website and the recommendation system in the general case is shown in Figure 2.1.

The website shown in Figure 2.1 can be either a collection of HTML pages residing on a web server or a web application written in some programming language which serves content in form of HTML pages. The usage of web recommendations usually assumes that the technology employed on the web server allows dynamic generation of HTML content. The recommendation system obtains information from the website. This information can include data about different aspects of the current situation on the website and of the past situations, which are deemed to be relevant to the task of providing web recommendations. Based on this information, the recommendation system generates a set of so-called web recommendations. Each recommendation is usually represented as a hyperlink, accompanied by descriptive information. These recommendations are shown in specially defined areas on the website, as depicted in Figure 2.1.

There are recommendation systems which do not follow the general schema shown in Figure 2.1. Examples of such systems are WebWatcher [JFM97] which operates as a proxy between the browser and the website and Letizia [Lieb95] where the presentation of recommendations is performed by an add-on to the browser. Such systems are however rare and have not attained recognition in commercial web applications.

A number of algorithms were developed for generating web recommendations by applying different statistical or data mining approaches to some available information, for example on characteristics of the current page, product, web user, buying history etc.

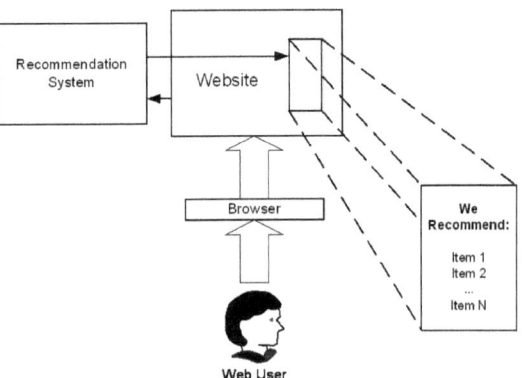

Figure 2.1. Schematic representation of the interaction between a website, a recommendation system and a web user

[Burk02][JKR02] However, so far no single algorithm uses the benefits of all the available knowledge sources and no single algorithm shows clear superiority over all others. Therefore, the need for hybrid approaches which combine the benefits of multiple algorithms has been recognized [Burk02].

In this part of the thesis, we present a new approach to creating a web recommendation system capable of combining many algorithms for generating recommendations (*recommendation generators* or simply *recommenders*). Our approach utilizes a central recommendation database for storing the recommendations coming from different recommendation generators and applies machine learning techniques to continuously optimize the stored recommendations. Optimization of the recommendations is based on how "useful" they are to users and to the website, i.e. how willingly the users click on them and how much profit they bring. The incentive for our optimization approach was the observation, that the popularity and perceived relevance of individual recommendations are not always well predicted by the recommendation generators.

The information about the website and the users is represented in the recommendation database in the form of ontology graphs. This allows us to semantically enrich the recommendations and bring in the knowledge from the additional sources, for example geographical databases or publicly available ontologies. It is also practicable for the adaptation of the system to the different types of websites.

The preliminary version of the architecture presented here was sketched in [GR04] and further developed in [GR05]. In this thesis we describe the architecture of the system, the prototype implementations of the system and present the evaluation results.

The focus of our work lies on providing a generic recommendation system architecture for commercial websites, designed in particular for usage with internet shops but also suitable for other types of websites.

We have implemented the prototype of our system on two real-life websites: a website of the Database Group, University of Leipzig http://dbs.uni-leipzig.de and an internet software shop http://www.softunity.com. The screenshots of the web pages presenting recommendations are given in Appendix 1. We have also performed experiments in a simulated environment modeled after http://www.softunity.com. To denote the origin of the examples and notions in this part of the thesis we mark them with EDU (educational) for the Database Group website, EC (e-commerce) for www.softunity.com or SIM for simulation. The detailed descriptions of our prototypes can be found in Chapter 4. We also use the examples taken from our prototypes throughout this part of the thesis to illustrate the incentives for our architecture.

The main contributions of the research work described in this part of the thesis are:
- The generic semantically-enriched recommendation architecture for e-commerce websites capable of combining different recommendation approaches.
- The online optimization algorithm for web recommendations based on user feedback.
- The evaluation of the architecture and the algorithm for real-life environments.

In the next chapter we explain the architecture of the system and its main components. We also describe some practice-driven incentives for choosing the described architecture, but leave the discussion in this chapter largely generic. The optimization techniques are presented in Chapter 3. In Chapter 4 we describe the implementation of our prototypes and the correspondence between the generic architecture and the design of the prototypes. In Chapter 5 we present the results of the experiments performed on real-life prototypes. Chapter 6 contains evaluations of different architectural decisions and optimization approaches obtained in the simulated environment. In Chapter 7 we provide an overview of the related work and discuss some selected approaches in more detail. Chapter 8 summarizes this part of the thesis.

2. THE GENERIC RECOMMENDATION SYSTEM ARCHITECTURE

In this chapter we propose and discuss the generic recommendation system architecture. We give an overview of the architecture and some relevant notions in Section 2.1. In the subsequent sections we discuss the selection of recommendations using the ontology graphs (Section 2.2) and the generation of the recommendation rules (Section 2.3).

2.1 Overview

The architecture of our recommendation system is shown in Figure 2.2. In this section we briefly describe each of the components depicted in Figure 2.2. More detailed descriptions follow in the subsequent sections. The *website* interacts with the web user, presents recommendations and gathers the feedback. The *web data warehouse* stores information about the content of the website (e.g., products and product catalog, HTML pages, etc.), users, and the usage logs generated by the web server or the application server. It serves as an information source for the recommendation generators and ontology generators and allows evaluations of the user behavior and the efficiency of recommendations using OLAP tools. The *recommendation database* stores the semantic information in form of *ontology graphs* and the recommendations in form of *recommendation rules*, which are described in the next section. The set of *ontology generators* is responsible for generating the *ontology graphs*. The set of *recommendation generators* generates the recommendations using the data from the web data warehouse. The combination of different recommendation generators which use different algorithms for generating recommendations makes our system a hybrid recommendation system. The combination of different recommendation generators is applied to avoid the drawbacks which most popular recommendation algorithms are known to have when used alone. The recommendation rules specify, which content items should be recommended in which situation, the situation being expressed using concepts contained in the ontology graphs. The ontology graphs and recommendation rules can also be created and edited by a *human editor*. The *optimizer* refines the recommendation database based on the feedback obtained from the website using machine learning. The refinement is done by adjusting the weights of the recommendation rules according to an *optimization algorithm*. The study of different optimization algorithms is an important aspect which is addressed in detail in Chapters 3, 5 and 6.

In our recommendation system we distinguish the generation loop and the optimization loop. The generation loop is represented by a larger ellipse in the background of Figure 2.2. It includes the website, the web data warehouse, the ontology and recommendation generators and the recommendation database. The generation loop is executed at regular intervals of time. It involves updating the web data warehouse using

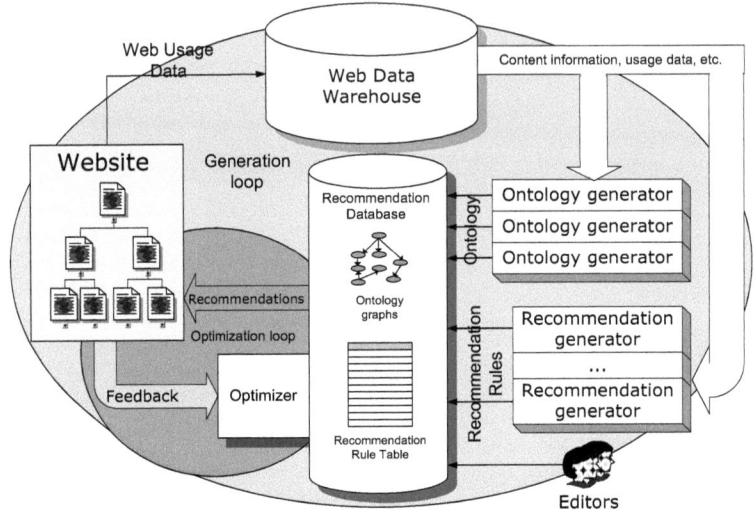

Figure 2.2. Generic recommendation system architecture

the data from the website and subsequent generating/updating of the ontology and the recommendation rules utilizing the information on the content and recent usage information from the web data warehouse. The optimization loop is executed continuously. It selects and presents the recommendations from the recommendation database. After the presentation system gathers the user feedback, i.e. user reactions to presented recommendations. The optimizer uses this information to refine the recommendations in the database and to influence the selection of future recommendations. The detailed descriptions of the components of the generation loop are presented further on in this chapter. The discussion of the optimization loop is presented in Chapter 3.

The online, i.e. real-time optimization of the recommendations is a distinctive feature of our architecture. Although a number of recommendation system architectures adjust or update their recommendation model at regular intervals of time, for example every night, we argue that online optimization and the resulting quicker reaction to the changes in the user interest can be significantly more beneficial in many cases. The direct incentive for implementing the online optimization was the buyer behavior observed on the e-commerce website http://www.softunity.com (EC) which we used for one of our prototypes. The buyer activity on this website is distributed very unevenly in time, featuring some dramatic activity peaks from time to time. This can be attributed to the fact, that many of the computer games and software products offered on the website are sequels of previously popular computer games and products. The release of such sequels is long awaited by the prospective buyers and the first release day usually brings overwhelmingly successful sales. For several successful products on the website the revenue generated on the first release day constituted up to 75% of the sales in the subsequent 12 months. In fact, 30% of the revenue generated by the website is generated by the products on their respective release day. In contrast, the second and third day bring only 1% of the revenue each. So, it is very important to optimize recommendations on http://www.softunity.com in terms of hours and minutes, for the most popular products even in terms of seconds. More information about the website http://www.softunity.com can be found in Section 4.1.

An even stronger incentive for the online optimization can be assumed for news websites. Indeed, although the content of news articles can stay on such websites for years, the peak of the interest is usually the first day or even several hours. The recommendation systems on such websites should therefore be able to learn the user interests and optimize the presented recommendations within this time span as well.

Since we intend to create a generic recommendation system architecture which can be used for many types of websites, we pay attention to separating the components which need to be implemented specifically for each website from the components which stay the same for all websites. So, the web data warehouse, the ontology generators and recommendation generators depend on the concrete website, since their implementation depends on the entities and entity attributes which are specific to each website (for example, software products or clothes or news articles). The recommendation rule database is generic and its structure can remain the same for all websites. The optimization loop is also generic, but can be configured via a set of parameters described in Chapter 3 to suit the needs of the concrete website.

The ontology graphs give our architecture the independence from the concrete website and the possibility to encompass the recommendations coming different recommendation algorithms, as discussed in the next section.

Some important notions which we use to describe different aspects of our recommendation system include *web user, item, page view, session, acceptance rate, session acceptance rate*[2]. *Web user* is a human which uses a web browser to access the website. Sometimes the web users are required or allowed to register on the website and enter some descriptive information about themselves. More often, however, web users remain anonymous and the information about them is obtained indirectly. The web users usually view one or more pages on the website. During each such *page view* the web user's browser sends a series of HTTP requests[3] to the website. Each request contains the information about the IP address of the user, the used browser and some other descriptive information. A series of page views coming from the same user in a limited interval of time is called *session*. Sometimes websites let users log in and log out on the website. Determining the user session in such cases is straightforward. More often, however, there's no possibility for the user to explicitly end the session and the end of the session has to be determined by timeout, i.e. time interval during which no HTTP requests are obtained from

---

[2] Definitions of some additional terms which are used to describe web activity can be found here: http://www.w3.org/1999/05/WCA-terms/
[3] Protocol HTTP is specified in RFC2616 (ftp://ftp.rfc-editor.org/in-notes/rfc2616.txt)

the web user's browser. The page views can contain presentation of the recommendations as illustrated in Figure 2.1. The user may click on such recommendation, i.e. *accept* it. The ratio of the number of times a recommendation has been accepted to the number of times a recommendation has been presented is called *acceptance rate* of the recommendation. *Session acceptance rate* is a ratio of the number of the sessions in which a recommendation was accepted to the number of sessions in which it was presented. We can speak about the acceptance rate or session acceptance rate for a single recommendation, for the entire recommendation system or for a group of recommendations unified by some common characteristic such as the recommendation algorithm used to generate them or the user group for which these recommendations are relevant.

2.2 Recommendation Selection Using Ontology Graphs

The information which the recommendation system needs in order to provide relevant recommendations can be manifold and complex. We do not deem it feasible to specifically name all possible reasons and consideration which can influence the recommendation decisions in different web applications. Obviously, an e-commerce website which sells automobiles would operate in different concept space when thinking about its users and its products than a website which sells clothing. A news website and an educational would also need their own concept spaces different from e-commerce websites. Striving to create generic recommendation system architecture, we have decided to introduce a special semantic layer between the website and our recommendation system. This architectural decision answers the following needs:

- To be generic, our architecture needs to be isolated from the implementation details of a given website.
- The concept spaces which contain knowledge about content, users, time and other relevant information often exhibit a complex structure. This complex structure needs to be represented in a way which allows the recommendation system to reason about it.
- The human editors of the website need a human-friendly view of the concepts which influence the presentation of recommendations. Very often the owners of the website need to impose business rules onto the recommendation system. The recommendation system needs to be able to represent these business rules internally in a way understandable both for the recommendation system and for humans.
- In cases when the recommendation system is unable to find recommendations for specific concepts on the website, it may be a meaningful decision to search for some similar, related or more general concept and present the recommendations relevant to these concepts.

An additional discussion about the role of ontologies in recommender systems and personalization can be found in [BMC+06].

In our system this semantic layer is represented using so-called *ontology graphs*. The ontology graphs are directed acyclic graphs. The concepts are represented with nodes and provided with labels. The edges can be provided with labels and weights. In the general case, we assume that three ontology graphs are relevant for making recommendations, one graph respectively for content, users and time. In some cases more or fewer graphs may be adequate. So, in our prototype EC we use three graphs and in the prototype EDU two graphs, as discussed in Section 4.2.2.

The ontology graphs are automatically generated by ontology generators and can be edited manually by the editors of the website. The ontology graphs for the website content can often be extracted with ease, since the navigation on a website is usually hierarchically structured.

Figure 2.3 shows the process of selection of recommendations using ontology graphs. To request recommendations to present, the website specifies the current *website context* and the desired number of recommendations. The website context is a set of parameters, which characterize the currently viewed website content, current web user and present point in time. An example of a website context is given below:

WebsiteContext{ ProductID="ECD00345"; UserCountry="DE"; UserOperatingSystem="Windows"; Date ="21.03.2005";...} (EC).

Obviously, the choice of suitable parameters in the website context depends on the specific website, especially with respect to the current content.

The recommendation system maps the provided website context into a *semantic context*, which consists of nodes of the three ontology graphs {ContentNodes, UserNodes, TimeNodes}. After the semantic context has been determined, our recommendations system is using a so-called *selection policy* to select the recommendations associated with the relevant nodes of the ontology graphs for the presentation on the website. This two-step selection process aims at supporting the application-oriented recommendation strategies and high flexibility. Assigning recommendations to semantic concepts is expected to be more stable than assigning them directly to the low-level website contexts whose values may change frequently (e.g. due to website restructuring). The selection policies may be as simple as selecting recommendations which are directly referencing the given context

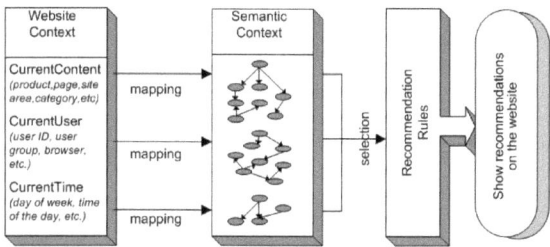

Figure 2.3. Selecting recommendations using semantic context

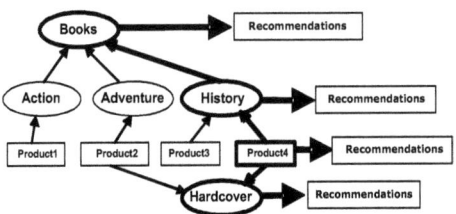

Figure 2.4. A sample ontology graph for content dimension (EC)

nodes. It is however also possible to do a more complex selection by traversing the ontology graphs and taking additional relevant context nodes into consideration. The algorithms for more complex selection policies should be tailored to the needs of the specific website.

Figure 2.4 shows an example of an ontology graph for website content. Ontology graphs for web users and time are built in a similar way. We use directed edges to point from more specific concepts to more general concepts, from subcomponents to aggregated components, etc. Recommendations can be assigned to any node in such a graph. Highlighted with thick lines in Figure 2.4 is an example of how the semantics stored in the ontology graph can be used to search for additional recommendations for Product4. We are able to retrieve the recommendations directly for Product4 as well the recommendations that are bound to some common property that Product4 possesses (in our case Hardcover) and the recommendations to some product catalog topics that Product4 belongs to (History, Books).

The mapping between website and semantic contexts is specified by mapping clauses. Mapping clauses are statements written in a simple predicate language which may be attached to nodes in the ontology graphs. The predicate language supports logical operators (AND, OR, NOT), comparison operators ($<, >, =, <>, >=, <=$) and the operator LIKE, which does string matching with wildcard, similar to the SQL-operator with the same name. Some of the nodes in the ontology graphs immediately correspond to a certain set of parameters and can be mapped using mapping clauses. Other nodes represent abstract notions. Such nodes can be reached only by traversing the ontology graph and have no associated mapping clauses. The predicate language is chosen to be compatible to SQL in order to be able to implement the mapping of the website context to the semantic context as SQL query over a table in a relational database. In combination with indexes created on the relevant columns this allows quick mapping even in case of very large number of nodes in the ontology graphs.

Each of the three ontology graphs is mapped separately. In our EC application, the ontology graphs are created by ontology generators using the product catalog, common properties of products and the business logic of the website. The application EDU uses the manually specified website content hierarchy and user groups determined by data mining. Most mapping clauses are automatically determined by the ontology generators together with the creation of the ontology and simply use an equality operator. Manually specified mapping clauses may be more complex. Examples of the mapping clauses are:

ProductID="ECD00345" -> ContentNode=1342 (EC)
UserCountry="DE"-> UserNode=3 (EC)
UserDomain LIKE '%.edu' OR UserDomain LIKE '%uni-%' -> UserNode =2 (EDU)

The recommendations associated to nodes in the ontology graphs are represented by the recommendation rules stored in the recommendation database. The recommendation rules have the form:

RuleContext{Content, User, Time} -> RecommendedContent, Weight

RuleContext refers to nodes in one or several of the three ontology graphs. These values can also be set to NULL, denoting that the rule does not depend on the corresponding dimension. RecommendedContent is the pointer to the content being recommended, e.g. recommended product or URL. The Weight is used as a criterion for the selection of the recommendation rules for presentations.

We have implemented and tested several recommendation selection policies in our prototypes. These policies include the default straightforward policy "direct match" and some more complex selection policies which use the additional semantic information contained in the ontology graphs. We discuss these policies in Chapter 4 in more detail. The ontological structure which we present here can also be used to implement the ontology-based policies proposed by other researchers. Some of these ontology-based selection techniques are discussed in Section 7.6.

2.3 Generating Recommendation Rules

The recommendation rules are generated by the recommendation generators and stored in the recommendation database. We think of recommendation generators as belonging to the website-specific part of our recommendation architecture. The algorithms used in the recommendation generators may be specific for the given website or generic. However, even the generic algorithms need tailoring to the data structures and peculiarities of the specific website so that the recommendation generators should in our opinion be considered in general website-specific.

The most popular approaches for generating web recommendations are content-based approaches and approaches based on collaborative filtering.

The content-based approaches exploit the content of the items to provide recommendations. A common example of the content-based approach is the recommendation generators based on text similarity between the items. Items with similar titles and/or descriptions are assumed to be good recommendations.

The approaches based on collaborative filtering attempt to match the current user to the other users based on the gathered information about the user preferences. The preferences of these other users are then used to generate the recommendations for the current user.

When used alone, each of these algorithms exhibit certain drawbacks. So, the collaborative filtering algorithms require statistical information about the items and the users to be gathered before the recommendations can be generated. This leads to the so-called "new user" and "new item" problems, which arise when such information is not yet available. Content-based recommendation approaches do not cause the mentioned problems. However, they are based on the assumption that the information contained in the content of the items is sufficient to generate good recommendation. This assumption may or may not be the true depending on the concrete items. Algorithms other than collaborative filtering and content-based, for example algorithms based on the domain knowledge, usually generate very specific types of recommendations and cannot be used alone as well. For more information about the different recommendation algorithms and their respective benefits and drawbacks please see the surveys [Burk06], [JKR02], [PSF02], [AT05]. By gathering the recommendations generated by different algorithms in one recommendation rule database and subsequent optimization of this database we intend to combine the benefits and avoid the drawbacks of the different recommendation algorithms.

A recommendation generator may supply an initial weight for every generated recommendation rule. The weight of a recommendation rule is a real number in the interval [0 .. 1]. If the recommendation generators generate a rule which already exists in the recommendation rule table with a different weight, the weight in the recommendation rule table takes preference over the weight supplied by the recommendation generators. We have explored two approaches to setting the initial weights of the newly generated recommendation rules. In the first approach, we simply set all initial weights to zero. The second approach uses normalized recommendation generator specific weights or relative priorities for the respective contexts. When several recommendation generators generate the same recommendation we use the maximum of their weights. The initial weights are expected to be relevant primarily for new recommendations since the weights for presented recommendations are continuously adapted in the optimization loop. In Chapter 4 we discuss the possibility of setting the weights for the new recommendations to stimulate their presentation in the initial period.

The individual recommendation rules may also be easily created, edited and deleted by a human editor. Trivial as it may seem, this possibility is very important for the operation of the recommendation systems on e-commerce websites. An example of situation where lack of such direct control over the presented recommendations has lead to a breakdown of the entire recommendation system is presented in [Flyn06]. In this New York Times article the author describes an incident with the recommendation system deployed at the website of the large US Company Wal-Mart. To commemorate the anniversary of Martin Luther King's birth, the company has brought out a boxed set of movies related to Afro-American themes and presented it in a prominent position on their web-site. In addition, the company employed automatic cross-selling recommendation system on their website which proposed a number of automatically selected products to be bought together with this special product. Some of the product combinations proposed by this recommendation system to the described commemorative movie set have been perceived as very offensive by the potential Afro-American customers. According to the New York Times article, the entire cross-selling recommendation system on the Wal-Mart website had to be taken down. If the recommendation system used by Wal-Mart provided the possibility of the manual control of the presented recommendations, the problem would have been solved by simply deleting the offending recommendations without the need to switch off the entire recommendation system.

3. FEEDBACK-BASED OPTIMIZATION

In the previous chapter we have discussed our approach of generating recommendation rules and storing them in the recommendation rules database. The recommendation generators provide the recommendation rules basing on different assumptions about the interests of the web users, more specifically about the correlation between the observable information and the web user preferences. These assumptions may or may not be true either in general or for some of the generated recommendations. In particular, none of the available single (i.e. non-hybrid) techniques of generating recommendations is able to use all possible information that is available. This leads us to a suggestion that all available recommendation models are too coarse when being used alone.

We can obtain a more fine-grained recommendation model in our architecture by gathering the recommendation rules from different recommendation generators and storing them in the central recommendation rule database. However, such recommendation rule database contains both the "tops" and the "flops" of any available recommendation generator. Now we can start using the recommendation rules and separate the "tops" from the "flops" by observing the user reaction to presenting recommendations. We do this using feedback-based optimization. We represent the user feedback in numerical form (reward value) and use it for adjusting the weights of the recommendation rules in such a way that the total reward is maximized. In this chapter we describe the model which we employ for our optimization, the issues which we have to solve in our optimization algorithms and the different approaches to solving these problems.

3.1 Modeling the Problem of Optimizing Web Recommendations as Markov Decision Process and Applying Reinforcement Learning

We model the process of selecting recommendations for presentation as a Markov Decision Process (MDP). The Markov Decision Process is a generic model of a sequential decision process which serves as a foundation for a large number of methods for solving optimization problems. Markov Decision Process assumes the existence of an agent which interacts with the environment. At any moment, the agent is deemed to be in some state s which belongs to the set of all possible states S. In any state s the agent may perform an action a from the set of possible actions A. After performing the action a, the agent's state may change from state s to state $s' \in S$. The agent may also receive a feedback from the environment, feedback being expressed numerically. Several terms are used in the MDP literature to describe the numeric value of feedback, such as "reward", "cost", "penalty" (cost and penalty being negative of reward). We use the term "feedback" to describe the user's reaction to the agent's action and the terms "reward" or "feedback value" to denote the numerical value which describes the feedback. The feedback is used by the agent for making decisions about taking one or another action in the future. In our case the recommendation system acts as the agent.

An MDP model is a four-tuple <S, A, R, TR>. In this tuple, S is the set of possible states and A is the set of possible actions. R(s, a, s′) is the reward function on <S, A, S> which describes the immediate reward which is obtained from the environment if the agent performs the action a in the state s and appears in the state s′ afterwards. TR(s, a, s′) is the transition function which describes the probability of transition from the state s to the state s′ after performing the action a. By performing actions, the agent usually strives to optimize some function of the received reward values. An MDP model is called finite MDP in case when the state and action spaces are finite [SB98]. We use a finite MDP to represent the task of making web recommendations.

The MDP states often correspond to combinations of different characteristics of the environment. In such cases the states are represented via a number of state variables. In our architecture we have three state variables respectively for the content, user and time parts of the context. Each of the variables can contain a reference to the node in the corresponding ontology graph or the value "NULL".

An MDP model should satisfy the so-called Markov property. The Markov property of the sequential decision task means that the conditional probability distributions of the future states depend only on the current state and not on any past state. The non-markovian learning tasks can sometimes be converted into MDP by using states of the form

$S_n^* = \{S_{n-m}, S_{n-m+1}, \ldots, S_n\}$,

i.e. by representing the sequence of last m states as a single state. An MDP which takes the last m states into account when making decisions is called an m-th order MDP. An MDP for which the Markov property holds without converting the sequence of states into one state is called first-order MDP. The use of the MDPs of higher order has been proposed to solve the problem of presenting web recommendations in [SBH02][SHB05]. The incorporation of the past states of the agent, however, leads to an explosion in the number of possible states in the resulting higher order MDP.

For practical purposes it is often useful to assume the Markov property to hold even when it is not the case in the reality. A reasonable prerequisite for such an assumption is that the current states have a much larger influence than the past states. The preliminary experiments with our prototype data have shown that we have relatively few situations where we could benefit from taking previous states into account. The majority of sessions in our prototypes has only one page view[4]; for the sessions which have two page views the first page view is usually the starting page of the website. In our system we use only the first-order MDP and take into account only the current state. We have not implemented or tested higher order MDPs in our prototypes. However with our generic architecture this could be implemented with little effort. The states in our system are defined on the nodes

---

[4] More details on the session length distribution for the EC prototype are given in Section 4.3

of the ontology graphs. The nodes can be configured to represent the combinations of current and past states.

In an MDP, the agent is usually taking one action in every state. In our case an action is equivalent to the presentation of a certain recommendation. A recommendation system, however, usually presents a list of several recommendations. A straightforward way to represent this behavior of the recommendation system in MDP would be to consider each combination of recommendations as one action. This however would lead to an explosion of the number of possible actions. To avoid this, we have made a simplifying assumption that the probability of a recommendation being clicked in our system does not depend on the other recommendations presented simultaneously. This allows us to treat the simultaneous presentation of N recommendations as N independent learning episodes in the sense of MDP. Such a simplifying assumption is often found in the literature, as discussed in Section 7.5.

The problem of learning the optimal behavior of the agent by learning from feedback provided by the environment using the framework of Markov Decision Process constitutes the *reinforcement learning problem*. There are several families of methods which can be used to solve this kind of optimization problem. Examples of such families of methods are *dynamic programming* [Bell57] *and reinforcement learning* [KLM96] [SB98][5].

Dynamic programming requires a complete model of the environment, in particular the transition probabilities and the reward function should be known a priori. The most prominent examples of dynamic programming are value iteration [Bell57] and policy iteration [Howa60]. Dynamic programming has been widely studied in application to a wide range of optimization problems, not only those expressed as an MDP. Dynamic programming is computationally expensive since it requires re-calculation of the entire state-action space after each step. There are synchronous dynamic programming algorithms which require waiting for the re-calculation of the transition probabilities after each step and asynchronous methods where the agent does not have to wait until the calculation of the entire state-action space completes. Although with asynchronous algorithms our system may be able to propose next action quicker, the total computation load the asynchronous dynamic programming algorithms put on the computer is still very large. Therefore, both synchronous and asynchronous dynamic programming methods are computationally prohibitive for online optimization.

In contrast to dynamic programming, reinforcement learning algorithms do not require the complete model of the environment and can implicitly learn the transition probabilities during optimization. In the task of making web recommendations, exact

---

[5] There seems to be a dual understanding of the term reinforcement learning in the literature[KLM96]. In the broader sense, this term relates to the set of problems which involve learning from feedback and the algorithms which can be used to solve these problems. Such algorithms include genetic programming and dynamic programming. In the narrower sense, the term relates to the set of approximative algorithms which focus on online learning (i.e. algorithms allowing realtime computation) without requiring the complete model of the environment.

transition probabilities are unknown and need to be learned. The reinforcement learning can be applied incrementally. The recalculations of the entire space-action space are therefore not necessary, making the online optimization possible. These characteristics make reinforcement learning algorithms particularly interesting for the task of optimizing the web recommendations. The most popular reinforcement learning algorithms are Q-Learning [Watk89] and SARSA [RN94]. The transition function is usually not learned directly but estimated using for example state-action value function $Q(s,a)$, which assigns weights to combinations of states and actions. In our recommendation system the state-action value function corresponds to the weight of recommendation rule $Q(r)$, since the recommendation rules contain information about both the state (i.e. recommendation context) and the action (i.e. recommended item).

The goal of the reinforcement learning optimization is to maximize the total amount of reward. Many of the reinforcement learning algorithms including Q-Learning and SARSA deal with delayed rewards. That means, that the agents decisions may be rewarded not only immediately after performing the action ("immediate reward") but also when a reward is received in some of the subsequent steps ("delayed reward"). This reward is usually discounted, i.e. multiplied by the discount ratio γ ($0 \leq \gamma \leq 1$). In the task of making web recommendations, however, our goal is to obtain the reward immediately. Indeed, the web recommendations are supposed to shorten the navigation paths which lead to interesting content. The low usefulness of the delayed reward in application to our prototypes is illustrated by the session length distribution of the EC prototype as described in Subsection 4.3. The number of the observed sessions with a given length falls at exponential rate as the session length increases. This leads to the intuition that the web users are reluctant about continuing navigation when they do not see the interesting content immediately. Because of this characteristic of our task, we are able to employ the simple single-step reinforcement learning approaches in our prototypes. However, our generic architecture can also support the usage of delayed rewards. Web recommendation systems utilizing reinforcement learning approaches with delayed rewards have been studied in [MR07][MR07a] and subsequent works from the same research group and also on [TKG07][TK07]. The first series of works utilizes Policy Iteration and the second Q-Learning. Both systems are discussed in Section 7.5 in more detail.

An interesting research direction in the field of reinforcement learning is *generalization of feedback*. A common problem in the feedback-based optimization is that the amount of feedback received by the system is small in comparison to the total number of possible states. Generalization attempts to alleviate this problem by employing the observation that the state space often exhibits some kind of internal structure or relation between states. These relations can be used to generalize the feedback obtained in a single state to the neighboring or similar states in the state space. A number of different approaches can be used to perform this generalization, including artificial neural networks, decision trees and multivariate regression [SB98]. Our recommendation system architecture provides an ontological representation of the state space which can be used to perform the feedback generalization. Currently, however, we use this representation only to perform the selection of recommendations and not for the feedback generalization. The study of the different feedback generalization methods in the context of our recommendation systems remains a matter for future research. Several other recommendation system architectures based on reinforcement learning use the generalization of feedback as discussed in Section 7.5.

There are formal proofs of convergence to the optimal values for a number of basic reinforcement learning algorithms like SARSA. However, as noted in [KLM96], the proofs of convergence for the reinforcement learning algorithms are of little practical value. Such formal proofs usually assume an infinite number of visits of each state. Practically, however, an algorithm that is proven to converge to the optimal values may be less interesting that an algorithm that achieves only near-optimal values but at a faster pace. So, the learning speed becomes the practically important metric for assessing the quality of a reinforcement learning algorithms. In Subsection 6.1.5 we present the comparative study of learning behavior in time for the optimization algorithms implemented in our recommendation system.

3.2 "Drift of Interest"

One of the characteristics of the problem of optimizing web recommendations is that this problem is a non-stationary problem. That means that the transition probabilities in the corresponding MDP do not stay constant over time. This is caused by the changes in the interests of the web user with respect to the recommended items. Products or content items may become obsolete, put into obscurity by new products or events happening in the world. Sometimes, on the contrary, old product or content may become interesting again due to some events. We can handle these temporal changes in the user's interest, the so-called "drift of interest" in several ways:

- Ignore the „drift of interest". We can consider older rewards and newer rewards to be equally important. In this case, the weight of the recommendation rule Q(r) is calculated using the formula for *arithmetic average*:

$$Q(r) = \frac{\sum Reward\ (r)}{N_{presented}\ (r)} \qquad (3.2.1)$$

where $\sum Reward(r)$ is the sum of rewards received by the recommendations r since its creation and $N_{presented}(r)$ is the number of times the recommendation r was presented. The "drift of interest" is not taken into account here. In case when we use Reward=1 when a recommendation is clicked and Reward=0 when a recommendation is not clicked, the Q(r) becomes equivalent to the acceptance rate of the recommendation rule.

- Consider only the last n reward values for each recommendation rule and generate the weights of the recommendation rules from them by using one of the following formulae:

$$Q_t(r) = \frac{\sum_{k=0}^{n-1} Reward_{t-k}(r)}{n} = Q_{t-1}(r) + \frac{Reward(r) - Reward_{t-n}(r)}{n} \quad (3.2.2)$$

or

$$Q_t(r) = \frac{\sum_{k=0}^{n-1} w_k Reward_{t-k}(r)}{n}, \text{ where } \sum_{k=0}^{n-1} w_k = 1 \quad (3.2.3)$$

In the formulae above, $Q_t(r)$ is the weight of the recommendation rule r after the presentation t, $Reward_t(r)$ is the reward the recommendation system receives after the presentation t, n is the number of last presentations which have impact on the weight of the recommendation rule. The first formula is known in the literature as *simple moving average*, the second as *weighted moving average*. In the first formula all n participating reward values have equal impact on the weight of the recommendation rule. In the second formula the impact which the reward from each presentation has on the recommendation rule weight can be controlled using the weights w_k. In practice, the weights w_k are chosen in such a way that for every k $w_k < w_{k-1}$.

These *simple moving average* and *weighted moving average* approaches, however, have drawbacks. So, the calculation of the recommendation rule weights is possible only after first n presentations of each recommendation. Both approaches also require additional memory in case of online optimization, since the last n reward values need to be stored for calculation.

We are not using the *simple moving average* and *weighted moving average* approaches in our system, since the next approach handles the „drift of interest" starting from the first presentation and without an additional memory overhead.

- Use *aging by division* (also called *exponential smoothing, exponential decay or exponential moving average* in the literature). Here, with every presentation the original weight of the recommendation rule is decreased by a fraction of its value:

$$Q_t(r) = \left(1 - \frac{1}{T}\right) * Q_{t-1}(r) + \frac{Reward(r)}{T} \quad (3.2.4)$$

In this formula, $Q_t(r)$ is the weight of the recommendation rule r at step t, T is the aging parameter (T>1). Reward(r) is the numerical value which describes a user's response to the presentation of the given recommendation. Multiplying the current weight by (1-1/T) implements the aging, since this way the latest presentations have the most impact on the resulting weight value while the contribution of past presentations decreases exponentially with each next presentation. Lower values of T lead to a decrease in the impact of the older recommendations presentations in comparison to the older presentations. The impact of the value of parameter T on the acceptance rate of different recommendation optimization algorithms is studied in Chapter 4. With aging by division, we do not need to keep the reward values from the previous recommendations and can start optimization from the first presentation.

3.3 Exploration versus Exploitation

In order to be successful in the long run, our recommendation system needs to pursue two goals. One goal is to gain the immediate profit from presenting recommendations, i.e. to exploit the recommendations which are known to be good. In order to achieve this, the recommendation system needs to present the recommendations with the larger utility. Another goal of our system is to learn how good the recommendations are, i.e. to explore the utility of the recommendations. In order to achieve this goal, the system needs to present the recommendations which have smaller number of presentations in the past. Balancing these two goals is an important issue for our adaptive recommendation system

There are formally justified algorithms for computing the Bayes-optimal way of balancing exploration and exploitation. These algorithms are however known to be computationally intractable [SB98]. The improvements of such algorithms in order to make them computationally tractable are a subject of current research [Wang06], however no generally accepted solution has been provided yet.

In order to balance the exploration and exploitation in practical applications, several heuristic methods have been developed and widely applied. One such technique is called ε-*greedy* in the literature [SB98]. This technique splits all recommendation presentations for a given context into two fractions. One fraction of the presentations is used to learn the utility of the recommendations. The recommendations in this fraction are selected using a pseudorandom number generator. Another fraction exploits the gained knowledge to maximize the acceptance rate of the recommendation system as a whole. This fraction always chooses the recommendations with the largest weight. Such behavior is called *greedy*. The explorative behavior is followed with probability ε (0<ε<1), the exploitative with probability 1-ε.

Another technique called *softmax* takes a different approach to balancing exploration and exploitation. The *softmax* technique selects the recommendations stochastically with probabilities which correlate to their weights. Many approaches can be used for correlating the weights and the selection probabilities. One common approach for the calculation of the selection probabilities is the Gibbs distribution, also named Boltzmann distribution:

$$P(r) = \frac{e^{\frac{Q(r)}{\tau}}}{\sum_{b=1}^{n} e^{\frac{Q(b)}{\tau}}}$$

where r is the recommendation rule for which we calculate the probability, Q(r) is the weight of the recommendation rule r, e is the Euler's constant and τ is a positive parameter called *temperature*. Higher values of the parameter τ lead to smaller differences in probabilities of selecting different recommendation rules. Lower values of τ cause the recommendation rules with higher weights to be strongly preferred to the rules with lower weights [SB98].

According to [SB98], there are neither theoretical results nor comparative experimental studies which prove the superiority of either ε-*greedy* or *softmax* technique over each other in general case. The choice of one or the other technique depends on the concrete problem. We have tested the *softmax* algorithm implemented using Gibbs distribution in our first informal experiments. We have found it very difficult to set the parameter τ for our experiments, because its influence on the learning process is less intuitive than the influence of ε. In our experiments the *softmax* technique has been able to achieve acceptance rate similar to ε-*greedy* only on a very narrow interval of the values of τ, being dramatically worse for all τ-s outside of this interval. If the values of τ lie below this narrow interval, the system pays too little attention to the weights of recommendations rules. If the values lie above the interval give non-proportional preference to the rules with higher weights to the disadvantage of rules with lower weights. This experience is in accordance with the following quote from [SB98]: "Most people find it easier to set the parameter ε with confidence; setting τ requires knowledge of the likely action values and of powers of *e*". Since this property of the softmax technique would impede the usability of our recommendation system on real-life websites, we have not used this technique in our further experiments.

It should be noted that the usage of aging as described in Section 3.2 also fosters exploration. Indeed, the idea of exploration is to avoid the so-called greedy behavior, i.e. the behavior which involves always selecting the best action according to the current knowledge, disregarding the fact that this knowledge may be incomplete and/or obsolete. Since aging gradually decreases the influence of the older knowledge on current decisions, it also alleviates the greedy behavior and makes way for exploration.

However, as opposed to the ε-*greedy* method, employing of aging cannot guarantee that sufficient exploration is performed in all situations. The benefit of such exploration is that we do not need to sacrifice a fixed fraction of presentations for exploration.

We would like to specifically mention some situations in the context of our recommendation system architecture, in which insufficient exploration can lead to systematic presentation of worse-than-optimal recommendations. These situations assume that the recommendation system is allowed to present N recommendations in one presentation.

Exploration Situation 1 (exploration blockage): We suppose that a new recommendation context is created and M new recommendation rules are added to this context simultaneously, M>N. If sufficient exploration is not provided for, then after any N recommendations receive positive feedback no other recommendations will ever be presented. Such situation can be circumvented by using optimistic initial weights [SB98] for the new recommendations, i.e. such weights which would enforce the presentation of the new recommendation in the initial period. A similar situation occurs when there are already M recommendation rules available for the context that we are investigating, M>N.

If a new recommendation rule is generated and its initial weight is lower than the weight of at least N other recommendation rules for the same context, this rule will never be explored, even though it might be possible that the new rule would have higher acceptance rate is presented. Such situation can be solved by using optimistic initial weights as well. One of the possibilities to implement optimistic initial weights is by using negative feedback values as described in the next subsection.

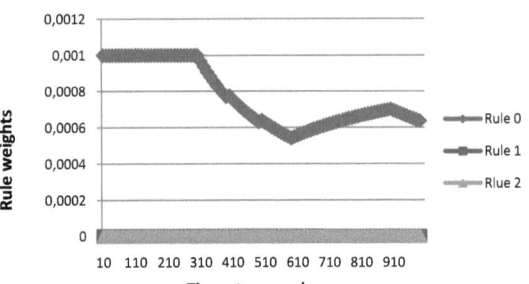

Fig. 2.5. Exploration vs. expoitation: lack of exploration

Exploration Situation 2 (unawareness of interest shift): Due to a shift of the users' interests one of the previously less popular recommendation rules becomes more popular than the others. If this recommendation has not previously been among the N recommendations with the highest weight, the recommendation system which prefers exploitation to exploration will never become aware of this shift of interest. This situation cannot be used by applying optimistic initial weights, since we are dealing with an already existing recommendation. Use of aging can alleviate this problem but it does not solve it completely, since aging is applied to all recommendation rules to the same degree.

These two situations are illustrated in Figures 2.5, 2.6 and 2.7. All three figures show development in time for one recommendation context with three recommendation rules. The learning process is iterated for 1000 steps. All rules have initial weights equal to 0. The number of recommendation which can be shown in one presentation N=1. The acceptance rates of the recommendations are set to change with time as follows:

Recommendation rule	Step 0 to 300	Step 300 to 600	Step 600 to 750	Step 750 to 1000
Rule 0	0.1	0.01	0.1	0.1
Rule 1	0.01	0.1	0.01	0.01
Rule 2	0.01	0.01	0.01	0.2

Table 2.1. Sample acceptance rates for different time step ranges.

Figure 2.5 shows the situation when the exploration is insufficient. The weights of the recommendation rules at each time step are calculated according to the formula (3.2.1). The recommendation system pursues greedy behavior. Figure 2.5 illustrates both the Exploration Situation 1 and Exploration Situation 2. As long as Rule 0 receives positive feedback, it blocks any further exploration. Although the algorithm detects that at step 300 the acceptance rate falls, it is unable to provide an alternative recommendation. When at step 750 the acceptance rate of previously unpopular Rule2 suddenly grows, the algorithm is unable to react adequately.

Figure 2.6 shows the development of weights with aging applied. The weights of the recommendation rules at each time step are calculated according to the formula (3.2.4) with parameter T=25. The weight of the recommendation rule Rule0 reacts quickly to the changes in popularity, but this is not enough to ensure exploration, since the weights of other recommendation rules are too low.

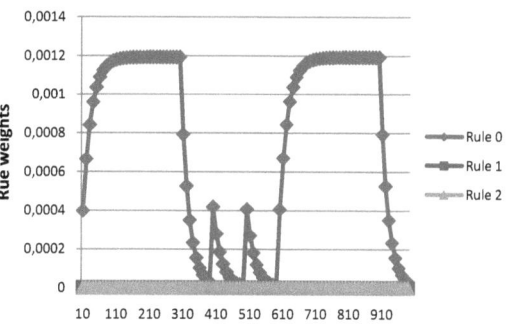

Fig. 2.6. Exploration vs. expoitation: aging applied

Figure 2.7 shows the case when Exploration Situation 1 is solved by using optimistic initial weights and Exploration Situation 2 is partially solved by using aging. When the system detects that the acceptance rate of the currently presented recommendation rule is falling, other recommendation rules are allowed to be explored. The behavior of the Rule2 illustrates why aging solves the exploration problem only partially. Indeed, although the Rule2 has gained popularity in step 750, it has only started to be presented after step 900 when Rule0 has become sufficiently unpopular. If the Rule0 keeps being sufficiently popular, Rule2 would not be presented even though its acceptance rate is higher. If ε-greedy balancing is in use, such issues do not arise. This however does not mean that ε-greedy balancing is guaranteed to achieve better results in general. Indeed, the ε-greedy balancing needs to show random recommendations at times, including the ones with the lowest acceptance rates.

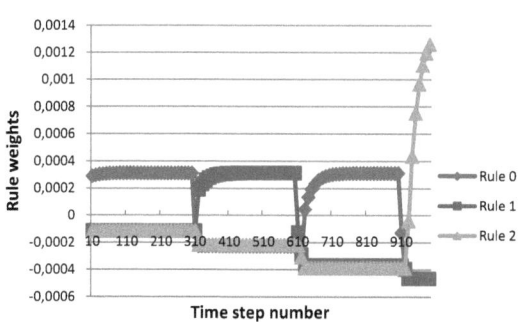

Fig. 2.7. Exploration vs. expoitation: problem of insufficient exploration partially solved

Recommendations presented by the aging-based balancing may not always be the best of all available recommendations but are usually sufficiently good. The best balancing method should be determined experimentally for a concrete situation. We have compared different ways of balancing exploration and exploitation experimentally in a simulated environment. The results of the experiments are provided in Section 6.

3.4 Feedback Values

Different events induced by the web users can be assigned different feedback values. Following are the typical cases which can result in feedback in an e-commerce environment:

1. Viewing a product as a result of recommendation (recommendation accepted/clicked)
2. Adding a product into to the shopping cart as a result of recommendation
3. Checking out the shopping cart which contains a product which was added as a result of recommendation
4. Successful payment for the product which was added to the shopping cart as a result of recommendations
5. Ignoring the recommendation

The first four cases generate positive feedback; the last case can be considered for either negative or neutral feedback. In our system, the feedback influences the weights of the recommendation rules, i.e. the individual recommendations presented in a certain context. It is also possible to use feedback in other ways, for example to influence the selection of the recommendation generators as described in [TR04][TGR04][6].

The selection of concrete feedback values is left to the person who is installing and configuring the recommendation system in the given environment. This person should decide, how important different events caused by the recommendation system are and to what extent they should influence the future behavior of the recommendation system. This relative importance could be for example expressed as follows:

- Recommendation clicked: 1
- Add recommended product to shopping cart: 5
- Check out shopping cart with recommended product: 5
- Received payment for recommended product: 10
- Recommendation not clicked: 0

---

[6] For detailed discussion and comparison please see Section 4.5

In this example, the same recommendation rule can obtain feedback several times for the same presentation. Some of this feedback will reach the recommendation rule with time delay. Such delayed feedback should however be distinguished from the delayed reward in the sense of full reinforcement learning problem [KLM96]. In full reinforcement learning problem the agent can make several steps until it receives reward in the so-called terminal state. Delayed reward in this sense is usually a discounted reward which is given to actions which have been taken in non-terminal states. In our recommendation system each step is a terminal step and receives undiscounted reward either immediately or after a time delay.

Alternatively to the static feedback values as mentioned above, we could use feedback values which reflect the revenue of profit generated by the product. Some researchers also consider the viewing time as a possible source for feedback, suggesting that if a web page is viewed for longer time, it means that it is more interesting to the web user. We argue that such intuition is unfounded, since longer viewing times can also be caused by other factors, such as web user being distracted or switching to another browser window.

Another alternative for setting the feedback values is using explicit feedback. Explicit feedback is gathered by asking the user on the website to rate the presented recommendations. Such feedback has been widely considered in the early research on recommendation systems and is rarely used in the recent research. The chief reasons for this are the additional burden put on web users (something which particularly e-commerce systems are striving to avoid) and possibilities for unfair manipulation of the recommendations. We do not employ explicit feedback in our system. For a discussion of the implicit and explicit feedback please see [Lawr03].

In our prototypes EC and EDU we have not been able to use all variants of feedback mentioned above. The EDU prototype was not an e-commerce website and therefore the cases 2, 3 and 4 were not relevant. In the EC prototype the shopping cart and payments were implemented in a separate system to which we did not have direct access. We also did not have access to the information which is needed to set the dynamic feedback values representing revenue or profit. Therefore, we had to constrain ourselves to cases 1 and 5, namely "Recommendation clicked" and "Recommendation not clicked". The feedback values in our prototypes are discussed in Chapter 4.

The absolute values of the feedback values are not important in general case, since the recommendation rules are selected for presentation by comparison to each other and not to some absolute value. The case when the absolute feedback values become important is when we need to relate it to the initial weights supplied by the recommendation generators. This is more important for optimization algorithms using aging and less important for algorithms using ε-greedy balancing without aging. Indeed, the algorithms without aging use the formula (3.2.1) which overrides the initial weights after the first presentation. On the contrary, in the formula (3.2.4) used by the aging-based algorithms the initial weights play significant role for many presentations in the initial optimization phase. To ensure sufficient exploration in the initial optimization phase, aging-based algorithms rely on initial weights being optimistic, i.e. high enough to be presented sufficient number of times in the initial phase. We find it convenient to control that by employing negative feedback values. Since our recommendation generators generate initial weights in the range [0..1], such initial weights should be optimistic in particular with respect to the already existing recommendation rules with lesser quality if negative feedback is used. How optimistic such initial weights are depends on the value of negative feedback. We investigate the different values of negative feedback experimentally in Subsection 6.1.4 basing on the simulated environment.

3.5 Optimization Algorithms

The generalized algorithm for optimized selection of recommendations is shown below:

N - number of recommendations needed, $\{P\}=\{P_1,...., P_K\}$ - set of parameters, describing the current context of the website
1:{C}=MatchContentNodes({P})   // Set of matching content nodes
2:{U}=MatchUserNodes({P})   // Set of matching content nodes
3:{T}=MatchTimeNodes({P})   // Set of matching content nodes
4:{R}=GetRecommendations(P,{C},{U},{T})   // applying selection policy P to obtain the set of recommendation rules {R}, |R|≤N
5: PresentRecommendations({R})   // Present the recommendations on the website
6: {F_R}=GatherFeedback()   // Get the feedback from user.
7: AdjustWeights({R},{F_R})   // Adjust weights of the recommendation rules according to feedback

The implementations of functions GetRecommendations(), GatherFeedback() and AdjustWeights() can vary depending on the chosen optimization technique. So, the implementation of the GetRecommendations() is responsible for having or not having the random exploration component. The function GatherFeedback contains the definitions of the numeric feedback values for different user actions. The function AdjustWeights() determines whether aging is applied to the weights of the recommendation rules.

Using the techniques described in the previous subsection to solve the problems of handling the "drift of interest" and balancing exploration versus exploitation, we have constructed several algorithms for optimizing the presentation of the recommendations:

- REWARD_ONLY. This algorithm uses ε-greedy technique to balance between exploration and exploitation. The "drift of interest" is not accounted for, i.e. no aging is used and the weights of the recommendation rules are calculated according to the formula (3.2.1).

- REWARD_DEC (reward-decay). This algorithm combines aging by exponential decaying according to formula (3.2.4) with ε-greedy balancing technique. Negative feedback values are not used since ε-greedy technique provides for sufficient exploration even in the initial phase, thus making optimistic initial weights redundant.

- REWARD_PEN (reward-penalty). This algorithm uses aging by exponential decaying and negative feedback values. The algorithm relies on aging for exploration and does not perform random exploration.

The detailed experimental analysis and comparison of the above algorithms is presented in the next chapter.

It is also possible to construct other recommendation optimization algorithms by combining or modifying the techniques we have described. However, in our preliminary experiments with these algorithms we have not been able to achieve improvement in comparison to the algorithms listed above. We discuss these algorithms here but do not further analyze them in Chapter 4. In particular, we have considered the following algorithms:

- The ε-*greedy* algorithm with negative feedback values.
- The algorithm combining aging by exponential decaying, negative feedback and ε-random selection of the recommendations for exploration.

In case of the first algorithm we have found out that the negative feedback values do not have any influence on the learning, since only the relative values are important for selection of recommendation rules. The optimistic initial weights are not relevant for the ε-*greedy* technique, since the ε-*greedy* technique always dedicates a fraction of recommendations to exploration.

The motivation for the second algorithm was the fact that the aging-based balancing technique does not guarantee sufficient exploration, in particular in Exploration Situation 2. There are cases, when all the recommendations currently presented on the website are clicked so often, that the aging with a given parameter T cannot sufficiently decrease the weights of these recommendations to expose other underexplored recommendations in the time interval between two clicks. To overcome this problem, we have investigated the possibility of augmenting the aging-based exploration with exploration implemented according to ε-*greedy* technique, i.e. introduce a fraction of the presentations in which the recommendations are selected according to a pseudorandom number generator.

According to our experience, the application of this algorithm increases the number of parameters which needs to be set but does not bring an improvement of the acceptance rate. Apparently, the deterioration of the acceptance rate caused by the random component is larger than the improvement achieved through guaranteed exploration.

4. IMPLEMENTATION OF THE REAL-LIFE PROTOTYPES AND THE SIMULATED ENVIRONMENT

To comprehensively evaluate our recommendation system approach, we have performed a series of experiments in different environments. So, the evaluations of the different recommendation generators were done on the EDU website. The recommendation system implemented on this website was a joint work with A. Thor [TR04][TGR04], who has been working on the optimization of recommendation systems based on selection of different recommendation generators as opposed to selection of individual recommendations which is described in this thesis. On this website, we have also tested the effects of presenting different recommendations to different user groups. The effects of the optimization of recommendations in an e-commerce environment were studied on the prototype EC. The simulated prototype SIM provided a platform for thorough investigation of different optimization algorithms and parameter settings.

In this chapter we describe the implementations of our real-life prototypes and the simulation environment. In the first sections of the chapter we describe the real-life experimental environments we used (Section 4.1) and the adaptation of our generic recommendation system architecture to these environments (Section 4.2). In Section 4.3 we provide a description for the simulated environment and the data from the EC prototype which were used to create it. Section 4.4 elaborates on the structure of relational databases used in our prototypes to implement recommendation rule database and web data warehouse.

4.1 Real-life Prototype Implementations

The prototypes of the adaptive recommendation system corresponding to the general architecture described in the previous chapters were implemented and applied at two real-life websites. The first one is the website of the Database Group, University of Leipzig (http://dbs.uni-leipzig.de, approximately 2000 page views per day), further denoted as EDU. It shows two (N=2) recommendations on all html-pages of the site. This prototype was developed as a joint work with A. Thor. In particular, the implementations of the recommendation generators used on the EDU website are due to A. Thor. This prototype was used to study the user group based recommendations and to compare two approaches to optimizing the web recommendations. Both optimization approaches are based on user feedback. In the first approach implemented by A. Thor the optimization was done by adaptive switching of different recommendation generators. In the second approach (the approach presented in this thesis) the optimization was done by combining the recommendations from different recommendations generators and adjusting their weights individually. The website EDU contains information related to teaching and research in the area of database technology at the University of Leipzig. This information includes for example study material, research papers, personal pages of the researchers.

The second real-life application of our architecture is a mid-size commercial online software store (http://www.softunity.com, approximately 5000 page views per day), further denoted as EC. The online store is run by the German company Koch Media GmbH (http://www.kochmedia.com/). Here, our approach is used to automatically select and present five (N=5) recommendations on the product detail pages. The products presented on the website include computer and console games, software for home use and supporting products such as solution books for games and accessories for home computers and game consoles. The product details presented on the website include pictures, screenshots and text descriptions. Sometimes a trial or protected version of the software product is offered for download.

Both websites have around 2500 content pages. The recommendation database contains about 60000 rules for (EDU) and 35000 rules for (EC).

All recommendation generators and the optimizer on the EDU and EC websites, as well as the websites themselves, are implemented using the PHP scripting language. The experimental data from the EDU website presented here were obtained in the period from April 2003 to September 2004. The experimental data from the EC website were obtained from December 2003 to May 2005.

The implementation effort for creating the EC prototype amounts to 2 man-months. The EDU prototype was created by porting the recommendation system used on the EC prototype in several days. Such swift development was made possible by the generic nature of our architecture as well as by the fact that the website-specific components such as web data warehouse and recommendation generators were already implemented by A. Thor.

4.2 Adaptation of The Generic Architecture to The Prototypes

Our generic recommendation system architecture has been adapted to two specific real-life websites. We have described some of the specific implementation details in the previous sections as examples of implementation of our generic architecture. In this section we summarize the correspondences between our generic architecture and concrete prototype implementations.

4.2.1 Web Usage Data: Crawler Detection, Data Cleaning

A crucial problem for a recommendation system which utilizes web usage data is the preparation and cleaning of these data. The most common source which provides web usage data is the log files of the web server. Although some researchers consider working directly with usage data represented in this form, for a number of reasons it is beneficial to transfer the usage data into a relational database. The following reasons speak for using a relational database to store the web usage data [RS03]:

- Large amounts of data. The amount of web usage data even on smaller websites grows very fast. If we need to analyze such data over longer periods of time, the amount of web usage data can grow to multiple Terabytes. Accessing such data for analysis in sequential manner, as usual for plain files, can be prohibitively slow. A relational database with its index structures ensures the feasibility of the analysis.
- Flexible analysis. Relational databases support a large number of possibilities for analyzing the data ranging from ad-hoc queries to interactive tools for OLAP analysis and data mining.
- Using a relational data representation, it is easy to establish relations with data coming from other data sources, for example with a database containing information about registered web users or about the products presented on the website.

In our architecture we follow the approach of storing the web usage data into a relational database. In constructing such relational database we adhere to the data warehouse technology, which offers a specially designed relational schema optimized for performing analysis of the large volumes of data. The resulting database is called web data warehouse and is shown as one of the components of our architecture in Figure 2.2. The relational structure of the web data warehouse is discussed in Section 4.4.

Before any analysis can be performed on the web usage data, the data needs to be prepared and cleaned. Sometimes this preparation is done during the process of loading the data into the data warehouse; sometimes it makes sense to prepare the data after they are loaded into the relational database. Usually the following tasks need to be performed:

- **Session reconstruction.** In case when the sessions are not supported by the web server or application server directly, it may be hard to determine whether different page views belong to the same sessions. Special algorithms have been proposed for accomplishing this task. These algorithms are however mostly heuristic and do not guarantee the gapless reconstruction of sessions. In the EDU prototype, the session reconstruction was implemented by A. Thor by combining several session reconstruction techniques [TR04]. The primary technique for maintaining sessions is so-called "HTTP cookies"[7]. If the HTTP cookies are not supported by the client web browser, a set of heuristics is applied. This set of heuristics analyzes the information contained in the HTTP Request which came from the web user, such as IP address, access time, browser type etc. and determines whether different requests belong to the same session. In the EC prototype, we make use of the ability of the application server to maintain sessions. The application server is able to maintain sessions both using cookies and, if cookies are not available, using a special parameter "session identifier" which is automatically added to the URL. Utilizing this application server feature does not require additional

---

[7] For specification of HTTP Cookies see RFC-2956, http://www.rfc-editor.org/

development effort in the web application. Instead of putting the usage information into log files in text format, our application puts all available information including the session id into a temporary database. The usage data are then transferred from the temporary database into the web data warehouse.

- **Crawler detection and removal of page views originating from crawlers.** Crawlers are programs which automatically surf the Internet and gather information. Crawlers are also known as "robots" or "bots". Most commonly the crawlers are used by search engines such as google.com and yahoo.com to update their search databases. The appearance of crawlers can distort the web usage data, since crawlers do not behave like normal web users. They usually follow all links found on the website and generate larger amount of usage data. Therefore, to obtain the correct picture of the web user behavior we need to detect and remove the sessions originated by crawlers. An interesting approach to the elimination of crawler sessions is proposed by [TR04][8]. The detection of the crawler sessions in [TR04] is done by placing a special hyperlink on the website, which is visible only to web crawlers and not to human website visitors. This approach can be used to reliably distinguish between the sessions coming from crawlers and human users after the complete page view history of a session has been captured. This approach is however not suitable for use with online feedback, since the access to the hidden hyperlink may occur later in the session. We discuss the online crawler detection in Section 4.2.4.

- **Page view detection.** An additional problem which needs to be solved in many web applications is the page view detection. Each page view usually consists of several HTTP requests. One of them is the main request which is triggered immediately by the user; other requests are sent by the browser to obtain supporting information, such as subdocuments, pictures and multimedia objects. In many web applications built with traditional technology this problem can be solved relatively easy, since the main HTTP request usually asks for an HTML-file and the auxiliary requests ask for other types of data. However in modern web applications built using so-called AJAX[9] technology such a straightforward solution doesn't work, since such applications also request auxiliary data in HTML format. In the EDU prototype we consider the requests for HTML documents to be the page views and all other requests to be auxiliary. In the EC prototype the web application takes care of logging only the main page view request and not the auxiliary requests.

---

[8] Discussed in more detail in Section 5.4
[9] For more information about AJAX technology please see http://www.w3schools.com/Ajax/ajax_intro.asp

4.2.2 Ontology Graphs and Ontology Generators in Prototypes

The ontology graphs have been specially designed to help incorporate the implementation-specific features into our generic architecture. Our prototypes EC and EDU make use of the ontology graphs as follows:

EC: The prototype EC features all three possible ontologies for content, user and time. The content ontology for the EC prototype contains all products and categories in the web shop, with relations between products and categories. There are several types of product detail pages on the EC website, for example normal product detail page or product highlight page (special page layout for best-selling products). For our recommendations system it is less important which layout is used to present the product; important is the product that is shown. The mapping clauses for the content ontology nodes in the EC prototype therefore use product ids for mapping, disregarding the URL under which the product is shown, for example:

ProductID='ECD000687K'

In case of the EC prototype, the content ontology is present in the website database in form of hierarchical product catalog and needs to be extracted and converted into the representation used by our recommendation system. The implementation of the content ontology generator is therefore quite straightforward.

The user ontology graph of the EC prototype consists only of three nodes which represent the countries in which the purchased products can be delivered: Germany and Luxembourg, Austria, Switzerland and Liechtenstein. This information is determined basing on explicit country selection by the web user and is instantly available for use in the mapping clauses. An example of the mapping clause is given below:

UserCountry='CH' or UserCountry='FL'

The time ontology of the EC prototype consists of several nodes which denote certain periods of time when some time-restricted sales offers are effective. These nodes are used for several manually specified recommendation rules. The nodes and the attached mapping clauses are also created manually. An example of the mapping clauses for the time ontology:

WeekOfTheYear=50 or WeekOfTheYear=51

EDU: The prototype EDU uses only two ontologies, content ontology and user ontology.

The content ontology for the EDU prototype contains the URLs of the web pages on the server. That means that even if the same content were shown on two pages with different URLs, this would be represented as two different nodes in the content ontology of the EDU prototype. In the EDU prototype, the content ontology is implicitly present in the directory structure on the web server. The ontology generator extracts this information and converts it into the format understood by our recommendation system. In the EDU prototype, the mapping clauses for the content ontology graph use the names of HTML (or PDF etc.) files. An example of the mapping clause is given below:

URL like '%/study/wintersemester0809/database_systems1.html'

The user ontology graph of the EDU prototype is created using a decision tree algorithm J48[10]. The decision tree predicts the interest area of the user based on the user's country. An example for the node representing users interested mostly in research topics is given below:

UserCountry in ('in','cn','us','ru','se','gr','jp','ca','id','kw','np','hk','nl','ua')

The value of UserCountry for each user is determined based on the lookup of his[11] IP address in the open database of IP addresses GeoLite Country[12].

Further details about the user ontology graph for the prototype EDU can be found in Section 5.3.

We have also considered creating the time ontology in the EDU prototype and utilizing it for making time-specific recommendations for students. Possible cases where the time-specific recommendations could be useful are for example recommending examination announcements at the end of each semester or study plan in the beginning of each semester. However, we have not implemented this feature in our prototype.

As can be seen from the examples in this subsection, the mapping clauses can be readily used as part of SQL queries to quickly select the relevant nodes from a table in a relational database. In Section 6.2 we further investigate the retrieval of information from the ontology graphs stored in a relational database and in main memory.

4.2.3 Recommendation Rule Generators in the Prototypes.

The following recommendation generators were used in our prototype implementations:

- Content similarity. This recommendation generator determines for each product (EC) or HTML page (EDU) the M most similar products using TF*IDF text similarity score. We have used the implementation of the normalized TF*IDF algorithm which is provided by the MySQL database server[13]. The parameter M is configured for the specific website. We have used M=5 on the EDU prototype and M=10 on the EC prototype. The initial weight of the recommendation rules is the TF*IDF similarity score as returned by the algorithm.

---

[10] Weka's improved implementation of the C4.5 algorithm [Quin93].
[11] In this thesis, the masculine pronomena are used to refer to both masculine and fenimine persons.
[12] http://www.maxmind.com/app/geoip_country
[13] http://dev.mysql.com/doc/internals/en/full-text-search.html

- Sequence patterns. This recommendation generator recommends products (EC) or HTML Pages (EDU) most often succeeding other products/pages in the same user session. The initial weight is set to the probability of one product or page succeeding the other one based on the historical information from the web usage warehouse.

- Item-to-Item collaborative filtering. (EC) Products, which most often appear together in one user's basket, are recommended for each other. Collaborative filtering is considered the most successful recommendation technique, although some limitation and drawbacks of this recommendation technique are known. So-called item-to-item variant of collaborative filtering eliminates some of the scalability problems which the classical collaborative filtering has. This type of collaborative filtering produces the recommendation rules of the format which fits well into our data structure. Item-to-item collaborative filtering is due to [LSY03]. The initial weights provided by the recommendation generator are based on cosine similarity as described in [LSY03].

- Search Engine recommendation generator (EDU). This recommendation generator is applicable to the users coming from a search engine such as Google. It extracts the search keywords from the HTTP Referrer field and uses the website's internal search engine to generate recommendations for each keyword. The recommendation generator was first described and implemented in [TR04]. The initial weights are set based on the relevance score which is provided by the website's internal search engine.

4.2.4 Capturing Online Feedback in Prototypes

In both prototypes the clicks on recommendations were considered as feedback with value 1. If negative feedback was not in use, we used the value 0 to denote that the user has not accepted the recommendation. If negative feedback was used, its value was different in different experiments as described later in this chapter. Theoretically, for the EC prototype we could have richer possibilities for feedback. So, for example, we could have additional feedback if the product is put into basket, when the basket is checked or when the transfer of the money for the purchased product is confirmed. We could also let our feedback values be influenced by the profit brought by the individual product. We were however not allowed by the website owners to access the data and programming interfaces needed to implement these additional kinds of feedback. Therefore the feedback for our EC prototype depends only on users clicking or not clicking the recommendation links.

An important issue for the online optimization is filtering out the feedback from crawlers. Not all crawler detection techniques which can be applied to the web usage data in general are applicable for online crawler detection. In particular the reliable technique utilizing a hidden hyperlink as proposed in [TR04] is not applicable here, since the order in which crawlers access the hyperlinks is different for every crawler and it is possible, that a recommendation hyperlink is visited and gets feedback before the hidden hyperlink is visited. In this case the recommendation would receive false feedback. For the online case we have to fall back onto the less reliable heuristic techniques. One such technique is checking whether the file "/robots.txt" is the first page view of the session. This technique relies on the "de-facto" internet standard [Kost96] which specifies the method for controlling the behavior of the web robots and crawlers by the website owners. This control method assumes that the first request a crawler should send to a website is a request for the file "/robots.txt". The file robots.txt specifies which areas of the website are allowed be indexed be the crawlers. Our recommendation system checks the first HTTP request of the current session. If request for "/robots.txt" was the first request of the current session, the session is ignored by the recommendation system. Another technique is based on the publicly available databases of robots and crawlers. These databases contain lists of IP addresses and values of HTTP-attribute "User-Agent", which can be used to detect crawlers and robots. To implement this type of online crawler detection in our prototype, we have combined the lists from the websites http://www.user-agents.org/ which contains the values of User-Agent attribute and http://www.robotstxt.org/ which contains both the values of User-Agent attribute and the IP-addresses of known crawlers.

4.3 Simulated Environment Overview

Initially, we were planning to perform all the experiments on the real-life websites. However, it has turned out that the amount of usage data generated by users of the EC and EDU is not sufficient to adequately explore various algorithms and algorithm parameters. To be able to comparatively test different approaches, we had to split the presentations between them. In one year, we could comparatively test only 5 combinations of different recommendation techniques and parameters, including the baseline technique without optimization.

To overcome the problem of insufficient usage data on the available real-life websites, we have created a simulation environment to extensively test the different combinations to determine the optimal parameter values. To implement the simulation environment, we have taken the usage data from the http://www.softunity.com (EC). The usage data were taken from a period of 12 months, January 2006 until July 2006 and September 2006 to January 2007 inclusive. August 2006 was omitted, since due to a server crash and subsequent website relocation very few data were available for August 2006.

During this period, the adaptive recommendation system installed on the EC website was disabled in order not to influence the obtained usage data. The following data from the EC website were used to perform the simulation:

- Start pages of all sessions, i.e. all pages from which the users have started a navigation session on the site, in chronological order of the sessions. The page views originating from web crawlers were eliminated from the usage data we are using for simulation. For the described period, there were 784,747 sessions with a total of 971,197 page views.
- The session length distribution. The session length distribution for the described period is shown in Figure 2.8. The average session length for the EC website in this period was ~1.237. There has been a small number of sessions containing more than 25 page views. We deem such sessions to come not from human users but from unknown crawlers. Such sessions are not used in the simulation.

For every month, the conditional probabilities of the product to be viewed after another product in one session are calculated based on the above data. The product information and the recommendation rules with their initial weights were also taken from the EC website.

To test the different optimization algorithms with different parameter combinations, we used simulation runs. For every experiment described later in this section, the average results obtained from 10 runs are presented. The user behavior in every run is reproduced by an agent based on a pseudo-random number generator. The agent is presented all session start pages from EC in chronological order. For every page, the agent is provided with a selection of several recommendations. The agent may select one of the recommendations or not select any. If the agent selects a recommendation, it is presented the page the recommendation was leading to. On this new page, it is presented a list of several recommendations again. The agent's decision whether to continue the session or not is based on the session length distribution as shown in Figure 2.8. The selection of the recommendations by the agent is based on the conditional probability of a product to be seen after another product for the month in which the page view takes place.

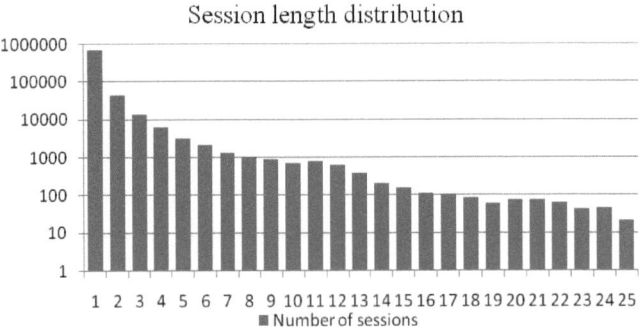

Figure 2.8. Distribution of the session lengths on the EC prototype. Number of sessions is shown on the logarithmic axis y.

To test the different parameters, the following routine is used: we generate a set of seeds for pseudo-random generator. For each algorithm/parameter combination we want to test, we make several runs, every time with a different seed from the set. To test another algorithm/combination, we use the same set of seeds. This way, different algorithms combinations are tested on agents behaving in a similar way; however any non-common behavior the specific agent may have is alleviated by averaging multiple runs. The simulation environment was implemented in Java programming language. In all experiments in this section the number of simultaneously presented recommendations N is set to 5, unless explicitly stated otherwise.

4.4 Database Structure

4.4.1 Recommendation Database

The recommendation rules are stored in a relational database. Both our real-life prototypes and the simulation environment use MySQL database server for the recommendation database. The relational schema of the recommendation rule database is shown in Figure 2.9. The rules are maintained in the table *Rules*. Some additional information is stored together with the rules, such as the number of times the recommendation was presented ($N_{presented}$), number of times the recommendation was clicked ($N_{clicked}$), the recommendation type (the recommendation generator which

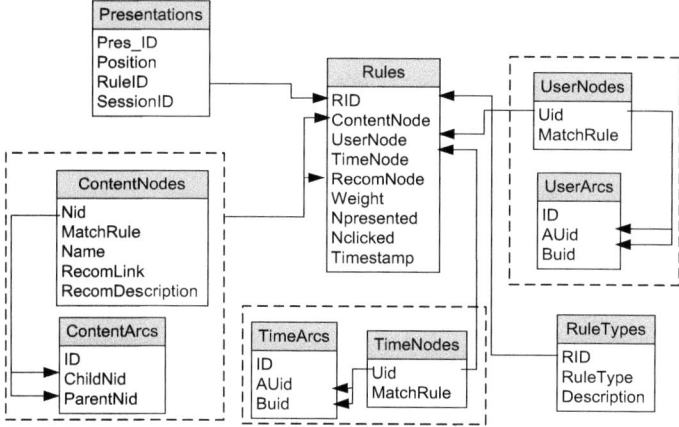

Figure 2.9. Structure of the recommendation database

generated the rule), and the creation time of the rule. The attributes ContentNode, UserNode and TimeNode are the foreign keys which uniquely identify the values of the respective context dimension (null values are allowed to cover the partially specified context information). RecomNode identifies the recommended content and thus also refers to the ContentNodes table.

The context dimensions are stored in pairs of tables ContentNodes/ContentArcs, UserNodes/UserArcs, TimeNodes/TimeArcs to allow the representation of ontology graphs. This representation of the ontology graphs is straightforward but has potential performance drawbacks. We discuss the ways of improving the performance of the ontology graph in Section 6.2. The node tables contain information on all relevant content items (products or URLs), users and time events that may occur in the context or recommendation part of a rule. The recommended content is represented by the fields Name, RecomLink and RecomDescription in ContentNodes.

The table *RuleTypes* specifies from which recommendation generator algorithm a given recommendation rule comes. The same recommendation rule may come from several recommendation generators.

The table *Presentations* is used to temporarily store the information about user recommendation presentations and the session identifiers. The data in this table is regularly moved to the web data warehouse to allow further evaluation.

4.4.2 Web Data Warehouse

The Web Data Warehouse was implemented using Microsoft SQL Server 2000. Microsoft SQL Server 2000 provides extensive functions and tools which simplify the creation of data warehouses and analytical processing of the data. The following functions are available in MS SQL Server 2000:

Partitioned tables. Partitioned tables simplify and speed up processing the large tables. The fact tables in our data warehouse are good candidates for horizontal partitioning on the date key. By partitioning the tables we can improve the speed of adding and removing the data. The adding of data to the data warehouse is accelerated due to the ability to first load the data and then to build the indexes, as opposed to the costly operation of index update. The removal of data is sped up by the ability to easily remove or move entire partitions, which is a typical operation for data warehouses where older data are regularly relocated to archive.

Bulk load facility. Bulk load facility allows faster loading of the large portions of data into tables in the database. Analogous to partitioned table, bulk load facility speeds up the loading by deferring the updates of the indexes until all data rows are loaded.

Microsoft Data Transformation Services (DTS). Microsoft Data Transformation Services is a powerful toolkit for data extraction, transformation and integration, suitable for flexible creation of the ETL (extract, transform, load) tools. Microsoft Data Transformation Services provide the possibility to graphically specify the workflow and data flow with data transformations. It allows scheduling of the data extraction, transformation and loading tasks.

Microsoft Analysis Services is providing the multidimensional database, the tools for creation of the OLAP cubes with different storage types (MOLAP, ROLAP, HOLAP) and the data mining algorithms, such as "Microsoft Clustering", "Microsoft Association",

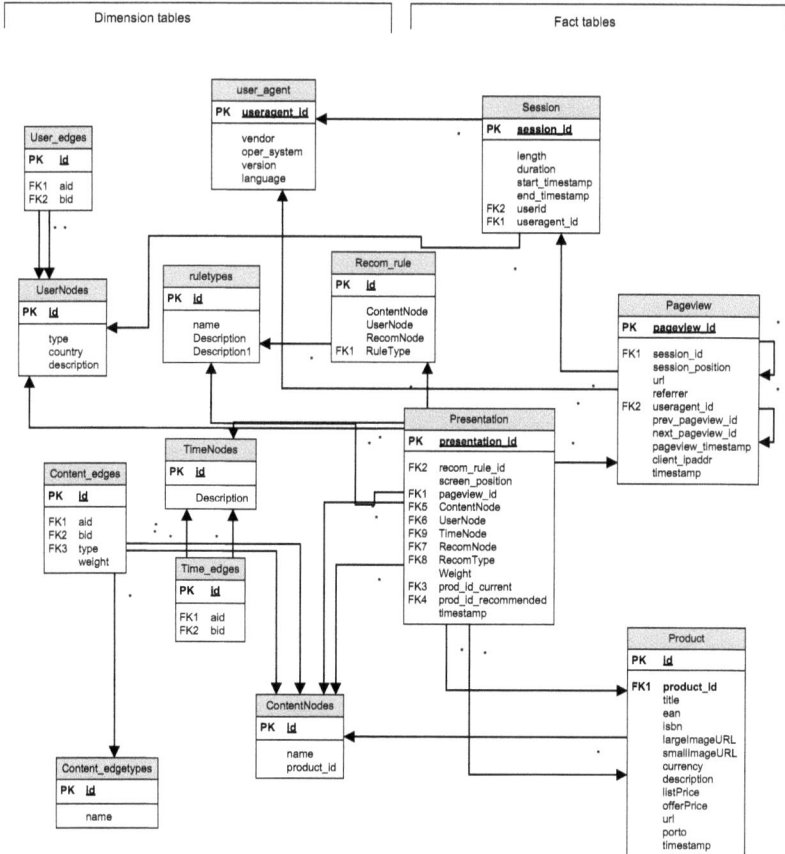

Figure 2.10. Database structure of the web data warehouse (EC)

"Microsoft Sequence Clustering" and others. Additional tools need to be used for visualization of the OLAP cubes. An example of such tool is the PivotChart/PivotTable COM-object supplied with Microsoft Office.

The relational database schema of the web data warehouse is shown in Figure 2.10. The schema shown here is the one that was used on the EC prototype. The data warehouse used on the EDU has a similar relational schema. However, it has some distinctions due to the fact that the recommendations were presented not on a product basis but on a HTML page basis. The data warehouse used for the EDU prototype also has additional tables and fields which serve to support the optimization approaches based on the recommendation generator selection and to perform comparative analysis of the approaches based on the recommendation generator selection and the approaches based on the optimized selection of individual recommendations.

The structure of the web data warehouse is specific to the domain of e-commerce as well as to the functions the data warehouse has to support. The data warehouse holds historic data about the web usage and changes in product assortment. The task of the web data warehouse is to support executing analytic queries, building the OLAP cubes and performing data mining. The data warehouse is based on a galaxy schema with several fact tables and multiple dimension tables which are shared between fact tables. We use an ETL process created using the Microsoft Data Transformation Services toolkit to import both web usage data and auxiliary data such as information about products. The ETL process is executed periodically. Although it has been a common practice in web usage mining systems to use the log files of the web server to update the data warehouse, we use the temporary table Presentations of the recommendation rule database to feed the data warehouse, since this significantly the data transfer and cleaning.

Most modern application servers and web development frameworks are able to maintain sessions automatically and transparently manage the propagation of session identifiers between individual page views. A common practice for session identifier propagation is by using cookies when supported by the browser. If the cookies are not supported by the browser, the session identifier is transmitted as a query parameter in the request URL. The session identifier is also exposed to the web application. We make use of this feature and store the server-supplied session identifier for every presentation in the temporary table of the recommendation rule database. This significantly simplifies the ETL process: for example, we do not need to identify sessions in the ETL process. Some transformations are applied to the session and presentation data when they are transferred to the data warehouse. So, the start, end and duration and the number of page views (length) of the session is calculated based on the information in the table Presentations. For our prototype applications we also assume that the user component of the recommendation context stays constant during the entire session and for the sake of simpler analysis associate every session with a certain user node. In general, however, it is possible for the user component of the context to change within one session, for example when the user has a possibility to specify some of its attributes, such as language, country etc. explicitly on the website.

We have created several OLAP-Cubes: Session, Pageview, Presentation and Product. The cubes are based respectively on the tables with identical names in the data warehouse as fact tables. The fact tables are shown on the right side in Figure 2.10. The tables Session and Pageview hold the information regarding the usage of the website.

The table Presentation logs the presentations of the recommendations and whether the user clicked on them. The table Products contains the historical information about the products shown on the website. Some tables have redundancy in order to eliminate the need for additional joins, which speeds up the processing of the OLAP cubes. So for example the table Presentations contains not only the reference to the recommendation rule id, but also some information which is already contained in the recom_rule table, such as ContentNode, RecomNode, TimeNode, Presentation. Both tables Pageview and Session have the field "useragent_id".

The tables which contain historical data, i.e. several versions of the same objects at different times have artificial keys unique to the data warehouse. Tables such as Datasource, Recom_Rules etc. have their own artificial keys in the recommendation rule database. These keys uniquely identify the respective objects throughout the system's lifetime both in the recommendation rule database and in the data warehouse.

We use HOLAP (hybrid OLAP) implementation provided by the Microsoft SQL Server. The HOLAP partitioning is vertical, i.e. the detail data stay in the relational structure whereas the aggregated data are stored in the multidimensional structure. The cubes are processed incrementally at regular time intervals. The hybrid OLAP implementation allows maintaining a reasonable trade-off between the size of the OLAP cube and the time needed to perform multidimensional queries on the cube. The OLAP cubes are used for human evaluation of the web usage and product data. Data mining algorithms are used to generate the web recommendations based on the data stored in fact tables.

5. EXPERIMENTS ON REAL-LIFE PROTOTYPES

5.1 Prerequisites and Effects of the Optimized Recommendations

Figure 2.11 shows that the number of clicks per recommendation rule is distributed according to a Zipfian-like law (in Figure 2.11, only the recommendations with at least 100 presentations are considered.). The data shows that a relatively small percentage of the recommendation rules brings the majority of clicks. This supports our optimization heuristic, since it shows that we may achieve overall improvement of the acceptance rate by presenting the most successful recommendations more often.

The analysis of the customer and purchase data has also shown that 3.04% of all purchased products were bought immediately after clicking the recommendation, and 3.43% of all purchased products were recommended in the same session.

In general, 2.07% web users of www.softunity.com are becoming customers (this metric is usually regarded as CCR – Customer Conversion Rate). For web users who clicked a recommendation this value is 8.55%, i.e. more than four times higher.

The absolute percentage values which are presented in the experimental data seem to be very small. The acceptance rates of recommendations lie within 1%, with improvements through optimization measured in fractions of a percent. However, it is important to note, that according to the study [Shop07] the average customer conversion rate for internet shops lies between 2% and 3%. Therefore, a variation of the conversion rate amounting as small as a fraction of percent can be of large importance for the commercial success of an e-commerce website. For a larger website, even an improvement of 1 percent can result in revenue increase of hundred thousand to millions of euro per year. Also, the absolute values of the acceptance rates are influenced by aspects such as the layout of the website and the number of recommendations presented simultaneously. Therefore, it is important to study not the absolute values of the acceptance rates but their relative values for different

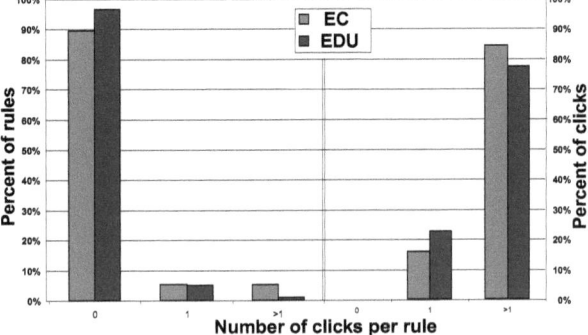

Fig. 2.11. A small percentage of recommendations brings the majority of clicks (EC, EDU)

algorithms.

Figure 2.12 shows the effects of our optimization algorithm in terms of buying behavior, in contrast to the non-optimized selection of the recommendations. The non-optimized algorithm uses the initial weights supplied by the recommendation generators as described in Section 4.2.3 to select the recommendations and performs no feedback-based optimization. Figure 2.12 shows that the optimized

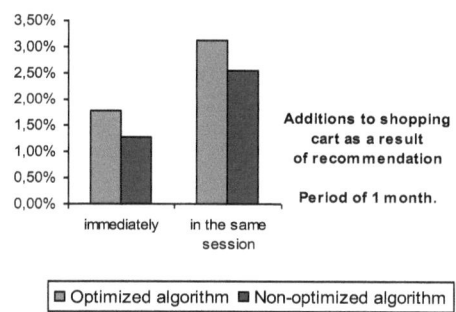

Fig. 2.12. Additions to basket as a result of recommendation (EC)

approach results in a noticeable increase of the number of additions to shopping carts.

The distribution of the number of presentations for the recommendation rules generated by different recommendation rule generators is shown in Figure 2.13. The average acceptance rate for the recommendation rules generated by the same generator is shown in Figure 2.14. Notably, the recommendations created manually have small number of presentations (due to the small number of manually created recommendation rules) but very high acceptance rate compared to the other types of recommendations, since they are based on human knowledge. An example of such manual recommendation on the EC website is the special "driving wheel" device for PC which is recommended as an accessory to the car racing games.

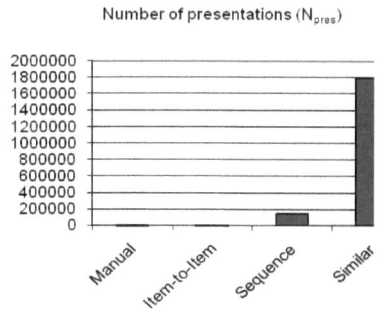

Figure 2.13. Presentation number for recommendation generated by different recommendation generators(EC)

5.2 Optimization Algorithms

To evaluate the effectiveness of the different optimization algorithms in the real-life environment, we have compared the performance of the reward-only and reward-penalty optimization algorithms with the selection of recommendations based on the initial weights supplied by the recommendation generators. For an evaluation period of several months the recommendation selection

5 Experiments on Real-Life Prototypes

algorithm on the EC website was chosen with equal probability from one of the following:

- REWARD_ONLY, ε-greedy balancing with ε=0.2 without aging
- REWARD_ONLY, ε-greedy balancing with ε=0.05 without aging
- REWARD_PEN, aging using exponential decaying with T=500 and negative feedback
- REWARD_PEN, aging using exponential decaying with T=200 and negative feedback
- without optimization, the recommendations are selected for presentation based on their initial weights as supplied by the recommendation generators

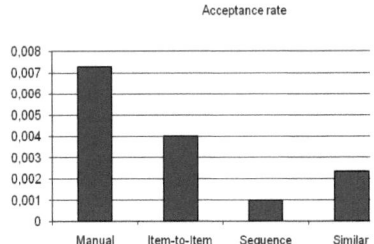

Figure 2.14. Acceptance rate of different recommendation generators (EC)

Originally we have been planning to conduct all experiments on the real-life prototype. However, it has turned out that the amount of feedback generated on the real-life website is not sufficient to thoroughly investigate all possible algorithms and parameter combinations. Therefore we have conducted the more thorough investigation in the simulated environment as described later in this chapter.

The comparison of the results obtained on the real-life website with the similar results obtained in the simulated environment can be used to judge about how well the behavior of our simulated environment represents the behavior of the real website. This comparison is presented in Subsection 6.1.8.

Figure 2.15 shows the comparison of the acceptance rate of different optimization algorithms as implemented in the real-life website. The results show that the optimized algorithms achieve higher acceptance rates than the algorithm without optimization.

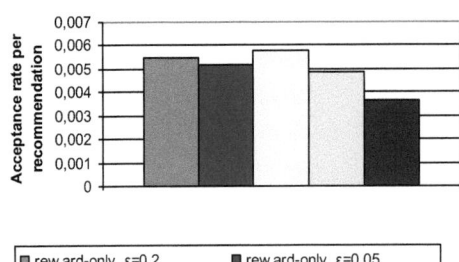

Fig. 2.15. Acceptance rate of different optimization algorithms (EC)

The algorithm which uses aging with T=500 was able to achieve somewhat higher acceptance rates than the algorithms which use ε-greedy balancing. The relatively small improvement of the reward-penalty algorithm can be attributed to the fact, that in our applications the successful and unsuccessful recommendations can be distinctly separated even by the simpler algorithms. The algorithm which used zero as initial weights for the recommendation rules was tested on the EDU website. Its acceptance rate was only 4% lower than that of the algorithm which used recommendation generator-specific initial weights. The feedback values for the algorithms based on ε-greedy technique were set as follows: 1 if the recommendation was clicked, 0 if the recommendation was not clicked. For the reward-penalty algorithms the feedback was set to 0 if the recommendation was clicked and to -0.01 if the recommendation was not clicked. A more elaborate discussion on the behavior of the individual algorithms is provided in Subsection 6.1.8.

5.3 User Groups

We have investigated the effects of automatically classifying users into user groups and presenting different recommendations to different user groups on our EDU prototype. Figure 2.16 shows the comparison of the acceptance rates for the different user groups. The user groups were built using a decision tree algorithm J48 over the usage data of several months from the EDU website. The EDU website is structured in several areas of interest, most important of which are Study and Research. For the decision tree algorithm, the area of interest (Research/Study) visited by the web user has served as a classification attribute; other attributes were "country", "browser" and "operating system" of the web user. However, after the tree was pruned, only the attribute "country" appeared to be of importance for predicting the area of interest. The resulting tree was transformed into the ontology graph nodes with mapping clauses. Figure 2.16 indicates that the acceptance rates differ substantially for the user groups and that for the website EDU the research-oriented users accept the presented recommendations almost twice as often as the study-oriented users. This behavior is explained by the fact that the research-oriented users are in most

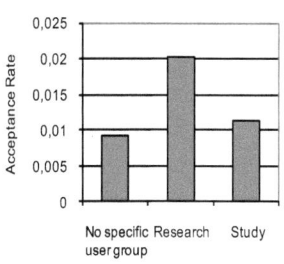

Fig. 2.16. Acceptance rates of different user groups (EDU)

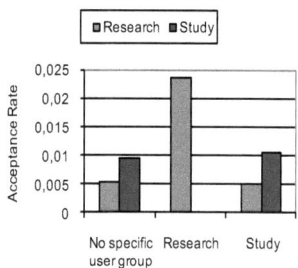

Fig. 2.17. Acceptance rates of user group based recommendation rules (EDU)

cases occasional users which are not familiar with the structure of the website and are therefore interested in recommendations which can quickly lead them from the start page to the desired content. Most study-oriented users, on the contrary, are students which come often to the website during the semester to check the information such as lecture scripts. After several visits such users usually memorize or bookmark the exact location of the content which is interesting for them and pay less attention to recommendations.

Figure 2.17 shows how good our user groups are in predicting the user interests. Here, differently colored bars show the acceptance for recommendations pointing to the content of different interest areas. The user group Research appears to be quite effective, since its users have only clicked the recommendations leading to the research area of the website. Users of the group Study preferred study-related recommendations but the corresponding acceptance rate is not much higher than for users not belonging to any of the two specific user groups.

In our EC prototype we are utilizing user groups as well. These user groups are also depending on the attribute "country". However, we are interested only in the three countries which are entitled to buy products on the EC website: Austria, Germany (with Luxembourg) and Switzerland (with Liechtenstein). The country (and therefore the user group) is determined in a straightforward way by the top level domain suffix: www.softunity.com and www.softunity.de are responsible for Germany, www.softunity.at is responsible for Austria and www.softunity.ch is responsible for Switzerland. The web users can also select their country manually on the website. The user groups on the EC website are also used to impose the country-specific restrictions on recommendations, since some of the products which can be sold in one country cannot be sold in another country (for example due to legal or trade restrictions). Therefore, such products can be recommended to users in one country and should not be recommended to users in another country. We do not provide the experimental results for the comparison of acceptance rates for different user groups on the EC prototype, since the aforementioned country-specific restrictions make the sets of recommendations for different countries incomparable.

5.4 Comparison of Recommendation Generator-Based Optimization and Recommendation-Based Optimization

Our prototype EDU was a project developed jointly with A. Thor. In this prototype we have implemented two different approaches to optimize web recommendations. In the architecture presented in this part of the thesis we use the optimization approaches which are targeted at individual recommendations, which can be classified as "mixed" according to [Burk02]. The approach proposed by A. Thor is the optimization of the selection of the recommendation generators based on machine learning, which can be classified as "switched" approach in terms of [Burk02]. This approach is described in [TR04][TGR04] and discussed in more detail in Section 7.4. In the prototype EDU the optimization approaches were tested on a rotating basis during the period from 1 April 2004 until 30

September 2004. The recommendation generators were identical for all tested optimization approaches.

Figure 2.18[14] shows the results of the experimental comparison of these two approaches and the approach "manual". The approach "manual" is a recommendation generator-based (i. e. "switched") approach, where the selection of one or another recommendation generator was specified manually with respect to

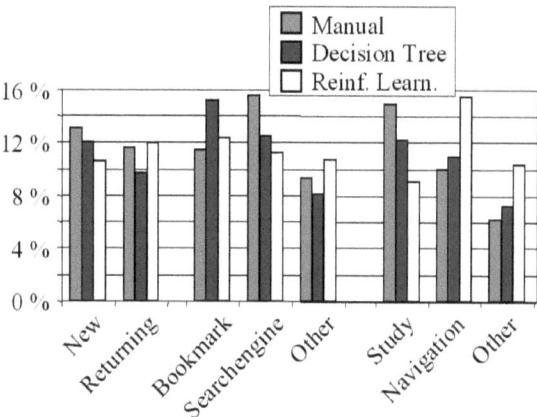

Figure 2.18. Session acceptance rates for different types of recommendattion generator based and recommendation based optimization (EDU)

the current context and basing on human knowledge. On the Y-Axis in Figure 2.18 we show the session acceptance rate for the different approaches. The session acceptance rate is the ratio of sessions which contain one or more accepted recommendations to the total number of sessions. In Figure 2.18 the approaches were compared using several independent criteria. The criteria are:

- whether the users were detected as new users or returning users.
- how the users came to the website: by using a bookmark (or directly entering the address of the website into the browser's address line), by using search engine or by following a link from another website.
- on which type of web page the session was started. There are two main groups of the web pages on the EDU website. The "navigation" pages are the main page of the website and the main pages of the sections of the website. These pages contain many hyperlinks to other web pages, for example to the "study" pages. The "study" pages contain the educational material, such as lecture notes. They contain large amounts of text and pictures and relatively few hyperlinks. Apart from "study" and "navigation" pages there were other types of pages which did not exhibit distinct differences in behavior with respect to the recommendation approaches.

It makes sense to analyze the different criteria together. So, the users coming from a search engine are likely to be new users and show accordingly similar distribution of the session acceptance rates. The success of the manual optimization approach for the users

---

[14] Figure 2.18 originates from [TGR04]

coming from a search engine is stipulated by the special "Search Engine" recommender, which intercepts the search terms entered by the user and shows the recommendations relevant for these search terms. The two automatic approaches show significant differences for sessions

Strategy	No. of rules	Acceptance rate	Session acceptance rate
Top-Rec	~2000	1.35%	10.27%
Decision Tree	~250	1.74%	11.13%
Reinf. Learning	~60000	1.92%	11.22%
Reinf. Learning Zero	~60000	1.87%	10.35%
Manual	5	1.97%	12.54%
Random	137	0.96%	6.98%

Table 2.2: Comparison of selection approaches

starting with a study page and a navigation page. As shown in Figure 2.18, the recommendation generator based approaches work better for "study" sessions; the reinforcement learning approach achieves better results for "navigation" and other types of sessions. The website where our prototype EDU was running contains a large number of study pages, whereas the number of navigation pages is rather small. However, the navigation pages receive almost 15 times more feedback per page than the study pages. Therefore, the recommendation-based selection approach can easily identify the best recommendations for the navigation pages but not for the study pages, since the feedback for the study pages is scarce. On the other hand, the feedback aggregation of the recommender-based approach can better handle this lack of feedback on the study pages, but is not specific enough to generate better recommendations for navigation pages.

An interesting parallel to this phenomenon constitutes the work [NM03]. The authors of [NM03] propose to choose the recommendation generators for the web page depending on the degree of connectivity of this page, i.e. the measure of how many outbound hyperlinks the web page has. In the EDU prototype, the degree of connectivity would be a good criterion for distinguishing the pages serving chiefly for navigation from the pages presenting the content.

Recommendation generator based optimization can be considered a type of generalization of feedback, since the feedback given by a click on the individual recommendation is generalized to all recommendations coming from the same recommendation generator. This is consistent with our experimental results, where recommendation generator based approaches perform better under scarce feedback. The benefit of the recommendation-based optimization is the relatively simple implementation of the generalization in comparison to our ontological structure. However, once implemented, the ontology-based generalization allows more possibilities than the generalization based only on the recommendation generators.

The Table 2.2[15] shows the overall performance of the different recommendation selection approaches on the EDU website. In addition to the approaches which already appeared in Figure 2.18 some additional strategies are shown in Table 2.2. So, the approach Top-Rec is recommender-based and employs statistical information for selecting the recommenders. This approach makes use of the web usage data warehouse to

---

[15] Table 2.2 originates from [TGR04]

determine the most popular recommender for every context which appears in the historical data. The approach Reinforcement Learning Zero is reinforcement learning with initial weights of all recommendations rules set to zero. The Random approach selects the recommender based on a pseudo-random number generator. As shown in Table 2.2, the approach Manual achieves the best results. This approach is based on the human knowledge of the website structure, different types of web users and their interests and on the results obtained by the manual OLAP-evaluation of the data in the web usage data warehouse. The approach Manual is followed by the strategy Reinforcement Learning which achieves the best results of all automatic optimization approaches. The Reinforcement Learning Zero and Decision Tree achieve somewhat lower acceptance rates than Reinforcement Learning. In case of Reinforcement Learning Zero this can be explained by the absence of the positive effect of the initial weights; in case of Decision Tree the slight superiority of Reinforcement Learning can be attributed to its online nature and quicker adaptation to the user's interests. The simple statistics-based approach Top-Rec achieves the worst results of all automatic algorithms, however its acceptance rates are still significantly better then the acceptance rates of the Random approach. It should be noted, that the random approach is recommender-based, i.e. rather than producing the random, possibly irrelevant recommendations it randomly selects one of the recommendation generators, which in turn produces recommendations it deems to be relevant for the current context.

6. EXPERIMENTS IN THE SIMULATED ENVIRONMENT

In this section we present the experimental results obtained in the simulated environment. Section 6.1 deals with the evaluation of the different recommendation selection algorithms. In Subsection 6.1.1 we present basic algorithms, which do not use optimization but give understanding of the usage data which is used for simulation and some of its important characteristics. In Subsections 6.1.2 through 6.1.4 we discuss the individual optimization algorithms, explore their parameters and present the corresponding experimental results. In Subsection 6.1.2 we discuss the reward-only algorithms without aging and explore how the acceptance rates change when the optimization parameters change. In Subsection 6.1.3 we explore the reward-only algorithms with aging and explore its parameters. In Subsection 6.1.4 we investigate the reward-penalty algorithms and its parameters. The Subsections 6.1.2 to 6.1.4 are structured in a similar way:

- We illustrate how the acceptance rate of the algorithms changes with different parameters specific to the algorithm.
- For each algorithm we test both the variant with initial weights as generated by recommendation generators and with initial weights set to zero.
- We find the near-optimal parameters and explain the impact of the parameters on the learning behavior.
- We also illustrate how the different algorithms improve their acceptance rates as they learn and optimize the recommendations.

To illustrate the improvement in time, we do not use the full session set. The full session set is not good for illustrating this behavior, since the user interests change over time. So, the increase of acceptance rate over time due to learning is compensated by the changing user behavior. Thus, the optimized algorithms do not show constant increase over time in this setting, instead the better algorithms have higher average acceptance rate than the worse algorithms. Also, the changes in the acceptance rates from month to month make it hard to distinguish what comes from learning and what is the change in user interest. In order to eliminate the influence of these interest fluctuations, we take the session set of one month and perform multiple iterations of our optimization algorithm using this session set.

In Subsection 6.1.5 we compare the learning behavior in time for the different optimization algorithms. Subsection 6.1.6 illustrates the influence which the number of simultaneously presented recommendations has on the acceptance rate. In Subsection 6.1.7 we compare the acceptance rates of the different optimization algorithms. Comparison of the results obtained on real-time prototype with the results obtained in the simulated environment is presented in Subsection 6.1.8. Subsection 6.1.9 discusses the ontology-based recommendation selection policies. Section 6.2 describes a standalone series of experiments which were performed to investigate the performance of different techniques for the retrieval of information from the ontology graphs.

6.1 Evaluation of different recommendation selection algorithms

6.1.1 Basic Recommendation Selection Algorithms

To give an understanding about the characteristics of the session set used for simulation, in Figure 2.17 we present the acceptance rates achieved by several basic recommendation approaches without the adaptive optimization in the experiments based on this session set. We will be using some of these acceptance rates as baseline for comparison of the optimized algorithms in the subsequent sections.

The baseline algorithms BEST_STATISTIC and WORST_STATISTIC rely on the statistical data gathered over the entire experiment period. The set of recommendation rules used for BEST_STATISTIC and WORST_STATISTIC is the original set of rules generated by the recommendation generators on the EC website. The weights of the rules are set to the conditional probabilities of one product following another in one session. The algorithm BEST_STATISTIC presents N recommendations for which the calculated conditional probabilities are maximal. The algorithm WORST_STATISTIC presents N recommendations for which the conditional probabilities are the lowest.

The statistical information which is used by BEST_STATISTIC and WORST_STATISTIC is relatively coarse. It is calculated for the entire evaluation period and does not account for possible changes in user interests during this period

The next two algorithms, STAT_CURRMONTH and STAT_PREVMONTH use more precise statistical information to make recommendations. The recommendation algorithm STAT_CURRMONTH uses the current month's conditional probabilities to select the recommendations for presentation. It is important to note, that this algorithm uses the conditional probabilities calculated for the entire month, not only from the beginning of the month to the current date in the simulation environment. The algorithm STAT_PREVMONTH uses the conditional probabilities for the previous month. As shown in Figure 2.16, the algorithm STAT_CURRMONTH has higher acceptance rate than BEST_STATIC. This shows that the drift of interest is an important issue which should be taken into account. However, it should be noted that the algorithm STAT_CURRMONTH (as well as BEST_STATISTIC) can be used only in the simulation environment and not on a real-life website, since it uses a-posteriori statistic information which is not available at a real-life website at the time when the decisions about presentation of recommendations need to be made. The algorithm STAT_PREVMONTH, on the contrary, can be used on a real-life website since it uses data which is also available on a real-life website. However, its acceptance rate is significantly lower than the acceptance rate of STAT_CURRMONTH. STAT_CURRMONTH and STAT_PREVMONTH are among the simplest approaches to using statistic information for selecting recommendations. These algorithms are shown here as the baseline for the future comparison. We will investigate more sophisticated algorithms in further subsections.

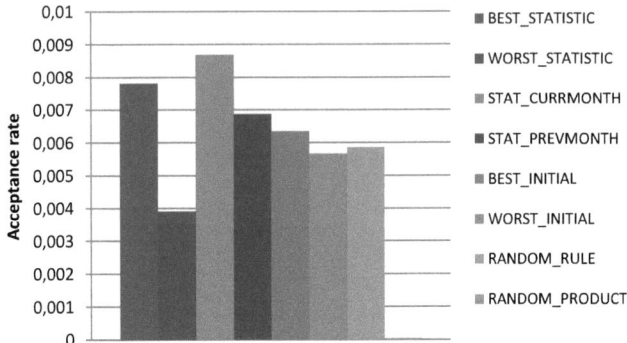

Figure 2.20. Acceptance rates for the basic algorithms without optimization

The algorithms BEST_INITIAL and WORST_INITIAL are also based on the set of recommendations generated by the recommendation generators on the EC site. The weights of the rules are the original weights generated by the recommendation generators. As shown in Figure 2.20, the BEST_INITIAL algorithm brings remarkably worse results than the statistics-based algorithms BEST_STATISTIC, STAT_CURRMONTH and STAT_PREVMONTH. However, the initial weights are predominantly interesting for the new recommendations, for which the statistic information is not yet available. For such recommendations the initial weights generated by the recommendation generators can be useful in the initial phase of the learning before sufficient statistical information can be gathered.

The algorithm RANDOM_RULE uses the same set of rules as the previous algorithms but assigns the weights by using the pseudo-random number generator. As shown in Figure 2.20, choosing random recommendation rules brings worse results than the BEST_STATISTIC and BEST_INITIAL algorithms but better results than WORST_STATISTIC and WORST_INITIAL algorithms.

The results for the algorithm RANDOM_PRODUCT is indistinguishable in Figure 2.20, since its value is very small in comparison to other algorithms. The recommendation acceptance rate for this algorithm is $4*10^{-5}$. This algorithm does not use the set of rules provided by the recommendation generators of the EC prototype. Instead, it presents N randomly selected products in any context.

Figure 2.21 illustrates on example of the basic algorithms how the user's behavior with respect to the recommendations has been changing throughout the period covered by our session set. The increase of the acceptance rate towards the end of the year is due to several highly popular products brought out shortly before Christmas sales.

6.1.2 Reward-only Algorithm with ε-greedy Balancing Technique without Aging (REWARD_ONLY)

The algorithms presented in the previous sections have not used any dynamic optimization, i.e. there was no exploration and learning of the weights of the recommendation rules along with the presentation of the recommendations. The algorithms presented in this subsection use a simple form of optimization. The weights of the

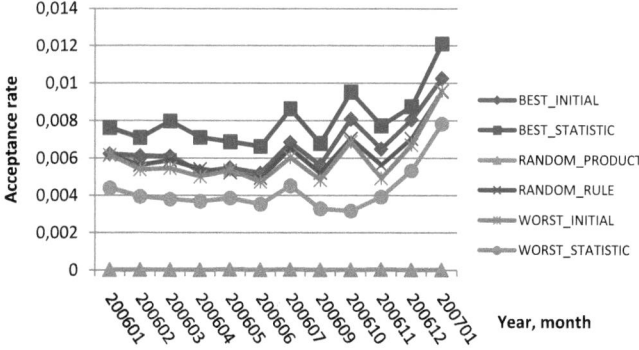

Figure 2.21. Acceptance rate of the basic algorithms changing with time

recommendation rules are set to the acceptance rate of the presentation rule according to formula (3.2.1). Additionally, a fraction of all presentations is used to perform the exploration of the recommendation rules. The intensity of exploration is managed by the parameter ε. With probability 1- ε the selection of recommendations is done according to their weights. With probability ε the selection of recommendations is pseudo-random.

The acceptance rate for this algorithm with respect to the value of the parameter ε is shown in Figure 2.22. The value ε=0 corresponds to no exploration, the value ε=1 means all recommendations rules are selected at random among the recommendation rules available in the recommendation rule database for the given context. The algorithms REWARD_ONLY_0 and REWARD_ONLY_I stand for reward-only with initial weights equal to 0 and reward-only with initial weights supplied by the recommendation

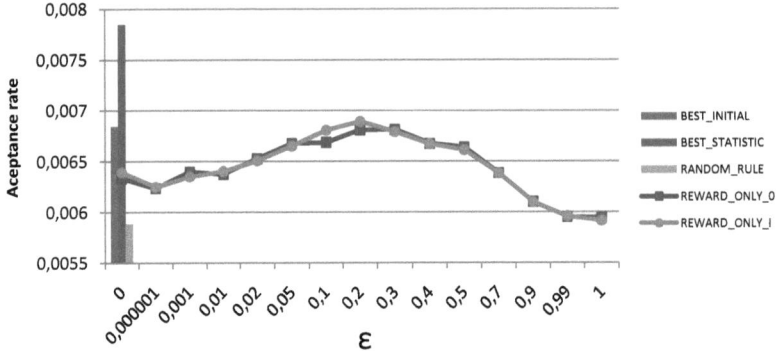

Figure 2.22. Correlation between the values of ε and acceptance rates for ε-*greedy* reward-only algorithms

generators. The algorithms BEST_INITIAL, BEST_STATISTIC and RANDOM_RULE are provided as a baseline for comparison and are represented with bars in Figure 2.22.

As shown in Figure 2.22, the optimal value of the parameter ε in our simulation lies around the value 0.2. Both excessive exploration and insufficient exploration lead to the deterioration of the acceptance rate. The acceptance rate with ε=1 is approximately equal to the acceptance rate of the algorithm RANDOM_RULE. Although the initial weights of the algorithm REWARD_ONLY_I are the same as the initial weights for the algorithm BEST_INITIAL, the acceptance of the REWARD_ONLY_I is lower than that of BEST_INITIAL. This is explained by the fact, that the initial weights for the algorithm REWARD_ONLY_I play a role in the selection of recommendations only on the first presentation of the respective recommendation. After the first presentation, the weights are replaced with values calculated according to the formula (3.2.1). Thus, the setting of the initial weights does not play a significant role for the acceptance rate of the reward-only algorithms without aging and therefore the algorithms REWARD_ONLY_0 and REWARD_ONLY_I behave in a similar way. This insignificant influence of the initial weights is also the cause for the fact, that the REWARD_ONLY algorithms in our experiment are not able to achieve notably better acceptance rates than BEST_INITIAL.

The improvement of the acceptance rate achieved through exploration depends how different the recommendation rules are in terms of popularity and how much time is allowed for learning. Most of the rules used in our simulation are quite similar in terms of popularity. The absolute value of the gain is therefore not large. The superiority of the REWARD_ONLY to algorithms based on the initial weights comes to light when the initial weights are inadequate or the REWARD_ONLY algorithm is allowed more time for learning. The second situation is illustrated in Figure 2.23.

In Figure 2.23 we show the learning behavior of the REWARD_ONLY algorithms in time. As shown in Figure 2.18, the overall recommendation acceptance rates in our

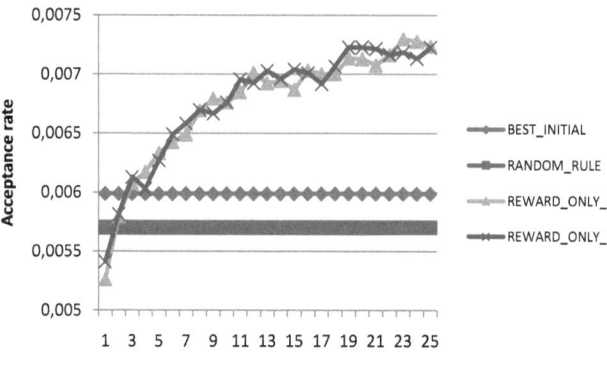

Fig. 2.23. The learning behaviour in time for the reward-only algorithms without aging

usage data fluctuate strongly from month to month. In order to alleviate this fluctuation of user interest and highlight the changes of the acceptance rate which are due to the learning behavior of the algorithms, we have taken the usage data from February 2006 and re-iterated our algorithm over these usage data 25 times without re-setting the weights of the recommendation rules.

As shown in Figure 2.23, the algorithms BEST_INITIAL and RANDOM_RULE are not improving with time since they have no optimization component. The algorithms with the learning component are significantly improving with time. As we already mentioned, the initial weights do not play a large role for our REWARD_ONLY algorithms, therefore REWARD_ONLY_0 and REWARD_ONLY_I exhibit very similar behavior. The small fluctuations of the acceptance rates in Figure 2.23 are caused by the pseudo-random exploration component of the algorithm.

In Appendix 2 we have provided two examples of how the recommendation rules weights change with respect to the presentations during the learning process (Figures A2.1, A2.2). The examples provided are for the algorithm REWARD_ONLY_0, which provides a good comparison since in this algorithm all the weights are the identical at the beginning. The parameter ε in Figures A2.1 and A2.2 is set to 0.2. As shown in Figures A2.1 and A2.2, a distinctive feature of the REWARD_ONLY algorithms is that in the beginning of the learning process the outcome of each presentation has a larger impact on the recommendation rule weights than later on. At any given presentation, however, all previous presentations have the same influence on the current value of a given recommendation rule. For our task of presenting recommendations on the website different behavior seems to be more reasonable. It seems that more recent presentations should have more impact on the recommendation rule weights than the older ones. This can be achieved by applying *aging*, as described in the next subsection.

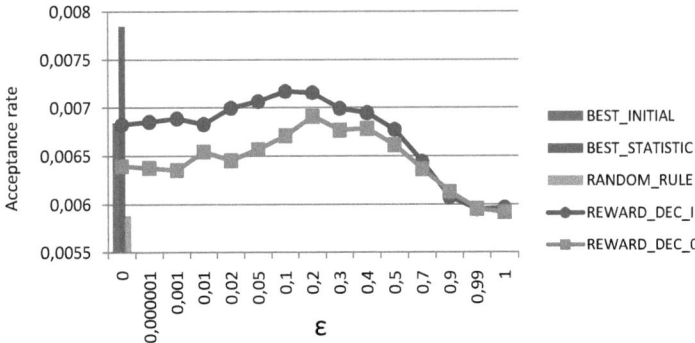

Figure 2.24. Acceptance rates for the REWARD_DEC algorithms
(aging with ε-greedy balancing) with respect to ε

6.1.3 Reward-only Algorithms with ε-greedy Balancing Technique and Aging (REWARD_DEC)

The reward-only algorithms with aging are an extension of the reward-only algorithms without aging, presented in the previous subsection. The weights of the recommendation rules are calculated according to the formula (3.2.4). When aging is in effect, the results of the older presentations have less impact on the current values of the recommendation rule weights. Similarly to the REWARD_ONLY, a fraction of the presentations is used to perform exploration. This size of this fraction is managed by the parameter ε. The acceptance rates of the algorithm with respect to the value of the parameter ε are shown in Figure 2.24.

The algorithms REWARD_DEC_0 and REWARD_DEC_I stand respectively for reward-only with aging (*decayed*) with initial weights set to 0 and reward-only with aging (*decayed*) with initial weights set by the recommendation generators. As shown in Figure 2.24, the initial weights play a more significant role for the REWARD_DEC algorithms than for REWARD_ONLY algorithms. This is due to the recommendation rule weight being amended, not replaced during the learning process. The algorithm using the initial weights supplied by the recommendation generators is able to achieve significant improvement compared to BEST_INITIAL. With ε=0 the acceptance rate is roughly equal to the acceptance rate of the algorithm BEST_INITIAL. As exploration increases, the acceptance rate of the algorithm REWARD_DEC_I also increases until the maximal value is reached at ε~0.2.

The behavior of the algorithms REWARD_DEC_0 and REWARD_DEC_I with respect to the parameter T is shown in Figure 2.25. The parameter ε for this experiment was set to 0.2. As shown in Figure 2.24, the value of T has little influence on the

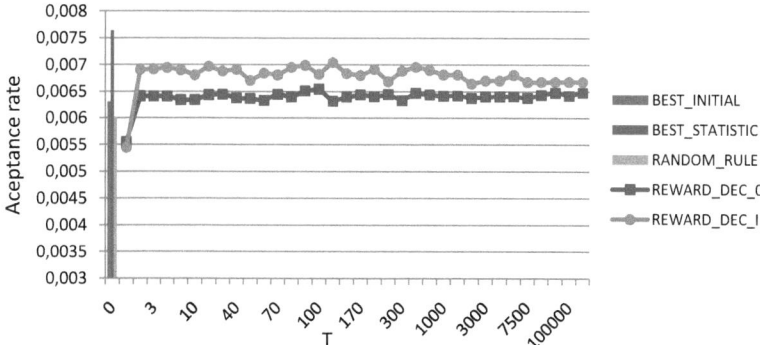

Figure 2.25. Acceptance rate of REWARD_DEC algorithms for different values of T

acceptance rate of the REWARD_DEC algorithms, with exception of T=1. In case when T=1 the formula (3.2.4) degenerates into replacement of the previous weight by the latest feedback value. The acceptance rate in this case is notably low. For other values of T the acceptance rate does not vary significantly. Such behavior is explained by the fact, that the recommendation rules are selected by comparing their weights to each other. As long as the value of T is the same for all recommendation rules, the relative significance of a recommendation rule compared to other rules also stays the same regardless of the absolute values of the rule weights.

For the algorithm REWARD_DEC_I this significance is also influenced by the initial weights of the rules. Because of this, the algorithm REWARD_DEC_I shows a slight decrease in the acceptance rate for higher values of T. According to the formula (3.2.4), higher values of T prolong the influence which the initial weights have on the relative significance of the recommendation rules. As seen in Figure 2.24, the learned recommendation rule weight can result in higher acceptance rates than the initial rule weights. Prolonging the influence of the initial weights can therefore lead to a decrease of the acceptance rate.

The learning behavior of the REWARD_DEC algorithms in time is shown in Figure 2.26. Comparison of Figure 2.26 with Figure 2.23 reveals that initial weights have more influence on the REWARD_DEC algorithms than on REWARD_ONLY algorithms. This influence is especially remarkable in the initial phase of the learning and gradually wears off later on. The fluctuations of the lines representing the acceptance rates of REWARD_DEC_0 and REWARD_DEC_I in Figures 2.25 and 2.26 are due to the behavior of the pseudo-random number generator which is used for exploration.

The examples of weight learning for the algorithm REWARD_DEC_0 are shown in Figures A2.3 and A2.4 in Appendix 2. For examples of the weight learning for the algorithm REWARD_DEC_0 the same two products were used as for REW_ONLY_0.

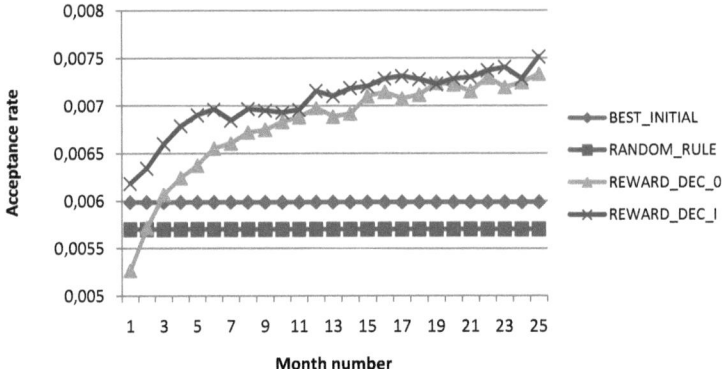

Figure 2.26. The learning behavior in time for the REWARD_DEC algorithms with aging

The value of the parameter ε in Figures A2.1 and A2.2 was set to 0.2, the value of parameter T to 1000. As the comparison of Figures A2.3 and A2.4 with Figures A2.1 and A2.2 shows, every new presentation has the same impact on the weight of the recommendations rules, regardless whether it appears in the beginning of the learning process or at a later time. The comparison of Figures A2.2 and A2.4 shows in particular, that the REWARD_DEC algorithms respond to the changes in the user behavior more promptly than the REWARD_ONLY algorithms. Figure A2.4 indicates that the product ECD008264M (Anno 1701 Limited Edition) was very popular as a recommendation in the beginning of the learning process. At a later point of time it suffered a sudden popularity loss. Subsequently the popularity has somewhat increased again. In Figure A2.2, however, this development of the product popularity is not reflected. In Figure A2.2, the weight of this recommendation steadily decreases after the initial peak.

6.1.4 Reward-penalty algorithm (REWARD_PEN)

The reward-penalty algorithm is a modification of the reward-only algorithm with aging. The same formula (3.2.4) is used to calculate the weights of the recommendation rules. However, as opposed to the reward-only algorithms, the feedback values in case the recommendation is not accepted are set to negative values (*penalty*). In contrast to reward-only algorithms, the reward-penalty algorithm does not need to sacrifice a fraction of the presentations to the exploration, since the exploration is provisioned by using penalty. We have made a series of experiments varying the values of all parameters to determine the optimal (or near-optimal) parameter values. The figures presented in this section illustrate the behavior of the algorithms with respect to the variation of the value of some parameter with other parameters set to near-optimal values discovered during the previous series of experiments.

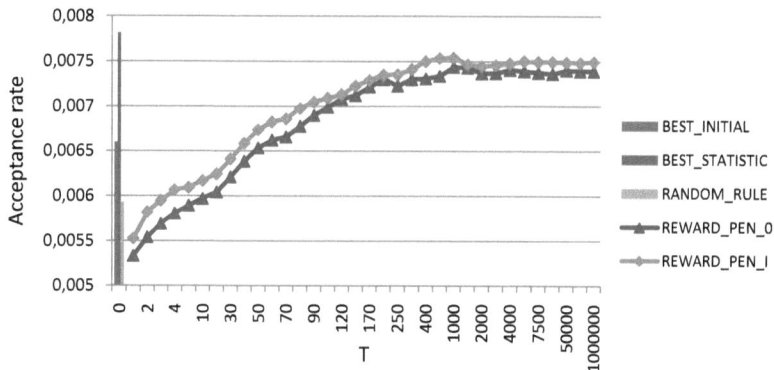

Figure 2.27. Acceptance rate of the REWARD_PEN algorithms with respect to the values of T

The correlation between the acceptance rate of the reward-penalty recommendation algorithms and the value of the parameter T is shown in Figure 2.27. The algorithm REWARD_PEN_0 uses 0 as initial weight of all recommendations. The algorithm REWARD_PEN_I uses the weights generated by the recommendation generators as initial

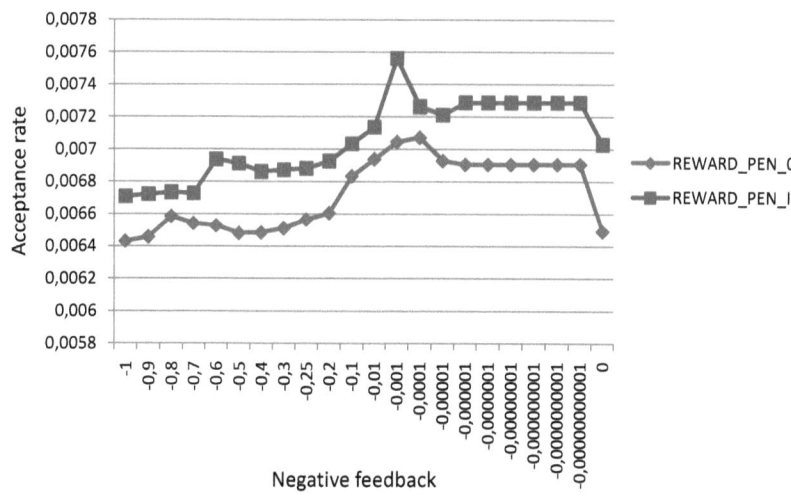

Figure 2.28. Acceptance rate of the REWARD_PEN algorithms with respect to the values of negative feedback

6 Experiments in the Simulated Environment

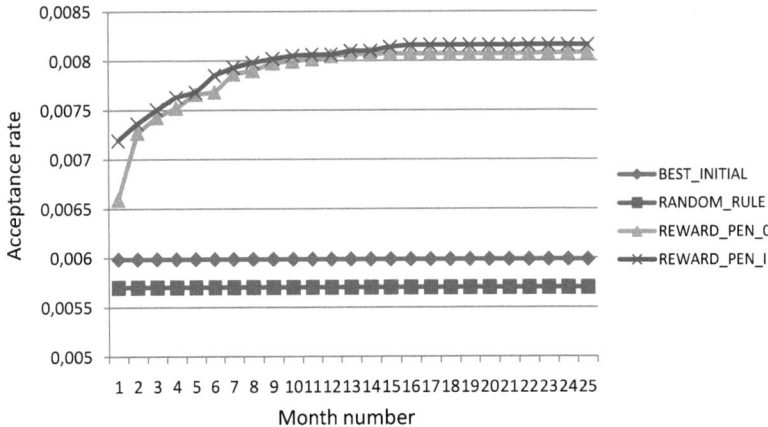

Figure 2.29. The learning behavior in time for reward-penalty algorithms

weights. In the experiments presented in Figure 2.27 the value of the negative feedback was set to -0.001. As shown in Figure 2.27, the acceptance rate of the REWARD_PENALTY algorithms with respect to the values of the parameter T behaves differently than the acceptance rates of the REWARD_DEC algorithms. In particular the smaller values of T lead to smaller acceptance rates. With smaller values of T the optimistic initial weights are wearing off too quickly and the learning is insufficient. REWARD_PEN algorithms do not have a separate exploration component to compensate this insufficient learning. For the values of T>=500 the acceptance rate is consistently high. In our subsequent experiments with the algorithms REWARD_PEN_I and REWARD_PEN_0 we use T=500.

Figure 2.28 shows the correlation between the value of negative feedback and the acceptance rate of the recommendation algorithms REWARD_PEN_0 and REWARD_PEN_I. For the values from -1 to approximately -0.001 the acceptance rate grows as the absolute value of the negative feedback decreases. The maximum of the acceptance rates for both algorithms lies between feedback values of -0.001 and 10^{-4}. Between the values 10^{-4} and 10^{-5} the acceptance rate somewhat decreases. Between 10^{-5} and 10^{-12} the acceptance rate stays constant. The negative feedback value -0.001 represents the optimum between optimistic initial values and aging. This holds also for the REWARD_PEN_0, since zero initial weights also become optimistic weights in the presence of negative feedback. For the negative feedback values from -1 to -0.001 the initial weights are too optimistic and allow too much exploration, which leads to a decrease in the acceptance rate. The values of negative feedback below -0.001 provide not enough exploration for all recommendations to be learned. The feedback value of 0 leads to a

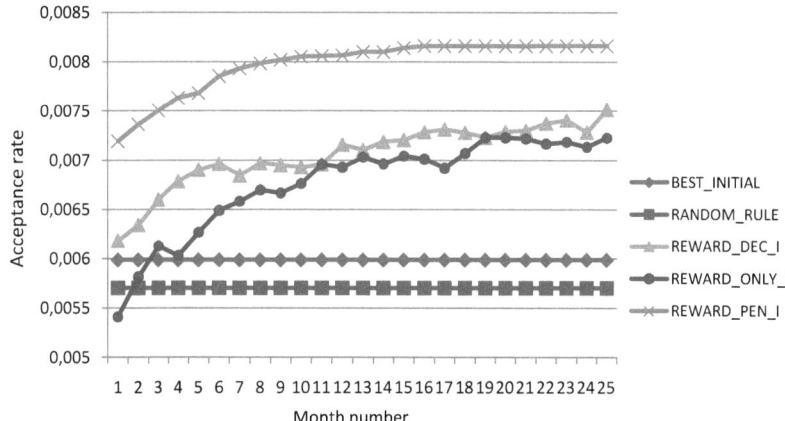

Figure 2.30. The learning behavior in time for different optimization algorithms

decrease in the acceptance rate for both REWARD_PEN_0 and REWARD_PEN_1. The remarkable "shelf" in Figure 2.28 from 10^{-5} to 0 shows that even the smallest absolute values of negative feedback allow to avoid the Exploration Situation 1^{16}, whereas feedback value of 0 does not avoid this situation. In our further experiments with REWARD_PEN algorithms we use the negative feedback value of -0.001.

The learning behavior of the reward-penalty algorithms in time is shown in Figure 2.29. Figures A2.5 and A2.6 in Appendix 1 show the examples of weight learning for the algorithm REWARD_PEN_0 on the EC website.

6.1.5 Learning Behavior in Time for Different Algorithms

We have shown the learning behavior in time for every algorithm in the corresponding sections. Now we would like to present and compare the performance of the best algorithms and parameter combinations together.

The evolution of the acceptance rates of the different optimization algorithms in time are shown in Figure 2.30. In this Figure we repeatedly employ the usage data of February 2006 to show how the optimization algorithms learn in the absence of the drift of interest. The algorithm BEST_INITIAL is used as a baseline for comparison. This algorithm does not use any optimization technique and its acceptance rate stays constant for all iterations. In contrast, the acceptance rate of the optimized algorithms increases with time. In the first iterations, the acceptance rate of the optimized algorithms grows quickly.

---

[16] As explained in Section 3.3.

The optimized algorithms surpass the BEST_INITIAL algorithm within the first iterations. In the later iterations, the acceptance rate of the algorithm REWARD_PEN stabilizes. The acceptance rate of the reward-only algorithms continues to fluctuate even after many iterations (the respective lines in the graphic are "jagged"). This is due to the pseudo-random exploration component of these algorithms. The "jagged" lines in the graphic are somewhat smoothed due to the fact that they represent the average acceptance rate of 10 runs of the experiments.

6.1.6 Influence of the Number of Recommendations on the Acceptance Rate

The quality of the recommendations candidates and the quality of the algorithm which

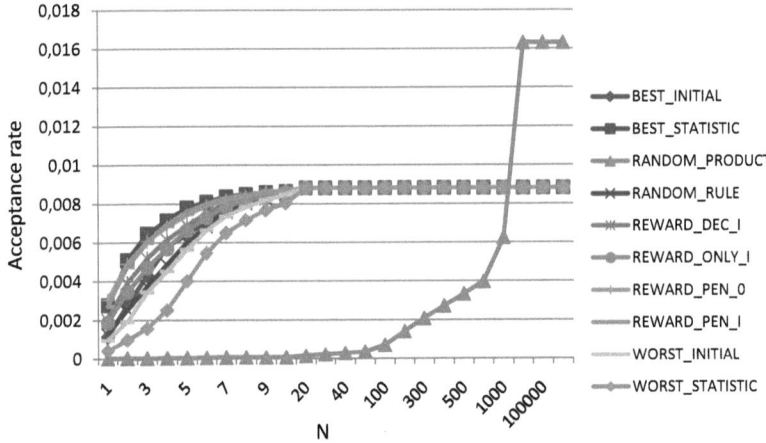

Figure 2.31. Influence of the number of simultaneously presented recommendations on the acceptance rate

selects the recommendations for presentations are not the only factors which influence the acceptance rates. The number of simultaneously presented recommendations N also influences the acceptance rate of the recommendations. Figure 2.31 shows the correlation of the maximum number of the recommendations presented in the same presentation with the acceptance rate of the different algorithms in the simulation.

It is not likely that the real-life data follow exactly the same pattern for large values of N. Large numbers of recommendations are expected to overwhelm the user. We did not have the possibility to conduct a real-life study of how a user reacts to the increase of the number of recommendations. The user reaction to the larger number of presented recommendations depends also on the layout of the website and the amount of other information presented on the website. However, it is realistic to assume that for smaller

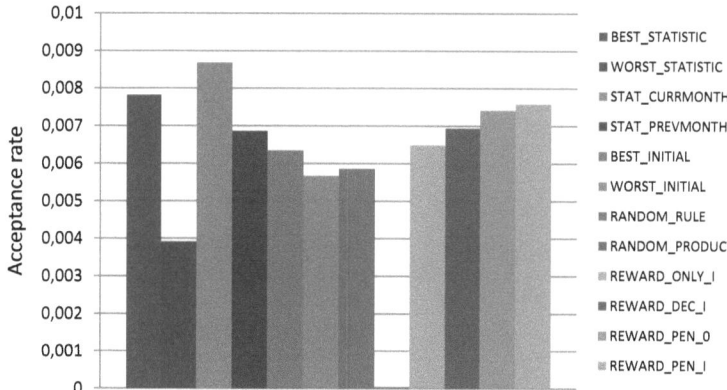

Figure 2.32. Comparison of the acceptance rate of the optimized recommendation algoritms based on the simulation data.

numbers of recommendations which do not overwhelm the users the increase in the number of recommendations should have a positive impact on the acceptance rate on real-life websites in the manner similar to presented in Figure 2.31.

The values of N higher than 30 are not very likely to be found on real-life websites because of the design and usability limitations. In Figure 2.31 these values are used to illustrate the theoretical limits of the acceptance rates which can be achieved by the discussed recommendation algorithms on our usage data. The algorithm RANDOM_PRODUCTS shows the limit of what can be achieved by using all products as recommendations. All the other algorithms show the limit of what can be achieved by using all the available recommendations rules which are generated by the recommendation generators. For these algorithms, the acceptance rate grows remarkably faster for the lower values of N. However, at a value of N~=20 all these algorithms reach their limit. This is simply due to the fact that the set of recommendation rules provided by the recommendation generators rarely contain more than 20 recommendations for every product. The maximal theoretically possible acceptance rate with our set of recommendation rules lies at 0.0088, maximal theoretically possible acceptance rate in case all products are used as recommendations lies at 0.0163.

6.1.7 *Simulation-based Comparison of the Recommendation Algorithms*

In Figure 2.32 we present the comparison of the basic algorithms (as shown in Figure 2.17) amended with the results obtained by applying optimization algorithms with near-optimal parameter values as described in the previous subsections. The algorithms

BEST_STATISTIC, WORST_STATISTIC, STAT_CURRMONTH, STAT_PREVMONTH, BEST_INITIAL, WORST_INITIAL, RANDOM_RULE and RANDOM_PRODUCT have been described in Subsection 6.1.1 and serve here as the baseline for comparison. The algorithm RANDOM_PRODUCT has a very low acceptance rate which appears as an empty bar in Figure 2.32. The algorithms REWARD_ONLY_I, REWARD_DEC_I, REWARD_PEN_0 and REWARD_PEN_I are the optimized algorithms. As shown in Figure 2.32, the REWARD_ONLY_I algorithm is better than the algorithm BEST_INITIAL based only on the initial weights supplied by the recommendation generators. However it is worse than the algorithms BEST_STATISTIC and STAT_CURRMONTH which use a-posteriori statistical data. The use of these statistical data explains their superiority to REWARD_ONLY_I and all other optimized recommendation algorithms, but also makes it impossible to use these algorithms on real-life websites. The superiority of STAT_PREVMONTH to REWARD_ONLY_I can be explained by the fact that it uses only more recent data to present recommendations, as opposed to the REWARD_ONLY_I which does not give the more recent data preference over the older data. The algorithm REWARD_DEC_I addresses this issue and achieves somewhat better results than STAT_PREVMONTH. The algorithms REWARD_PEN_0 and REWARD_PEN_I achieve remarkably better results by eliminating the pseudo-random component in the presentation of recommendations. The algorithm REWARD_PEN_I which utilizes the initial weights generated by the recommendation generators performs better than REWARD_PEN_0 which does not use the initial weights generated by the recommendation generators. Thus, the algorithm REWARD_PEN_I achieves the best results among the algorithms which do not use a-posteriori knowledge and can be used to generate recommendations on real-life websites.

6.1.8 Comparison of the Results Obtained from the Real-life Website and the Simulation

We have developed the real-life prototypes EDU and EC before the development of the simulation environment. To justify the results obtained in the simulated environment and show that they can be used to reason about the real-life user behavior we have repeated the same set of experiments which is shown in Figure 2.12 on our SIM prototype. The results for the experiments repeated in the simulated environment are presented in Figure 2.33. The comparison of the figures shows great similarity of the real-life results and simulated results, despite the fact that the usage data for the SIM environment was taken from the different periods of time compared to the EC evaluation. In the period from which the usage data employed for simulation originate the website EC became more popular and the overall recommendation acceptance rate (as well as the purchase rate) has increased.

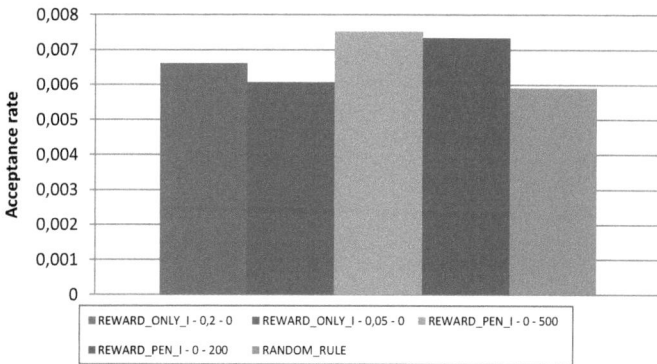

Figure 2.33. Acceptance rate of the algorithms and parameter combinations used in the prototype EC as measured in the simulation environment SIM.

As shown in Figures 2.12 and 2.33, in both real-life and simulated environments the reward-penalty algorithms achieve better results than the REWARD_ONLY algorithms. As expected, the RANDOM_RULE algorithm performs poorly both in real-life and in the simulation. In the case of reward-only algorithm the value of the parameter $\varepsilon=0.2$ brings better results than the value $\varepsilon=0.05$ for both real-life and simulation-based experiments. Also, for both real-life and simulation-based experiments the reward-penalty algorithm with T=500 performs better that with T=200. However, the difference between the acceptance rates of reward-penalty with T=500 and reward-penalty T=200 in the real-life experiments is larger than in the simulation-based experiments. In general, the comparison of the acceptance rate for the different algorithms for the real-life and simulation-based data shows that the simulation behaves similarly to the real-life website and therefore the simulation can be used to draw conclusions about the behavior of the real-life website.

6.1.9 Ontology-based Recommendation Selection Policies

We have tested different ontology-based recommendation selection policies in the EDU and SIM environments. The primary goal of the tested selection policies was to provide the recommendations for the cases when not enough recommendations can be supplied for a presentation by a straightforward selection policy which provides recommendations directly matching the current context. The following ontology-based selection policies were tested on the EDU site: DIRECT, DIRECT+PARENTS, ONLY_PARENTS, ONLY_SIBLINGS. For the SIM environment, we have analyzed the drawbacks of the policies used in the EDU environment and have created improved selection policies PARENTS_SIM and SIBLINGS_SIM. The ontology selection policies we have evaluated are based on the content ontology.

Figure 2.34 shows the session acceptance rates (number of sessions where at least one recommendation was accepted divided through total number of sessions) for the selection policies tested on the EDU prototype. The policy ONLY_PARENTS ignores the direct matching recommendations and takes only the recommendations from the higher levels of content hierarchy. The policy ONLY_SIBLINGS searches for the recommendations among the hierarchy siblings (nodes having a common parent with the current node), also ignoring the direct matches. According to the test results, the DIRECT policy performs better then the policy DIRECT+PARENTS. The DIRECT+PARENTS policy is able to find recommendations even in cases when no directly matching recommendations are available. However, since the weights of the directly relevant recommendations are not given any preference over the recommendations relevant to the parent ontology nodes, this leads to a decrease in the acceptance rate. Also, there are some pages which have no directly assigned recommendations and therefore no recommendation presentations have been registered for the DIRECT policy, which may have lead to the increased acceptance rate. These experimental results were published in [GR05].

We have analyzed the weaknesses of the ontology-based selection policies and performed further experiments in the SIM environment with improved selection policies. In the SIM environment, we have tested the following ontology-based selection policies: DIRECT, PARENT_SIM and SIBLINGS_SIM. The policy DIRECT uses only the recommendations of the given context and is equivalent to the DIRECT policy used in the EDU experiments. The policy PARENT_SIM uses the recommendations assigned to the parent nodes of the current content context node in addition to the recommendations assigned directly to the current content context node. The policy SIBLINGS_SIM uses the recommendations assigned to the sibling nodes of the current content context node in addition to the recommendations assigned directly to the current content context node. The policies PARENT_SIM and SIBLINGS_SIM work in a different way than the parent-based and siblings-based policies used in the EDU environment. The recommendations not directly associated with the current content context node are used only in cases, when the

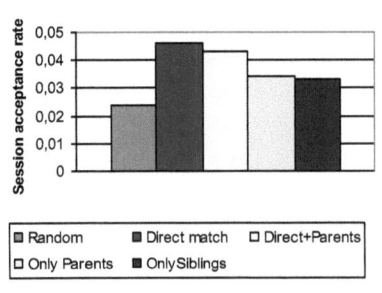

Figure 2.34. Session Acceptance rate of the ontology selection policies (EDU)

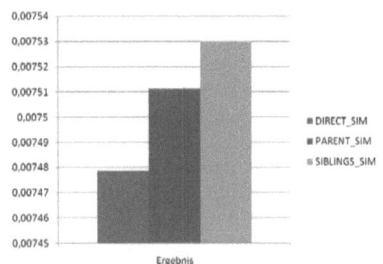

Figure 2.35. Acceptance rates for different ontology selection policies (SIM)

number of recommendation rules assigned to the current node is less than the number of recommendations N which are to be presented according to the design of the website. Also, these recommendations are always shown in the list below the recommendations directly relevant to the current node, regardless of their weight. If such recommendation is clicked, its weight is not changed. If this recommendation turns out to be steadily successful for the given context, the recommendation generator based on association rules should notice this and create a new recommendation directly assigned to the current context. This new recommendation will then participate in the weight optimization process. Thus, the policies PARENT_SIM and SIBLINGS_SIM help explore and find additional recommendations for the contexts which do not have a sufficient number of recommendations. As shown in Figure 2.35, both PARENT_SIM and SIBLINGS_SIM lead to an increase in the acceptance rate. The effect of the selection policies PARENT_SIM and SIBLINGS_SIM on the acceptance rate can be greater or smaller depending on how many contexts have insufficient number of recommendations. For our SIM environment only about 30% of the contexts have less than N recommendations (N=5). This is due to the fact that the similarity recommendation generator is able to provide enough recommendations for the majority of contexts. Therefore, the impact of our policies on the acceptance rate is moderate.

6.2 Optimizing The Retrieval of Information From The Ontology Graphs

In our web recommendation architecture we use the ontology graphs for the flexible representation of the concepts which can influence the recommendations presented on the website. The ontology graphs are stored in the relational database. The straightforward method of storing the graph information which is shown in the database schema in Figure 2.9 is by using two tables, one for the ontology graph nodes and another for the ontology graph edges. This method of storing graph information in the relational database shows significant drawbacks with respect to the performance of the retrieval of the data. The most frequent and most time-critical usage of the ontology data in our system is the retrieval of the ancestors of a given ontology graph node. In case the ontology graphs are stored in the relational structure shown in Figure 2.9, every such retrieval requires several queries with joins. Depending on the total number of edges, nodes and on the average length of the paths in the ontology graphs, such operation may be lengthy and put significant load on the database server. In our prototypes, the size of the ontology graphs, the maximal length of the paths in them and the number of the page views per second are low. Therefore, in our prototypes we use the straightforward technique based on the relational database structure presented in Figure 2.9. However, we have also investigated the possibilities for optimizing the retrieval of the ontology data for the websites with larger ontologies and more page views per second. We have explored two performance optimization techniques. The first technique relies on computing the transitive closure of the graphs [DCES04]. The second technique makes use of the main memory to store the graph. It is also possible to combine the two techniques and store the ontology graph's transitive closure in main memory.

Figure 2.36 shows the results of the experimental comparison of the different optimization strategies. The operation performed in the experiments was the retrieval of all ancestors of a given node. The ontology used in the experiments is a consolidation of three e-commerce ontologies which are also extensively used in the Part III of this thesis: Softunity.com ontology, Amazon.de ontology and eBay.de ontology. For our experiments, all the above ontologies were restricted to the interest areas Software, Video and Games. The consolidated ontology is a forest. The total number of nodes in the consolidated ontology is 3432; the total number of edges is 10435. The maximal length of the paths between nodes in the consolidated ontology graph is 5.

The following optimization strategies are shown in Figure 2.36: straightforward implementation with ontology graph stored in the relational database, transitive closure stored in the relational database, straightforward implementation with ontology graph stored in the main memory, transitive closure stored in main memory. For the selection of the ancestors we selected different number of nodes from the ontology using a pseudo-random algorithm. The implementation of the memory-based techniques was done in Java. Standard Java class java.util.HashMap was used to store the data in main memory. The standard Java implementation of a hashing algorithm used for retrieval provides for the high retrieval performance. The memory needed to store the ontology graph in our example is relatively low (around 50KB). Since the time needed to perform the same operation on a computer may be different depending on other conditions, for example on the activity of the garbage collector in the Java Virtual Machine, the experiments used to compare the performance of the retrieval was repeated 10 times. The execution times presented in Figure 2.36 are the average times calculated over 10 experiments. The computing of the transitive closure for large ontology graphs may become a problem in general case as well as specially for the relational databases. Several algorithms were proposed for efficient solution of this problem in general, for example [NUU95]. Some of the commercial relational database implementations, such as Oracle and IBM DB2 provide extensions to the SQL language to allow transitive closure computation [DCES04]. The computation of the transitive closure is an additional step which needs to be performed during the updates of the ontology graph data. In our setting, the update of the ontology graphs is a negligibly infrequent operation. We used a machine with 1 GB main memory and one 1.7 GHz CPU. The database server used to store the ontologies in our tests is MySQL Server 5.0.

The Y-axis in Figure 2.36 is logarithmic with base 10. As shown in Figure 2.36, the transitive closure is about 3 times faster than the straightforward approach when both methods use relational database and about 2 times faster when both methods are memory-based. The memory-based algorithms are up to 100 times faster than their RDBMS-based counterparts. Although the memory-based systems are less scalable with respect to the size of the ontologies, they are sufficient for the ontologies which are currently used on the largest e-commerce websites. Therefore, performing the graph traversal in memory is the most effective way to speed up the selection of the relevant ontology nodes.

As shown above, we have several ways of significantly optimizing the use of the ontology graph in our system, making it suitable for use on the large real-life websites. While we deem this level of optimization to be sufficient for practical applications, the authors of [CM05] go even further and propose a method which guarantees a constant-time retrieval of the relevant recommendations from an ontological structure similar to ours. This work is discussed on more detail in Section 7.6.

6.3 Summary: Prototypes and Experiments

In this chapter we have discussed the implementation of our recommendation system architecture on several prototypes and presented experimental results and evaluations. We have talked about the issues which need to be solved during implementation and illustrated our architectural decisions with real-life examples.

The experiments and discussion presented in this chapter indicate that our recommendation system architecture demonstrates some beneficial properties which make it suitable for use on commercial websites. Although the achieved increase of the acceptance rate due to optimization is not large compared to the total number of visits on the website, but as we have discussed this relatively modest increase of the acceptance rate can bring a significant increase of profit in the monetary equivalent especially on the large e-commerce websites.

7. RELATED WORK

The research work in the field of recommendation systems is ample and manifold due to the important practical incentives such as the continuous growth of the Internet and the commercial success of the recommendation systems used by the large e-commerce websites. The problem of making web recommendations was investigated by many researchers from different research fields. We are not able to describe every work related to the task of making web recommendations here. Here we describe the works which reflect the different aspects of the architecture of the recommendation systems in the most expressive way. We particularly focus on the works which are relevant not only to the task of making recommendations but also to the architectural decisions which we present in this thesis. The examples of such decisions are in particular the use of ontologies to represent the semantic information used for making recommendations, use of data warehouse technology or use of machine learning. We also present some works which are less related to our work but are characteristic for specific applications of recommendations or specific research areas. For the other works, we give a more general description and refer to the surveys.

Recommendation systems are sometimes placed in the more general research field of personalization. Recommender systems can be considered one of the methods to implement personalization. Since this is also the method most often found in practice, the overlap of these research fields is large and some researchers use the terms "personalization" and "recommendation systems" as interchangeable.

One of the important characteristics of our system which is common to our work

Characteristic	Nr
Surveys and classifications of recommendation systems, techniques and supporting tools (Section 7.1)	1
Hybrid recommendation systems, combination of multiple recommendation algorithms (Section 7.2)	2
Evaluation and comparison of recommendation systems (Section 7.3)	3
Web data warehousing, web usage mining and other database-related technologies (Section 7.4)	4
Systems based on Markov Decision Process and reinforcement learning (Section 7.5)	5
Recommendation systems employing concept hierarchies or ontologies (Section 7.6)	6
Personalization in broader sense	7
Construction and usage of user profiles	8
Commercial systems and systems for e-commerce	9
Feedback-based learning and optimization	10

Table 2.3. Important characteristics of the related research work.

Research work (Project name and/or authors)	Characteristics
Adomavicius and Tuzhilin [AT05]	1;2
Anand and Mobasher [AM03]	1;7
Perugini et al. [PSF02][PSF04]	1;8
Burke [Burk02][Burk06][Burk07].	1;2;3
Goy at al.[GAP07]	1;7;9
Pierrakos et al.[PPS03]	1;4;6;7;9
Schafer, Konstan and Riedl [SKR01]	1;7;9
Fab (Balabanovic) [Bal97]	2;10
WindOwls (Kazienko and Kolodziejski) [KK05][KK06]	2;9;10
Hayes, Massa, Avesani and Cunningham [HMAC02]	3
Herlocker, Konstan, Terveen and Riedl [HKTR04]	3
Yang and Padmanabhan [YP05]	3
CourseRank (Koutrika et al.) [KIBG08]	2;4;6
RQL (Adomavicius and Tuzhilin) [AT01][AT01a]	4;8
Web Utilization Miner (WUM, Spiliopolou et al.) [SF98][BS00][SP01]	4
WebSIFT (Cooley et al.) [CTS99a][CTS99b]	4;3
Rahm, Stöhr et al. [SRQ00][RS03]	4;1
Thor and Rahm [TR04]	4;1;2;10
Shani, Brafman and Heckerman [SBH02][SHB05]	5;10
Mahmood, Ricci et al. [MR07][MR07a][MR08] [MRVH08][MR09][MRV09]	5;10
Preda and Popescu [PP04][PP05]	5;3;6
Prudsys RE [Prud06]	5;2;9;6;10
Taghipour, Kardan et al. [TKG07] [TK07]	5;3
Acharyya, Ghosh [AG03]	6
Chen, McLeod [CM05]	6
Mobasher, Jin, Zhou.[JM03][MJZ03]	6;3
Quickstep and Foxtrot (Middleton et al.) [MRS01][MASR02][MSR03][MSR04]	6;2;8

Table 2.4. Characteristics of the research work in order in which it appears further in this chapter (For description of numbers in column Characteristics see Table 2.3)

and a large number of other works in the field is combining of multiple recommender algorithms, i.e. hybrid recommendation system architecture. Combining different recommender algorithms has become a widespread technique for increasing the quality of recommendation systems. A survey of the hybrid recommendation systems including a list of strengths and weaknesses of the different recommendation generator algorithms and a classification of the hybridization methods can be found in the [Burk02][Burk07].

In particular we would like to mention the work of A. Thor and E. Rahm. The prototype presented in their work and the prototype EDU presented in this thesis share a number of components which were developed in close cooperation. Another work which deserves a special mention is the Prudsys RE. The distinguishing feature of this work that it has been from the beginning developed as a commercial product rather than a research project. According to the authors, their architecture was inspired by our work and by the work [SBH02].

In the next section of this chapter we list several surveys, which can be consulted for a broader overview of the related work. In further sections we present research work subdivided by a number of prominent characteristics, such as combination of multiple recommendation algorithms, use of data warehousing technology and data mining, use of Markov Decision Process and reinforcement learning and use of ontologies. In case when the presented work possesses more than one of the listed characteristics and could be placed into several sections, we choose the section which corresponds to the more prominent characteristic or to the characteristic which deserves special discussion in comparison to our approach. An overview of characteristics which we deem to be important in the related work is given in Table 2.3. Important characteristics highlighted in bold cursive also serve to define corresponding subsections. Table 2.4 shows the characteristics which are exhibited by the related research work presented in this section.

7.1 Surveys

A good survey of the state of the art in the research on recommendation systems and a comprehensive overview of the possibilities for extension of such systems are given in [AT05]. There are also several extensive surveys which target either the more general field of personalization or more specific subareas within the field of recommendation system research like hybrid recommendation systems [Burk02], recommendations in e-commerce [SKR01], recommendation systems for travel and tourism [FGJ+06], explanations in recommendation systems [TM07]. We review some of these surveys below in more detail.

Adomavicius and Tuzhilin

In the survey [AT05] the authors classify the recommendation systems into three large categories (citing the earlier work [BS97]): content-based recommendation systems, collaborative recommendation system and hybrid recommendation systems. The collaborative recommendation systems are further subdivided into memory-based systems and model-based systems. The authors also present classification for the different hybrid recommendation approaches; this classification is however less elaborate than the classification of hybrid recommendation systems provided by the survey [Burk02][Burk06][Burk07]. The knowledge-based recommendations which are often referred to by other authors are not included in the classification. The reason for this may be that the knowledge-based recommendations are rarely used alone. Usually the knowledge-based recommendations are used as a part of a hybrid recommendation system.

The authors discuss the relative strengths and weaknesses of the collaborative and content-based recommendations. They point out that in several research projects the hybrid recommendations have been shown to provide better quality recommendations and to alleviate the common problems of both content-based and collaborative filtering.

Furthermore the authors provide an overview of the promising extensions to the basic approaches. They mention the possibilities for the richer representation of the information about users and items, using the mathematical approximation theory, tackling the multidimensionality problem, applying multi-criteria optimization and providing flexible manual control of the recommendations.

Anand and Mobasher

The work [AM03] is a survey of the more general field of web personalization[17]. The work features a strict definition of the personalization process, a classification of the intelligent techniques which can be used to implement personalization and a discussion of the different classification criteria for such techniques. The authors view web personalization as an application of data mining and machine learning techniques to the task of predicting user needs and adapting the website with the goal of improving user satisfaction [AM03]. Quite interestingly, the authors also state that the goal of the personalization process is to recommend items to users, thus blurring the distinction between the concepts of personalization and recommendation system. Throughout the work [AM03], the authors sometimes refer to a personalization system as a recommendation system.

The authors postulate that the personalization process consists of two stages: offline stage which concentrates on learning the necessary knowledge and online stage which utilizes the knowledge obtained in the first stage for personalizing the website. In our work, we enhance this concept by performing learning both in the offline and in the online stage.

The classification of the personalization techniques according to [AM03] can be performed using many criteria. For example, the distinction between reactive and pro-active techniques corresponds to the distinction between explicit and implicit feedback as discussed in this thesis. The authors note that in practice web users are often reluctant to provide explicit feedback even in cases when it can significantly improve the subsequent browsing experience. Among other criteria are collaborative versus individual (for example content-based) personalization, client-side versus server-side personalization, model-based vs. memory-based personalization etc.

The authors also discuss issues which commonly need to be solved in personalization systems. Such issues include "cold start" problems ("new user", "new item"), data sparseness, context-sensitivity, dynamics in user interests ("drift of interest"), and usage of domain knowledge. These issues are also explicitly addressed in our system. The authors point out that the problem of scalability is usually alleviated by using a model-

---

[17] [AM05] and [AM07] are later versions of the same survey

based approach as opposed to a memory-based approach. In our system we are taking the model-based approach as well. The issues not addressed in our system explicitly include robustness against malevolent manipulation and promotion of user trust in recommendations provided by the recommendation system. With respect to the latter issue the authors cite the study [SS01] which states that in general a recommendation should generate two types of recommendations, *useful recommendations* and *trust-generating recommendations*. In our system we do not provide special trust-generating recommendations. However, manual recommendations can to a certain degree serve for increasing trust in recommendations provided by the recommendation system, since they usually exhibit high quality and are based on sophisticated domain knowledge.

Perugini et al.

The authors of the survey [PSF04] (an extended version of [PSF02]) provide an unusual perspective onto recommendation approaches. They call their survey a "connection-centric" survey. The connections which the authors place in the center of their analysis are the social connections, i.e. connections between people. The authors argue that the social aspect is an essential but previously underrepresented aspect of the recommendation system research. The survey concerns largely the collaborative-filtering approaches and the knowledge-based approaches. Content-based systems are omitted in the survey, since they do not fit well into the connection-centric perspective.

The authors concentrate on different approaches to modeling the user profiles and the calculation of similarities or connections between different user profiles. They also review the possibilities of establishing a connection between the user profiles created by the recommendation systems and user profiles contained in the different social networks which are already available on the Internet. Another interesting research direction is "mining" of the explicit user networks from the implicit information contained for example in shared bookmark systems or in recommendation systems. The authors survey different aspects of interaction between a recommender system and the society, such as evaluation of recommendation systems in social context, targeting of the recommendation systems to different social groups, issues of privacy and trust. The work also identifies some of the possible future research directions, such as distributed recommendation systems, formal modeling of recommendation systems, new designs for human-computer interaction with recommendations, "recommendation appliances" – recommendation systems pre-installed on hardware devices which can be configured and utilized in any environment where recommendations are desired.

Burke

The author provides a very elaborate study of the different hybrid recommendation systems. There are several versions of the survey: [Burk02], [Burk06] and [Burk07]. The earlier version [Burk02] concentrates on classification issues, the latest version [Burk07] provides comparative evaluation of different hybrid systems. The version [Burk06] is a technical report which contains a more detailed version of the comparative evaluation presented in [Burk07]. In the latest version of the survey [Burk07] the author studies 41 implementations of hybrid recommender systems compares them to each other. The survey provides a classification of the basic recommendation techniques and a classification of the different approaches to creating a hybrid recommendation system by combining the basic techniques. According to [Burk02], the basic techniques can be classified as collaborative, content-based, demographic and knowledge-based techniques. The following classification of the possible ways of combining the basic techniques is proposed in [Burk02]:

Weighted: the recommendation scores returned by different recommendation techniques are numerically combined into one score.

Switching: the recommendation system automatically chooses which recommendation technique to apply in which case.

Mixed: recommendations provided by the different recommendation techniques are presented together on the website.

Feature Combination: the data from different knowledge sources (for example collaborative and content-based) are combined and given to a single recommendation technique as input data.

Feature Augmentation: the output of one recommendation technique is used as input to the next technique.

Cascade: recommendation techniques are assigned priority. The results of the recommendation techniques with lower priority are used to distinguish between the recommendations for which the recommendation techniques with higher priority return equal scores.

Meta-level: one recommendation technique creates a model, which is then used by another recommendation technique.

For each of the categories listed above the authors provide a schematic architecture description and several representative implementations in [Burk07]. We refer to this classification when describing hybrid recommendation systems further in this section. With respect to this classification, the architecture presented in this thesis possesses combined characteristics of a "mixed", "feature-combination" and "meta-level" system, with "mixed" property expresses more prominently. The implementation of a weighted approach within our system would be straightforward.

The authors also identify common problems which need to be addressed for implementing of a recommendation system. One of these problems is the so-called *cold-start problem*, also known as new item or new user problem. Another is the problem of *stability vs. plasticity*, which we call *drift of interest* in this thesis. In our architecture we address both of these problems.

In the comparison part the authors evaluated the different hybridization techniques by creating a series of two-component hybrid recommendation systems and comparing their performance on the same input data set. The evaluation was performed in a simulated environment using data from a real-life website. The components have been chosen in such a way that each component represents a different class of recommendation techniques, so that all meaningful combinations of the basic techniques and all hybridization types. According to [Burk07], the systems based on feature augmentation hybridization technique achieve the best performance on the used dataset. The authors note that it is not clear to which extent the results obtained on a given dataset can be generalized and to which extent the peculiarities of the implementation of the basic recommendation techniques have influenced the results of the hybrid algorithms. This is however a relevant critique for our experimental evaluation and for many other experimental evaluations as well. The authors make a number of observations that certain hybridization techniques are better suited to certain combinations of the basic techniques. These observations are likely to be valid also in the general case, independently of the specific input data and implementation details of the basic techniques. The one observation which is shared by many researches is that the hybrid approaches can achieve better results than those which are possible by applying only the basic recommendation techniques.

Goy at al.

The survey [GAP07] deals with personalization for e-commerce applications. Personalization is a broader term compared to recommendation systems, however there's no distinct border between the recommendation systems and other personalization techniques. The authors consider E-commerce in the narrower sense of Business-to-Customer (B2C) E-commerce. The survey considers commercial software which can be used for creating e-commerce systems with personalization as well as research prototypes of such systems. The authors note that the personalization possibilities implemented in commercial systems are rather simple, in contrast to the rich possibilities for management of content such as products, product catalogs, prices. The survey explores the connection between personalization techniques and modern technologies such as CRM (Customer Relations Management) and CDI (Customer Data Integration). [GAP07] classifies the personalization systems into adaptable systems and adaptive systems. The former are giving the user opportunities to adjust the system to his taste, the latter are trying to adjust themselves automatically. The authors then study the adaptive systems in more detail. They investigate what information can be used to create adaptive systems and common work steps of such system: acquisition of data needed to decide about adaptation, representation of these data and inference of the required adaptation, production of adaptation, i.e. making adjustments to the user interface. Web recommendations are the most known example of the possible adjustment, but there are also other possibilities for adaptation. Such adaptation possibilities are for example dynamically changing product catalogs. A promising application area of personalization is the adaptive representation of complex products with a large number of feature combinations, such as automobiles which allow different types of color and additional equipment to be selected. It is often hard for the users to find the suitable combination. The personalization can help to determine the configurations which certain kinds of users find interesting. The authors investigate the types of advantage which personalization brings: improvement of customer relations, quality of service, usability of the website, integration of data from different suppliers.

Pierrakos et al.

The work [PPPS03] is a survey of the approaches which combine data mining and knowledge discovery techniques applied to web usage data with web personalization. They discuss different ways to personalize websites and different *personalization functions*. One example of a *personalization function* is a recommendation system. Other personalization functions include user salutation, personalized layout, personalized pricing scheme etc. The authors provide an overview of the most important aspects which need to be addressed in order to personalize a website based on the analysis of the usage data. They also define several steps which need to be implemented to provide personalization: data collection, date pre-processing, discovery of patterns, knowledge post-processing. For data collection, they review different possibilities for gathering the data, such as gathering data on the server side, on the client side and on the intermediary level such as proxy servers and firewalls. Data cleaning, crawler elimination, session detection and user identification are named among the tasks which need to be solved by data pre-processing. For the pattern detection step, the authors describe and compare different approaches found in the literature such as clustering, classification, association rules and sequential patterns. For each method they discuss the specifics of its application to the task of automatic personalization. The knowledge post-processing is a process which is performed by humans. The authors describe several possibilities for knowledge representation which should simplify the task of knowledge post-processing.

The authors have selected a number of works in the field of web personalization for more detailed discussion. They subdivide the personalization systems presented in these works in single-function systems and multi-function systems. The authors describe personalization systems originating from research institutions as well as commercial systems such as Oracle AS Personalization[18].

They also identify open issues in web personalization, such as scalability with respect to large volumes of data and possibility of incremental updates. They specifically point out the problem of users' behavior changing over time, i.e. "drift of interest" and indicate that this problem has not been sufficiently addressed in the research.

They also indicate that the common representation of the knowledge obtained by web usage mining tools is an important practical issue and suggest using W3C knowledge representation standards such as RDF. In the architecture presented in this thesis we address this issue by using ontologies stored in a relational database to represent the knowledge. Such internal representation of the knowledge is superior in terms of retrieval

---

[18] http://www.oracle.com/personalization

performance to the internal representation in RDF format. However, the import and export of knowledge between relational format and RDF format are straightforward.

Schafer, Konstan and Riedl

Similarly to the survey [GAP07], the survey [SKR01] concentrates on personalization of e-commerce applications. Although the title of the work explicitly specifies the focus on recommendation systems rather than more general term "personalization", the perspective of the work is almost as broad as the perspective of [GAP07]. The authors survey the personalization and recommendation techniques used on several large e-commerce websites. They consider systems such as amazon.com, cdnow.com, ebay.com, drugstore.com, reel.com and compare different personalization techniques found on these websites. [SKR01] presents a taxonomy for recommendation techniques based on the input data received by the techniques and the output data provided by them. The aspects such as degree of personalization, different methods of delivery of recommendations to the user in e-commerce applications are analyzed in detail. The authors concentrate on the economical side of the personalization. They point out that the recommendation systems are at the moment used rather as "virtual salespeople" and not as marketing tools [SKR01]. Indeed, the recommendation systems can be used not only as sales instrument within the framework of a given website but also as a marketing instrument used in the framework of a company's marketing policy. The authors suggest using the recommendation systems for marketing campaigns or to capture a certain market segment.

7.2 Hybrid Recommendation Systems

Hybrid recommendation algorithms have been a fruitful research area in the recent time. Considerable amount of research work in this area has been published and a number of architectures of hybrid recommendation systems have been proposed. For most of them we refer to the surveys [Burk02][Burk07]. However, some of them deserve special attention in the context of this thesis and we therefore discuss them in this subsection in more detail.

Significant amount of research work deals with combining the collaborative filtering with content-based algorithms. Such architectures are proposed in [CGM99], [PZ03], [BH04], [Bal97] and other research works. Their approaches strive to combine both algorithms in one algorithm in an algorithm-specific way. The Fab system of [Bal97] is described below in more detail as an early example of such systems. Our approach, in contrast, implements the collaborative, content-based and knowledge-based algorithms as independent recommendation generators, but dynamically combines their results in a way which is optimized for a given website and the taste of a given web user.

Fab (Balabanovic)

The Fab recommendation system [Bal97] is one of the early hybrid adaptive recommendation system architectures which was the first to possess some of the features which we also used and extended in our architecture. The system in [Bal97] combines collaborative filtering and content-based recommendations. One distinctive feature of the Fab system is the usage of a central repository to store the recommendations. The repository is filled by so-called collection agents, which implement various recommendation algorithms. The selection agents select recommendations from this central repository and present them to users. Both collection and selection agents have own profiles. Each user is assigned its own selection agent. The profile of this selection agent serves as a profile of the user. Differently from our architecture, the system Fab relies on explicit feedback to adapt its behavior. The explicit feedback is used to adjust both the user profiles and the profiles of the collection agents. The adaptation is done on the level of recommendation algorithms, not on the level of individual recommendations. The author points out the need to perform both short-term and long-term learning in an adaptive recommendation system.

WindOwls (Kazienko and Kolodziejski)

The work presented in [KK05][KK06] presents a hybrid recommendation system architecture able to combine recommendations from different recommendation algorithms in one website. The authors target particularly e-commerce websites. In the terminology of [Burk02] the hybridization method is "weighted", i.e. the recommendation scores returned by different recommendation algorithms are combined numerically in one score. Two sets of numerical values are used to select the recommendations for presentation. One set of values contains the scores provided by the recommendation algorithms. In case when the same recommendation comes from several recommendation algorithms, the maximum score value is used. Another set of values contains the relative weights assigned to the different recommendation algorithms. In order to obtain the score of concrete recommendations, the scores provided by the recommendation algorithms are multiplied by the weights assigned to the respective recommendation algorithms. The sets of weights of the recommendation algorithms are individual for every user and are calculated statistically basing on the number of recommendations generated by the given recommendation algorithm which have been accepted by the user. The recommendation system also maintains a base set of weights, which represents the arithmetic average of the weights calculated over all sets of the individual users. The base set of weights is used to initialize the individual sets of weights for the new users.

In some aspects the work presented in [KK06] can be considered a middle ground between the approach followed by [TR04] and the approach followed by our architecture. The architecture presented in [TR04] is a "switched" architecture in terms of [Burk02], which means that the different recommendation algorithms generate and present their recommendations separately and independently. The user feedback is used to learn the optimal way of switching between the different recommendation algorithms. In the "mixed" approach presented in this thesis, the individual recommendations are detached from the recommendation algorithms which generated them to be learned and presented together. The feedback is used to influence the weights of the individual recommendations. In the architecture of [KK06] the recommendations are also detached from the recommendation algorithms and presented together. However, the feedback which they receive from the website is used to learn not the weights of the individual recommendations but the weights of the recommendation algorithms which generated them. In our opinion, the architecture of [TR04] has a major advantage over the architecture of [KK06]. In [KK06], the decision to give preference to one or another recommendation algorithm depends on the current user. In [TR04], this decision can be made basing on a large number of parameters of the so-called recommendation context, such as current user, current content and other information. The feature that associates [KK06] and [TR04] is that the feedback-based learning is done on the level of recommendation algorithms and not on the level of individual recommendations as in our architecture. This can be seen as both advantage and disadvantage, as discussed in Section 5.4 of this thesis. Our experimental data obtained on the EDU prototype show that the feedback-based learning of individual recommendations can be more sensitive to the user's interest and achieve better acceptance rates, but it also suffers much more from the scarcity of feedback compared to the feedback-based learning on the level of recommendation algorithms.

The authors present an evaluation of their system on a sample e-commerce website. The sample website is an internet shop that sells windsurfing equipment. With the total of 65 users and 42 purchased products the website is significantly less representative than the websites we used to evaluate our architecture. Using the data collected on the sample website, the authors investigate the behavior of the acceptance rates of different recommendation algorithms in time.

In [KK06] the authors polemicize with some of design decisions used in our architecture. In particular, they question the usage of the element CurrentUser in the rules of general form:

<CurrentContent, CurrentUser, CurrentTime> => <RecomendedContent, Weight>

This critique, however, is based on the mistakenly simplified understanding of our concept. So, the authors assume that the element CurrentUser represents an individual user in terms of the website. In our concept, however, this element represents the node in the ontology graph, which describes the semantic characteristics of the current user. If these semantic characteristics are shared by many individual website users, a node could be common for all these users, thus representing a user group rather than an individual user. Further, the authors assume that this element is mandatory. In our system, it is possible to employ the recommendation rules not depending on parts of the context or even completely independent of the context. Thus, any of the three context elements may be omitted in our recommendation rules.

7.3 Methods of Evaluation of Recommendation Systems

There is a series of works which deal specifically with the evaluation of the performance of recommendation systems. This notorious interest is caused by the fact that such evaluation is has proved to be a complicated issue. Several aspects make evaluation of recommendation systems complicated, for example insufficient willingness of real-life websites to run experimental systems and lack of a universally accepted single performance measure. The works presented in this section study these and other aspects of the evaluation of recommendation system in detail.

Hayes, Massa, Avesani and Cunningham

The authors of [HMAC02] review different ways of evaluating the recommendation systems. They utilize the subdivision between to online evaluation and offline evaluation introduces first presented in [KR99] and give several examples of both evaluation types. The meaning of terms online and offline in [KR99] is different than the meaning they have in the description of our architecture. Online evaluation in [KR99] is understood as an evaluation performed on a real-life website with real users, whereas offline evaluation is an evaluation performed in a simulated environment. The data set used for offline evaluation usually also comes from a real-life website. In [HMAC02] the authors argue that the only reliable way to evaluate a recommendation system is by using an online evaluation on a real website. The authors name examples of factors which can significantly distort the experimental results provided by an offline evaluation. [HMAC02] describes the architecture of a framework for online comparative evaluation of the recommendation systems. Their framework consists of a real-life web application visited by web users, two competing recommendation systems and a special component which controls the presentation of the recommendations generated by the different recommendation systems according to a policy. The authors discuss the steps which need to be taken in order to guarantee a fair competition between the recommendation systems. They also discuss different ways to consider the user feedback and propose different policies for presenting the recommendations, such as merging all recommendations in one result set and presenting them together, presenting two result sets simultaneously on the web page or presenting recommendations from different systems alternately in different presentations. Interestingly, the authors propose the use of reinforcement learning during the evaluation in order not to negatively impact the trust of the users of the real-life system. Reinforcement learning in their approach should assure that only a small fraction of recommendations comes from the worse recommendation system.

The evaluation approach proposed in [HMAC02] is in many aspects similar to the evaluation we present in this thesis. We perform evaluation using metrics which represent the attitude of the real web users towards our system. We agree that an online evaluation of a recommendation system on a real-life is more convincing than an offline evaluation. We have tried to use the online method as much as possible while evaluating our recommendation system. However, we have found out that even after overcoming the obvious obstacle of obtaining access to a real-life website willing to test an experimental implementation – an obstacle which is considered to be very serious by most researchers including [HMAC02] – one more serious obstacle appears which makes online evaluation quite difficult. This obstacle is the scarce feedback which is does not suffice to achieve reliable results for the multitude of the possible modifications of the recommendation algorithms.

A significant drawback of the proposed evaluation framework is that no implementation of the proposed evaluation framework has been done. Therefore it has not been possible to validate the theoretical considerations of the authors of [HMAC02] in practice. Also, there may be issues which become apparent only during the operation of the evaluation framework and which have not been mentioned in [HMAC02].

Herlocker, Konstan, Terveen and Riedl

The authors of [HKTR04] concentrate on evaluating one common type of recommendation systems – the recommendation systems based on collaborative filtering. They point out three major difficulties of the evaluation:

- Different datasets are used for evaluation of the recommendation systems. It is often unclear, to which degree the measured performance of a recommendation system depends on the design of the system and to which degree it depends on the characteristics of the dataset used for evaluation. To address this problem, in this thesis we used two datasets for the evaluation of our recommendation system. However, the question of whether our results apply to all or majority of possible datasets still cannot be answered with sufficient confidence.

- Different recommendation goals – some websites want better prediction of the user's interests, other websites deliberately want to propose something else than the user would most probably choose, if it serves the interests of the website's owner, for example increases the profit. For example, of the two websites which we used to test the architecture presented in this thesis, the EDU website is interested in providing comfortable navigation for the user while the EC website concentrates on increasing commercial profit.

- Different combinations of measures are used in different recommendation systems. In the work described in this thesis we use acceptance rate and session acceptance rate as performance measure for our systems. However, it is not possible to directly compare our architecture to many other architectures, since they use other measures such as precision and recall [CK68], ROC curve [Swet63], NDPM [Yao95] etc.

According to [HKTR04], most of the performance measures currently used for evaluating recommendation systems are so-called accuracy-based measures, i.e. measures which describe the predictive accuracy of a recommendation algorithm. The authors note that a "magic barrier" to the increase of the accuracy-based performance measures seems to exist. This "magic barrier" represents the degree to which a user himself is uncertain about what he wants to choose. If the different algorithms are tuned to the optimum, argue the authors, the improvements in terms of "accuracy" of the more complicated algorithms over the basic ones are tiny, since they approach the "magic barrier". This is why the improvements to the algorithms should not concentrate on the accuracy measures, but rather on additional characteristics of the recommendation systems. Among such characteristics the authors name the ability to communicate the reasons for a certain recommendation to the users and the amount of data the recommendations systems need to make recommendations.

These observations of the authors are consistent with our experience. The acceptance rate metric used in our work is a variation of the "accuracy" metric. That is why we concentrate not on the improvement of the specific recommendation algorithms but on the automatic optimization of the recommendations independently from the algorithms which generate them, thus ensuring that the performance of our system always stays as close to the "magic barrier" as possible. We also provide some additional characteristics which we perceive to be important for modern e-commerce websites, such as the ability to generate the recommendations online, flexibility in changing the recommendations manually and in representing different concepts of the websites.

In [HKTR04] the authors describe the difficulties listed above in more detail and propose the ways to tackle these difficulties: they categorize the goals of the recommendation system; discuss the selection of the datasets for evaluation; survey the evaluation metrics and study the behavior of different metrics on the same dataset, showing that the metrics can be divided into classes of correlated metrics. They also introduce and discuss some metrics which are not based on "accuracy", such as novelty, serendipity and coverage of recommendations. The marketing-related evaluation metrics such as offer acceptance and sales lift as well as the usability-related metrics and computational performance metrics are deliberately not considered in [HKTR04], although the authors admit that such metrics are important for the comparative evaluation of recommendation systems.

Yang and Padmanabhan

Similar to the other work listed in this section, the work [YP05] points out that the current situation with the evaluation of recommendation systems is unsatisfying. They argue that especially the relative easiness of implementing the different types of recommendation systems leads to a possibility of unforeseen problems and complications. ([Flyn06] gives a good example of such unforeseen complication). This makes the reliable evaluation of recommendation systems very important. Contrary to [HMAC02], the authors indicate that the evaluation on the real website is though welcome but rarely possible and even if possible then with limitations which make the obtained results weak. So, even if there is a real website willing to implement an experimental system, it is usually not willing to implement the relatively mediocre recommendation algorithms which could serve as a "control group". This is also the case with the real-life evaluations we present in this thesis. For example, we have not been allowed to use the recommendation algorithms which provide pseudo-randomly selected products as recommendations. We could use the algorithms which either pseudo-randomly switch the recommendation algorithms or pseudo-randomly select the recommendation candidates pre-selected by some non-random recommendation algorithm. For the common case when the real-life evaluation cannot be performed or cannot be used with reliable enough settings, the authors suggest a knowledge-based approach which can alleviate the weakness of previously used evaluation schemes. They introduce the notion of so-called distinguishing sets. Distinguishing set is a set of statements which can be evaluated on the data and represent our understanding of what a "good" recommendation system in a given domain should be. It is not a requirement that this understanding should be complete and exhaustive. To be qualified as a distinguishing set, a set of statements should have a characteristic of leading to a certain outcome (i.e. a certain set of recommendations) while ruling all other outcomes out. They also introduce the notion of minimal distinguishing set for a given outcome, i.e. such distinguishing set which doesn't contain any other distinguishing sets as a subset. The evaluation of the recommendation system is then performed in the following way:

- Determining the set of minimal distinguishing sets using the algorithm provided by the authors in [YP05].
- Testing whether these minimal distinguishing sets hold on the experimental data.

The technique described by authors is a systematic approach to evaluating the recommendation systems. It forces us to specify our assumptions about what is a good recommendation system in an explicit manner. It is also possible to include the previously used metrics in the statements describing knowledge in the distinguishing sets. This approach allows performing continuous evaluation and validation of a running recommendation system.

[YP05] also provides an example of how such evaluation system can be implemented. The authors use a simple case with real-life data, formulate a distinguishing set of rules and show how the performance of a recommendation system can be evaluated against these rules.

The authors of [YP05] acknowledge that their approach has a serious problem, namely that the evaluation depends now not only on how good the recommendation system is but also on how good the domain knowledge is. The problem of assessing the quality of the domain knowledge used in this evaluation framework is however a hard problem if attempted to be solved as a computational problem. This problem is more suited to be solved on the organizational level while implementing the recommendation system, for example by cross-validating the domain knowledge by several human experts in the given domain.

[YP05] explicitly does not advocate the use of the proposed evaluation method in case when possibilities for performing comparative experiments on real-life systems with a control group exist. In the common case, however, such experiments are not possible and the approach [YP05] represents a valuable contribution to the solution of the demanding problem of evaluation of the recommendation systems. Although in our system we had the possibility of using a real-life evaluation, the aspects discussed by the authors are also relevant for our evaluations, since our control groups are relatively weak and are only representative of how good our optimization algorithms are, not how good our recommendation system as a whole is.

7.4 Web Data Warehousing and Web Usage Mining

In this subsection we review the connections between recommendation systems and database-related technologies. Such database-related technologies include data warehousing, online analytical processing (OLAP) and data mining. In some cases, new technologies have appeared on the intersection of these two fields. In particular, the application of data mining techniques to the data describing the user navigation on a website is termed "web usage mining". Web usage mining is a sub-concept of the more general concept "web mining" which denotes the application of the data mining techniques to the data found on the World Wide Web. Other types of web mining include web Content mining and web structure mining [BL99][MBNL99]. Web usage mining and web data warehousing provide the foundation for the research presented in this thesis, in particular for the implementation of the recommendation generators.

CourseRank (Koutrika, Ikeda, Bercovitz, Garcia-Molina)

The system CourseRank [KIBG08] is used at Stanford University in order to help undergraduate students select their courses. Similarly to our approach, CourseRank suggests courses to the users relying on a rich data model which is stored in a relational database. The authors argue that using only a single type of recommendations, i.e. only collaborative or only content based recommendations brings a number of drawbacks and propose using hybrid architecture. The combination of different approaches is achieved by specifying so-called *flexible recommendation workflows*, which can provide recommendations based on a set of input parameters and on the domain knowledge contained in a relational database (*rich data* in the authors' terminology). The authors stress that the recommendation workflows are specified using a high-level definition language. This high-level definition language includes operators commonly used for accessing relational data, such as selections and joins, as well as operators which are specific for the generation of recommendations. The latter include the operator *extend*, which allows accessing additional relations in the database, the operator *recommend* for generating recommendations and the operator *top-k* for filtering the set of generated recommendations. The combination of match clauses and ontology selection policies which is presented in this thesis is comparable to the recommendation workflows as described in [KIBG08]. However, it should be noted that the recommendation workflows are more generic and therefore more flexible than the approach based on mapping clauses and ontology selection policies. The authors also report that they are working on the mechanism for automatic optimization of the recommendation workflows; however no results are yet available.

The system CourseRank does not gather implicit user feedback and performs no feedback-based optimization. Instead, CourseRank provides user with the interface which allows adjusting various parameters of the recommendation workflows in order to obtain personally tailored recommendations. Such approach potentially allows better fine-tuning. However, it expects the user to have at least a basic understanding of how the recommendation system works and how the different parameters affect its behavior.

RQL (Adomavicius and Tuzhilin)

Adomavicius and Tuzhilin present the use of data warehousing technology for generating web recommendations in two works [AT01][AT01a]. They point out a number of improvements which can be introduced by such symbiosis, for example the aggregation of the data used for generating recommendations and creation of profiles basing on these data. In particular the creation and use of hierarchical profiles and groups is possible. The use of data warehousing technology can help the recommendation system to tackle the problem of multidimensionality. The authors propose to use a special recommendation warehouse, i.e. a data warehouse designed especially for making web recommendations. They also propose a special language RQL (Recommendation Query Language). RQL can be used both to define a recommendation warehouse and to select recommendations from it. RQL allows flexible management of the recommendations. Statements expressed in RQL can be used by the website owners to specify which recommendations should be used in which situation.

The authors present an implementation of their architecture. In their implementation, the recommendation warehouse is implemented using a relational DBMS and the RQL language is translated to SQL. The authors indicate that such implementation can be a performance bottleneck in a production system and suggest that the recommendation warehouse be implemented as custom software in this case.

The architecture presented in [AT01] and [AT01a] has a number of contact points with our architecture. These contact points include using the data warehousing technology, advocating of the need for use of groups and hierarchical profiles, using rules for making recommendations, giving the website owners the possibility for flexible adjustment of the recommendation rules. There are also significant differences. For example, the direct use of a data warehouse to select recommendations for presentation as proposed in [AT01] does not seem to be a plausible solution for a real-life recommendation system. Indeed, data warehouses usually contain large amounts of data and the queries posed to a data warehouse put considerable load onto the database server. This is especially pertinent since RQL allows almost arbitrarily complex queries. Performance problems are likely to arise when such architecture is used on a real-life website. In our architecture we use rules of a simpler kind. We generate recommendation rules basing on the information from the data warehouse and then store them in a recommendation rule database which is specially optimized for quick access. Other differences between our architectures include the absence of the automatic selection of the recommendations from [AT01] – the RQL statements should be entered manually by the website owners. The possibility of automatic optimization of the recommendation rules using feedback received from web users is also absent from [AT01] [AT01a].

Web Utilization Miner (WUM, Spiliopolou et al.)

Web Utilization Miner is a specialized tool for web usage mining described in [SF98][BS00][SP01]. WUM is comprised of two components. The first component is called aggregation module. This component prepares and aggregates the web usage data for analysis. The second component is the mining processor which performs the recognition of significant navigation patterns in the usage data. WUM architecture does not contain a special personalization component. The authors suggest that the personalization should be performed manually by the website owner, after the user preferences are understood with the help of WUM. The mining of the usage data is controlled manually using an SQL-like mining language named MINT. Human experts need to use MINT to specify what types of behavioral patterns are being looked for. MINT processor can be used to explore the behavioral patterns of the web users or to monitor the changes in the user behavior. [BS00] discusses an extension of the system which allows mining usage data for dynamic websites where HTML-Pages are results of form-based queries over a relational database or some other source of data. The authors propose creating the concept hierarchies for such "hidden" data and investigating the user behavior with respect to these conceptual hierarchies. An interesting approach is taken by the authors with respect to storing the usage data for analysis. Although they do not use a relational database, they recognize that such analysis is not possible without a suitable data structure. WUM uses specially structured data storage called Aggregated Log with special indexes based on *trie* algorithm [Brian59].

WebSIFT (Cooley et al.)

The system WebSIFT is described in [CTS99a][CTS99b]. WebSIFT is a framework for web usage mining. The distinctive feature of WebSIFT is the usage of the domain knowledge as auxiliary source of information for the usage mining. WebSIFT employs web content mining and web structure mining to automatically extract domain knowledge which can be helpful in detecting interesting patterns in the usage data.

The domain knowledge in WebSIFT is used to assess the "interestingness" of the pattern. The authors relate "interestingness" of a usage pattern to its "unexpectedness". For example, a strong usage pattern connecting the items which belong to unrelated areas (according to the content hierarchy) or have highly dissimilar content are considered especially interesting.

We would like to note that such definition of "unexpectedness" is focused on the website owner and not on the web user. Indeed, the behavior patterns which cannot be easily predicted basing on the domain knowledge provide the most interesting insights for the website owner. However, since the web users do not necessarily possess sufficient domain knowledge, even the patterns which can be easily predicted from the domain knowledge may be quite unexpected and interesting for the web users when used as recommendations.

The system WebSIFT relies on the relational database technology for storing the usage data and the domain knowledge. However, no task-specific techniques such as data warehousing methodology or special types of indexing are applied.

Rahm, Stöhr et al.

The authors of [SRQ00][RS03] discuss the problem of evaluating the web usage data and designing personalization systems from the point of view of relational database technology and data warehousing. They come to the conclusion that the use of the database technology for personalization is inevitable given the characteristics of modern websites and the characteristics of the usage data which needs to be stored and evaluated. In [RS03] the authors first theoretically analyze the possibilities for database-supported processing of web usage data and point out that data warehousing technology is particularly suitable for this task, despite of the relatively high implementation effort. The authors then present the architecture of a web data warehouse and extensively study the different practical aspects of the processing of web usage data in a data warehousing environment. [RS03] also contains an overview of the tools for preparing and analyzing the data. In general, [RS03] can be used as a practical instruction for creating a web data warehouse.

The works [SRQ00] and [RS03] concentrate on the processing and analysis of the usage data. The possibility of creating an automated adaptive personalization system is suggested but no specific architecture of such a system is proposed. However, the architecture proposed in this thesis as well as architecture proposed in [TR04] are based on the ideas and results presented in [SRQ00][RS03] and can be regarded as the continuation of this work.

Thor and Rahm

The work described in [TR04] employs a data warehouse to store the usage information and implicit user feedback. In [TR04] the feedback is used to learn how to switch the different recommendation generator algorithms, which work independently from each other, whereas in our approach the feedback influences the weights of individual recommendations ("switched" approach vs. "weighted" approach according to the classification in [Burk02]). [TR04] describes several strategies, according to which the best recommendation generator can be chosen, including an adaptive strategy based on a decision tree algorithm. The selection of the recommendation generators is influenced by the current context, i.e. current situation on the website. The work also contains a classification of recommendation algorithms.

[TR04] proposes an interesting technique of filtering out the page views originating from automated web crawlers. The filtering is performed by including special hyperlinks into the HTML code of the web pages. These hyperlinks are specially formatted to be invisible for the human user but are still visible for the crawlers. The sessions in which such links were visited can therefore be safely excluded from the analysis of the navigation behavior of the human users.

The implementation of the system described in [TR04] and the system presented in this thesis were performed in close cooperation. So, some of the recommendation algorithms developed by Mr. Andreas Thor were used to create the recommendation rules in our EDU prototype. Particularly interesting is the highly successful search engine based recommendation algorithm, which utilizes the keywords forwarded by the search engine in order to provide relevant recommendations. In the EDU prototype, a common data warehouse was used for both approaches. A joint paper [TGR05] containing the description and comparative evaluation of both approaches was published.

7.5 Markov Decision Process and Reinforcement Learning

[Sutt96] was the first to mention the possibility of employing reinforcement learning to solve the task of presenting web recommendations. Specially to mention are the work of Shani, Brafman and Heckerman [SBH02][SHB05] which described an MDP-based recommendation system. They also referred to the possibility of applying reinforcement learning but did not implement it in their architecture. At a later time, several research teams presented systems based specifically on reinforcement learning. The systems described in this subsection take different approaches to representing the recommendation problem as an MDP and solving it.

Shani, Brafman and Heckerman

The work of Shani, Brafman and Heckerman described in [SBH02][SHB05] exhibit a number of common points as well as a number of principal differences with our work. So, they also argue that the problem of making web recommendations should consist of creating the initial model and the part which optimizes this model based on the usage. The authors employ the MDP (Markov Decision Process) model. Our approach is based on reinforcement learning which in turn also employs MDP model to describe the problem to be solved. Although they use the term "online", but their use of this term is different from the online learning as presented in this thesis. Our online learning is performed after every presentation. They authors of [SBH02][SHB05] understand using relatively recent feedback as "online" learning. So, on their prototype they update the model only once every several weeks.

The prediction model used by the authors is based on the usage data. This means that the discussion for of "new item" problem arises for the cases when usage data is available. The authors mention that in case when new items appear and have no associated usage data the recommendations for these items are learned online. The authors point out that their online optimization approach does not depend on the implementation of the predictive model, i.e. some other algorithm which is not necessarily based on MDP can be used to generate the predictive model.

The authors use not only a currently viewed page to describe the current MDP state, but also a history of previous states. The history length is variable; the history can contain a combination of a maximum of 5 previous states. Since this may lead to explosion in the number of states, the authors apply special techniques to reduce the number of states. Our architecture also allows considering the previous states for making recommendation decisions. However, after a preliminary analysis of our data we have decided to restrain ourselves from using the previous states. The sessions with many page views are relatively rare in our data, so the benefits of using previous states didn't seem to justify the increased difficulty of handling much larger number of states.

The work of Shani, Brafman and Heckerman takes into account not only the immediate feedback, but also the prospective feedback of all subsequent states. This approach stands in contrast to our approach, which takes only immediate feedback into account. The authors point out that there are both benefits and drawbacks of considering not only the immediate but also expected subsequent feedback. The benefit is that we can maximize the reward beyond the reward which can be obtained by considering only immediate feedback. The drawback is that considering non-immediate feedback may lead to recommendations with low perceived relevance. This may lead users to losing confidence in the recommendation system and starting to ignore the recommendations in general. Another drawback of considering subsequent feedback is that it significantly increases the computational complexity, making it barely possible to learn recommendations in real time.

Noteworthy is that Shani, Brafman and Heckerman also presented the evaluation of their system on a real-life commercial website, which is encountered only in few works in the literature.

Mahmood, Ricci et al.

The authors of the extensive series of research works [MR07][MR07a][MR08][MRVH08][MR09][MRV09] use Markov Decision Process to model the recommendation problem and apply reinforcement learning to solve this problem. The use of an adaptive recommendation system in these works represents an interesting contrast to how a recommendation system is used in most other work presented in this subsection. In the described application, the adaptive recommendation technique is applied to the search queries entered by the user on a website. If the recommendation system detects that too many results would be returned by the query, it suggests some keywords which could be added to the query in order to reduce the number of returned search results. So, the recommendation system tries not to suggest how to extend the information currently presented to user, i.e. present him new products or content, but rather how to further constrain the amount of presented information to reach precisely the content the user is interested in (Query Tightening Process). The system also provides the opposite functionality, i.e. auto-relaxing of the search query in case when it returns no results. The recommendation problem described by the authors appears on many websites which offer search function, for example on the website www.ebay.com. The authors use two travel planning websites as examples for the application of the proposed architecture. A significant part of the experimental results was obtained using simulation.

In the proposed architecture the state and action spaces of the MDP are richer than in most other architectures presented in this subsection. So, the possible actions include moving from one page to another, showing the query form, suggesting additional query terms for tightening the query, accepting or rejecting a recommendation. Taking an action without reaching a goal is punished by negative feedback. The authors investigate how the different negative feedback values influence the behavior of the recommendation system and find out that the different values of feedback lead to different optimal recommendation policies.

The representations of the state models have been given special consideration in the described research work. The authors represent the state space as a set of feature variables. They argue that one particularly important issue for such recommendation system is the selection of the relevant features in the state representation [MR07a], since otherwise the size of the state space can make the recommendation problem computationally intractable. Therefore, including additional features to state variables may not always be beneficial for a given recommendation task. The authors propose two criteria for judging about the relevancy of features, namely Policy Diversity (i.e. the ability of a certain feature to produce a different optimal policy if taken into account) and Policy Value (based on the total reward achieved by the system). The authors demonstrate how an evaluation of the feature relevance can be performed in a simulated environment [MR07a]. In [MR08] the authors perform further experimental evaluations of feature relevance and show in particular that the selection of the relevant features depends also on the user behavior with respect to recommendations (i.e. how often the users are willing to accept a recommendation in general). The proposed architecture utilizes the Policy Iteration algorithm [SB98] which belongs to the dynamic programming family of reinforcement learning algorithms in order to calculate the optimal recommendation strategy.

Another important contribution of the research team is the design of the recommendation system for a real-life website [MRVH08] and the online evaluation of the proposed system on this website [MRV09][MR09]. The evaluation shows that the proposed adaptive recommendation system helps the users to reach their goals more quickly compared to the none-adaptive recommendation approach. It also shows that the acceptance rate of the different system requests has increased on the average due to the adaptive nature of the recommendation system.

Preda and Popescu

In the works [PP04] and [PP05] the authors employ Reinforcement Learning to solve the problem of providing web recommendations and perform experiments on a small real-life website. Their sample application is a website of a school library with ~500 users.

The authors employ the algorithm SARSA(λ) from the family of so-called TD(λ) reinforcement learning algorithms [RN94]. The value of parameter λ in their system is ser to 0.5. The value of parameter $\lambda <> 0$ denotes, that not only the immediate reward after taking an action is considered, but also the future rewards in the discounted form. This is different from our approach where we consider only the immediate feedback. In terms of a TD(λ) algorithm our approach would correspond to $\lambda=0$. The TD(λ) algorithms with $\lambda <> 0$ are significantly more expensive computationally then the algorithms used in our architecture.

The authors do not consider the problem of making web recommendations to be non-stationary, i.e. they do not account for the "drift of interest". Their algorithms are designed to handle the model in which the transition probabilities T(s,s′) remain the same throughout the entire lifetime of the recommendation system. In the sample application used in [PP04][PP05] this may be a plausible assumption which doesn't negatively affect the quality of recommendations, since it can be expected that the user interests on a website of a school library change slower than for example on an e-commerce website or a news website.

The authors devote much attention to the selection of states for the MDP which serves as a foundation for their reinforcement learning approach. In the face of the scarcity of feedback they see strong need for generalization. The generalization approach they employ relies on the domain knowledge. The authors approach bears some similarity to the approach which we present in this thesis. In [PP04] the authors represent knowledge in an ontological structure which imposes a partial ordering on the concepts of the website. The authors present their model as an ontological directed acyclic graph with weighted edges. The authors propose using content similarity (i.e. text similarity) as a metric for setting the weights of the edges in the ontology graph, but also mention that it is possible to use other metrics to set the weights. In fact, in their sample application the weights are specified manually by a human editor. To be able to generalize the knowledge in the face of large number of states and scarce feedback, the authors apply the technique of linear function approximation. Linear function approximation allows generalizing the feedback obtained by a particular state also to its neighborhood. The linear function approximation technique used in [PP04] is the CMAC (Cerebellar Model Articulation Controller) technique [SSR98][SB98], which represents a type of a neural network. In [PP05] the concepts presented on the website and the relations between them are represented via logical programs. The logical programs also serve as states for the MDP model. Some parallels can be drawn between the logical programs presented in [PP05] and the mapping clauses presented earlier in this thesis, since both consist of logical statements representing domain knowledge. The usage of the logical programs of [PP05] is however different from the usage of mapping clauses. The mapping clauses in our architecture have simple syntax and are used to map the information expressed in technical terms of the web application to the domain knowledge represented in the ontological structure. The semantic expressiveness of our mapping clauses is relatively weak. The logic programs of [PP05] constitute the states in the ontological graph. They are semantically rich and can be reasoned about. The authors propose an original method for calculating the similarities between the logic programs and thus the weights of the edges in the ontological graph.

In general, the approach investigated in [PP04] and [PP05] has a number of common design solutions with the approach presented in this thesis, however with a different focus. The focus in [PP04] and [PP05] lies on investigating different knowledge representations. In this thesis we concentrate on the software architecture and review engineering aspects which enable the application of the reinforcement learning approaches on the real-life websites. We provide architectural means for different representations of complex knowledge needed to select the web recommendations, but leave the details of the knowledge and exact representation up to the concrete application. Although in [PP04] and [PP05] the knowledge representation is discussed in much more detail than in this thesis, many issues are also left open, since they are usually domain-dependent and implementation-dependant. For example, the generation of the models in [PP04][PP05] is an open issue which is left up to the concrete application. In particular, it is not clear whether and how the logical programs of [PP05] can be generated automatically. In both [PP04] and [PP05] the sample application relies on the domain knowledge being generated manually by a human editor. The different knowledge representations in [PP04][PP05] are investigated from the mathematical perspective as opposed to the software engineering perspective assumed in this thesis. The authors present the results of the experimental comparison of three different recommendation systems on their sample website: item-to-item collaborative filtering, top N items from the category, reinforcement learning. Reinforcement learning achieves the best results, closely followed by the item-to-item collaborative filtering. Top-N achieves considerably worse results. The authors present the experimental values for the session acceptance rates similar to those observed in our experiments.

Prudsys RE

The recommendation engine Prudsys RE developed by the company Prudsys AG, (Chemnitz, Germany) is an industrial strength implementation of a recommendation system based on reinforcement learning. This recommendation engine is now used by a number of large German companies, including Quelle AG, BAUR Versand and Metro Group (Metro Future Store). The implementation of the Prudsys RE was done independently from the work presented in this thesis. However, according to Dr. Michael Thess, Managing Director of the Prudsys company, the ideas presented in our paper[GR04] and in the paper [SBH02] have inspired the architecture of Prudsys RE. The Prudsys RE extends our dimensions of <Content, User, Time> by two additional dimensions Price and Channel. However, they also state that in particular the dimensions Price and Channel can be fixed, i.e have the same value for all contexts possible in the system. The library of data mining algorithms Xelopes[TB07] developed by the company Prudsys is used to create the initial model. This model is then optimized using reinforcement learning algorithms which are also integrated into Xelopes. It is possible to operate the recommendation engine in three modes: Offline, when the recommendation weights are generated by the recommendation algorithms and not adjusted during the interaction with web users; Online, when the recommendations are learned immediately from the user interaction, and Offline+Online, when the recommendations are generated by learning from historical data and then adjusted online. The Prudsys RE is targeted not only for web recommendations, but also for recommendations in conventional stores, for example at cash counters or information kiosks. According to the joint statement of Prudsys AG and Quelle AG, after the introduction of the Prudsys RE on the website of Quelle AG the proportion of cross-selling products to the total sales has increased by more than ten times [Prud06]. Prudsys RE also has several interesting extensions which enrich the service provided by Prudsys RE. For example, Prudsys RE provides simulation analysis ("what-if" analysis) based on historical data. Another interesting feature of the Prudsys architecture is the dynamic price optimization. The product price can be adapted dynamically using regression-based methods to increase the profit.

Taghipour, Kardan et al.

The architecture presented in [TKG07] and its enhancements described in [TK07] apply Q-Learning to the problem of making web recommendations. Q-Learning is a popular Reinforcement Learning method. In two main aspects the model used in [TKG07] is different from ours and closer to the one used in [SHB05]. The first aspect is that the authors consider not only the current web page but also the history of the last web pages as states in their Markov model. Similar to [SHB05] they use the notion of N-Grams to represent the states in the Markov model. The application N-Grams in [TKG07] is however somewhat different than in [SHB05]. They used fixed N for all their N-grams representing states, whereas [SHB05] uses varying N for different states. Their states however consist not only of an N-Gram containing the last pages visited by the user as in [SHB05] but also of N-Grams containing the history of recommendations shown to user (or, more exactly, of M-Grams, since the sizes of page view history and recommendation presentation history can be different). The second aspect is that they take into account not only the immediate rewards but also the expected rewards for the subsequent states during the calculation, as the classical Q-Learning does. The corresponding discussion of the [SHB05] is also pertinent here. The authors favor using time which web user spends on a particular web page as reward value. We oppose such connection between time spent on the website and reward, as described in Section 3.4. Like most known systems, the authors consider multiple simultaneously presented recommendations as independent from each other and treat each presentation of a recommendation as a separate action. The difference between [TKG07] and both our system and the system described in [SHB05] is that the authors do not make distinction between the algorithms for creating a model and optimizing the model. Rather, the same algorithm is used to first train the system on the historical usage data and then to continue simultaneous training and exploiting of the system on the real website. The states and the actions are created basing on the training data. The balancing between exploration and exploitation in [TKG07] is implemented using ε-greedy technique. As we discussed earlier, the ε-greedy balancing always sacrifices a fraction of presentations to exploration, leading to inherently suboptimal recommendation presentation.

In [TK07] the authors realize some shortcomings of their architecture and propose enhancements which can alleviate these shortcomings. One shortcoming is that their model based on states and actions which are generated from the observed historical usage data during the training phase is not able to provide recommendations for the states which have not occurred in the training data. In [TK07] they address this shortcoming by employing a content-based algorithm to amend the initial model and enrich it with semantic information. This makes their architecture more similar to our approach. Another shortcoming of [TKG07] is that using both page view history and recommendation history in the states of the MDP leads to an explosion in the number of states. To solve this problem, the authors in [TK07] remove the recommendation history from the states and compensate the effects of this removal by using a special reward function which takes history of recommendation presentations into account.

The authors provide results of experimental analysis of some aspects of their architecture, such as sizes for page view history and recommendation presentation history, different reward functions. They have also conducted comparative evaluation of their approach and two other approaches based on association rules and collaborative filtering. The recommendation system based on reinforcement learning has performed better than the other two systems. The evaluations were done on simulated data and not on a real-world website. Therefore it's hard to tell whether this is possible from the point of view of the system performance, given the relatively complex structure of the state space in [TKG07] and [TK07].

7.6 Recommendation Systems Employing Ontologies

Acharyya, Ghosh

Although the work [AG03] does not present a complete recommendation system architecture, it deals with the issue which is very relevant to creating a semantically enabled recommendation system. The authors describe a method of representing the navigation of the web users through the pages of the website as navigation in the semantic concept space. The authors of [AG03] represent the semantic concept space as a tree. The generation of such a concept tree is left outside the scope of [AG03], where the authors assume the concept three to be already provided. The authors propose a probabilistic model which represents the surfing behavior of the users. They discuss the learning of the transition probabilities between the concepts in the concept tree and using these probabilities to predict further navigation of the users. Being able to predict the next step of the user is a crucial functionality for building a recommendation system. The model described by the authors can be for example implemented within our framework relying on the ontological structures we provide.

In [AG03], the interest of users for a specific area is determined by the time during which the user occupies certain pages certain areas of the concept graph. As already discussed in Section 3.4, we do not consider using the viewing time as a measure of user's interest to be an assumption which can be accepted unconditionally.

Chen, McLeod

The authors of [CM05] propose a semantically enriched recommendation system based on collaborative filtering. The authors point out the computation complexity which arises when taking semantic information into account. In [CM05] the authors focus on developing the algorithms and data structures which allow exploiting of the semantic information while reducing the computational overhead. In fact, they propose an algorithm which is able to perform the selection of recommendations based on the ontological structure in constant time. While the work [AG03] deals only with tree-like representation of the semantic concepts, [CM05] allows a directed acyclic graph representation. Unlike our architecture, which expects the ontology graphs to be supplied in the way which makes them suitable for selecting recommendations, the authors of [CM05] transform the supplied ontology graph into a special structure which allows constant-time recommendation selection. The transformation algorithm relies on geometry-inspired distance metric to convert the original ontology graph into a set of groups of concepts. The geometric proximity of the concepts to each other is considered to be equivalent to "hierarchical similarity". Every group of concepts is characterized by the "geometric" proximity of the member concepts to each other. Such groups are used during the recommendation selection process to quickly perform semantic-based generalization. The authors describe the application of their recommendation approach to a geosciences information system.

Mobasher, Jin, Zhou.

In [JM03][MJZ03] the authors employ the semantic information in form of an ontology to enhance a recommendation algorithm based in item-to-item collaborative filtering [LSY03]. The extraction of the ontologies is performed using an automatic ontology extraction algorithm based on text mining and heuristic rules. In [MJT03] the ontology classes are represented as tables in a relational schema. The class instances are stored in the table rows. Additionally, the instances are converted into vector representation in order to enable the computation of item similarities. The vector representations of the instances are combined into a similarity matrix. Thus obtained similarity matrix is however large and sparse. To reduce the dimensionality of the matrix and thus make it suitable for the item-to-item collaborative filtering algorithm, latent semantic indexing technique is used.

The authors have performed an experimental evaluation of their approach in a simulated environment using the data set from a real website. They compared their semantically-enriched collaborative filtering algorithm with standard item-to-item collaboration filtering recommendation algorithm. The authors report significant improvement in the predictive quality of recommendations which could be achieved by semantically enhancing the collaborative filtering recommendation system.

Quickstep and Foxtrot (Middleton et al.)

In a series of works [MRS01], [MASR02], [MSR03] and [MSR04] the authors propose the ontology-based hybrid recommendation systems Quickstep and Foxtrot. The recommendation systems are aimed at helping researchers quickly find research papers in the fields of interest. The Foxtrot system is an extension of the Quickstep system and shares the general architectural decisions with it. The system Quickstep is a pure recommendation system, while the system Foxtrot also provides facilities for search and user profile visualization. The recommendation systems make use of the external ontologies provided by the project *dmoz* (http://www.dmoz.org) and the project AKT (http://www.aktors.org/). The ontology AKT is also used to bootstrap the user profiles in the recommendation system, since it also contains personal information about some researchers. The relation between the individual research papers and the concepts in the ontology are determined using a modified version of the classifier algorithm [AKA91]. In Quickstep and Foxtrot, both explicit feedback and implicit feedback is used. The explicit feedback is obtained from the web users by offering them to rate topics in the ontology as more or less interesting, while implicit feedback is gathered from the clicks on individual recommendations. In Quickstep and Foxtrot, both explicit and implicit user feedback influences the weights of ontology topics and not the weights of the individual recommendations. While selecting the recommendations for presentation, the weight of the individual recommendations is obtained by combining the weight of the ontology topic with the confidence score of the classifier, which indicates how strong the relation between the individual recommendation and the given ontology topic is. Since the system is designed for internal use, the authors are able exploit not only the web logs from the website with recommendations but also the web proxy logs containing the complete browsing behavior of the internal users. The authors suggest that the use of ontologies can bolster the cooperation between independent knowledge bases. They however also point out that complications of legal nature may appear when establishing such cooperation. This is also pertinent to the gathering of the complete web navigation logs using web proxy. Three small-scale experiments with up to 260 users have been performed to assess the quality of the recommendations generated by the recommendation systems Quickstep and Foxtrot. The algorithms show the superiority of the ontology-based approaches over the recommendation approach using the unstructured flat topic list.

8. SUMMARY

In this part of the thesis we have described the architecture, implementation and use of a novel recommendation system. Our recommendation system uses multiple techniques to generate recommendations, stores the generated recommendations in a semantically enabled recommendation database and then refines the recommendations using online optimization. We present the evaluation of our architecture not only in a simulated environment but also on two real-life websites, which is rarely found in the literature. Our results for two real-life websites showed that feedback-based optimization can significantly increase the acceptance rate of the recommendations. Even the simple optimization techniques could substantially improve acceptance of recommendations compared to the non-optimized algorithm. In comparison to the overall buying behavior on the website, the overall impact of web recommendations stayed modest. However, if we have in mind that success of a website is a result of the joint efforts in the areas of pricing, product assortment selection, marketing, website maintenance, customer support etc, with each area bringing its share towards the common success, the share brought by a web recommendation system can be a valuable addition to this joint effort.

PART III. WEB RECOMMENDATIONS IN THE INTEGRATED DATA ENVIRONMENT

9. INTRODUCTION

In Part II of this thesis we have described the architecture of the adaptive recommendation system which is designed for a single website. The recommendations generated by that system were used to adaptively support navigation in the data coming from a single data source. In this part we study the case when the data shown on the website comes from different data sources. This happens for example when two or more e-commerce websites enter a partnership and offer complementary products to each others' assortment. Another example is provided by integrated e-commerce portals, which do not have their own product assortment but present data gathered from other e-commerce websites augmented with some additional services, for example with an overview of the market, customer reviews, price comparison for identical products from different sellers and comparison of characteristics for similar products. In this part we describe how such websites can be created and how web recommendations can be instrumental in implementing the user navigation for such integrated data environments. The data integration problems which arise in such situations are given particular attention in this part. As a proof of concept, we have implemented a prototype of an integrated e-commerce portal using data from several e-commerce websites.

To integrate the data from e-commerce websites, we have used the data integration platform iFuice [RTA+05]. iFuice enables integration of data based on the relations between data instances, so-called *mappings*. We called our prototypical integrated web portal EC-Fuice ("e-commerce web portal based on iFuice") and describe it in this part of the thesis.

The data presented in an integrated e-commerce website can be typically split into two parts: content items (product data) and the ontology (product categories), which describes the semantic structure of the data. The same is true for many other types of websites – digital libraries, news archives, online art galleries, encyclopedias and others. In this thesis we focus on the e-commerce applications. The role of content items in our setting is played by sets of information describing a product, which includes for example product title, prices, extended textual description of the product etc. Subsequently, we will call this set of information "product instance". We will use the terms "node in the product ontology" or simply "ontology node" to refer to a product category.

To provide smooth navigation between the data from different data sources we have to determine the relations between ontology nodes and product instances from different data sources. Such relations can be identity relations, in case when ontology nodes or product instances represent the same real world objects. However, the analysis of the real-world data shows that the identity relations found in real-world data are often not sufficient for implementing practicable navigation. Such relations often involve only a small fraction of the instances and nodes, usually require elaborate data cleaning but are nevertheless not completely error-safe. According to our experience additional, usually domain-specific types of relations are needed to implement the navigation. A convenient way of presenting such domain-specific recommendations is by using web recommendations. This way, recommendations become important means of navigation between the data from different data sources.

These are the main contributions of the research described in this part of the thesis:

- We study the problems which arise during the development of integrated e-commerce website, more specifically extraction and integration of the data and navigating in the integrated data. We propose the architecture for creating such integrated e-commerce websites. Integrated e-commerce websites are becoming increasingly popular. However, to our knowledge, the presented work is the first study of the data integration problems which are posed by such integrated e-commerce websites.

- We propose a new combined method of matching ontology and instance data in the context of e-commerce environment.

- We evaluate different methods for matching ontology and instance data and present evaluation results.

- We classify the types of recommendations which can be used on the integrated websites and propose new types of recommendations.

The part is organized as follows. In Chapter 10 we present the general architecture of EC-Fuice, outline the architecture of the web portal and the supporting services. We also give a detailed overview of the two systems which are used for data integration. The fist of the systems is the iFuice system which provides the website with data from the different data sources. The second is COMA++, the tool which we us to match ontologies in our system. In conclusion we explain how these tools work together to perform data integration in EC-Fuice. Chapter 11 describes the experiments on integrating product data and ontologies using iFuice and the semi-automatic ontology-matching system COMA++. Here we also evaluate experimental results regarding the application of different matching methods to the problem of ontology matching. In Chapter 12 we discuss the details of the EC-Fuice implementation, such as structure of the databases used in EC-Fuice, the web interface of EC-Fuice, the generation of recommendation on the integrated data and the different kinds of recommendations which can be presented on an integrated website. Chapter 13 gives an overview of related work and positions our approach within the research field of data integration and ontology matching. In Chapter 14 we summarize our work on recommendations in the integrated data environment and discuss possibilities for further research.

10. ARCHITECTURE OF EC-FUICE

10.1 Overview of the EC-Fuice Architecture

The general architecture of the EC-Fuice system is shown in Figure 3.1. Here, we show two types of the user interface our system supports. The first is the Web Portal interface, targeted for end users with common usage possibilities, such as keyword search, browsing etc. The second is the OLAP interface, which is devised for more complex analytical usage. In Figure 3.1 we show two interoperating databases: Web Portal Operational database and EC-Fuice Data Warehouse. These databases are served with integrated data, which come from the data sources through the data integration platform iFuice. iFuice has its own internal database which is used during the data integration process. The structure of the databases used in EC-Fuice is described in Chapter 12.

The data sources are shown in the lower part of Figure 3.1. For the sake of demonstrativeness, in Figure 3.1 we depict the specific data sources we used for our prototype. Our architecture in general, however, is in no way limited to these specific data

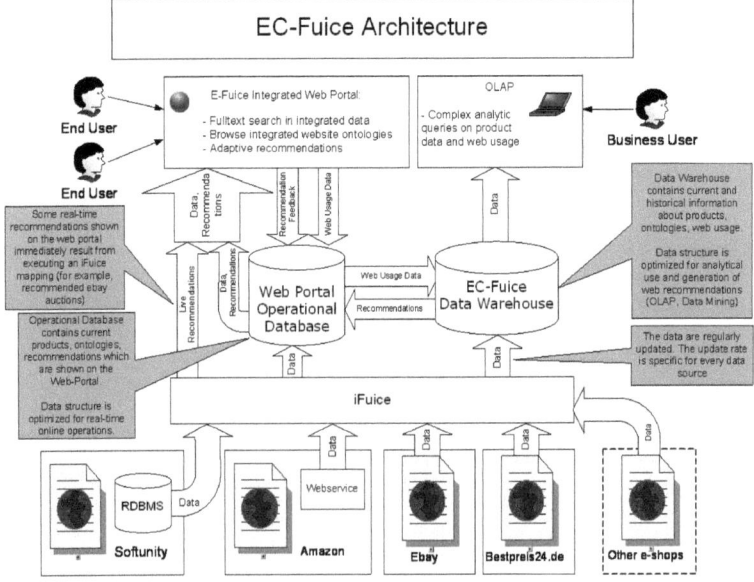

Figure 3.1. Overview of the EC-Fuice architecture.

sources but allows plugging in any other data source as well. In our prototype we have used the following data sources:

- Softunity – a German internet shop located at http://www.softunity.com and specializing in the distribution of software products. Books, DVD-Movies and some other products are also present in the product assortment.
- Amazon – "the world's largest online bookstore" (From Amazon advertisement). However, Amazon offers not only books, but also a wide range of other products, such as electronics, music, video products, household products etc. The German version of Amazon is located at located at http://www.amazon.de.
- eBay – eBay is an auction website. Because of this most data coming from eBay are very short lived. For most of the auctions there's no firm price. However, some of the data (auctions marked with "Buy it now /Sofort kaufen", "Best offer", "Sofort und neu") are similar to the usual e-commerce data in that they have firm price and remain listed for longer periods of time, from several weeks to several months. eBay has a very broad, practically unlimited assortment spectrum. The German version of eBay is located at http://www.ebay.de
- Bestpreis24 – German internet shop located at http://www.bestpreis24.de, which gathers products from other suppliers. Bestpreis24 specializes in computer- and office-related products.

The textual information contained in the data sources is mostly in German language.

We have also used some auxiliary data sources, for example the US version of the Amazon website. In contrast to the data sources listed above, the product data from these auxiliary data sources are not integrated into our framework. The auxiliary data sources are used to provide web recommendations leading to the external websites. The use of these additional data sources is discussed in Section 12.3.

Due to the huge amount of data, which is contained in the data sources listed above, and the modest (in comparison to the above sites) computational capacity of the equipment, on which our prototype runs, we limited the data to topics "Software" , "Video" and "Games". The topic "Software" is comprised of different types of consumer software for personal computers. The topic "Video" contains various video materials on DVD, VHS etc. The topic "Games" includes games for PC for different operating systems as well as games for game consoles. The topics usually also include some accompanying products, which are provided by the data source in the same interest area. For example, the topic "Software" also includes computer accessories, such as mouse pads and keyboards, the topic "Video" – film posters, the topic "Games" – game consoles, joysticks, books with game solutions etc.

The import of data is done according to the paradigm of the iFuice framework [RTA+05]. Access to data in the data sources is implemented using *executable mappings*[19]. An executable mapping can connect data sources to iFuice using many possible methods – by executing calls to a web service (Amazon), by querying a local SQL database (Softunity), by performing HTML-scraping (eBay, Bestpreis24). Other methods can be implemented by writing a wrapper in Java programming language. We will talk more about the implementation of the executable mappings in the next chapter. Several executable mappings are usually implemented for every data source. In most cases the data source provides at least executable product mappings and executable ontology mappings. There may also be other executable mappings to allow integrating additional information provided by a data source.

The integrated data produced by iFuice are used to regularly update both the web portal operational database and the EC-Fuice data warehouse. The update intervals can be set individually for each data source, since the rates at which information changes are specific for each data source.

The Web portal operational database stores the data and recommendations to be presented on the web portal. It also stores recommendation feedback and temporarily stores usage data before they are transferred to the EC-Fuice Data Warehouse. The web portal contains a module which performs optimization of the presented recommendations using the approach presented in the Part II of this thesis. In contrast to Part II, in this part we do not further study different approaches to generating recommendations. Instead, we investigate how the recommendations can be helpful in building navigation on an e-commerce website based on integrated data. However, in this part we also introduce a novel art of recommendations – live recommendations. Live recommendations are recommendations, which are requested by the web portal directly from iFuice avoiding the operational database. Live recommendations are can be provided by invoking individual iFuice mappings or iFuice scripts. The incentive for live recommendations is that some information is most valuable for a very short period of time. Examples for such information can be latest news or (as in our case) web recommendations based on last-second eBay auctions. Web portal contains a special module for live recommendations.

The web portal provides the following navigational features:

- Browsing in categories – the navigation in the link structure which connects categories with each other and with products within the same data source. The links in the browsing structure are characterized by their unambiguousness. The semantics of each link are strictly defined. For example, a link in the

---

[19] Between the works [RTA+05] which describes iFuice and the work [TR07] which describes the successor system MOMA, the use of the term *mapping* has changed. In iFuice *mapping* is an executable routine, which returns a set of correspondences between objects. This set of correspondences is called *mapping result* in iFuice. In MOMA, the term *mapping* is used to denote a set of correspondences which are returned by executable matchers. In this work we use iFuice terminology. In this thesis, we use the term *executable mapping* or *iFuice mapping* to refer to the executable mapping routine. The term *mapping* in this thesis is equivalent to *mapping result* in [RTA+05].

browsing structure can lead to a product in the current category, to a subcategory of the given category etc.

- Full-text search – allows searching product instances based on the relevance to the given query string.

- Recommendations – recommendations are computed based on different algorithms, they can be adaptive or not adaptive, pre-computed or live, lead from content of one data source to content of another data source or to external website. Recommendations make up a significant part of the navigation. As opposed to the unambiguous links in the browsing structure, the semantics of the recommendation links are "fuzzy". So, a recommendation link can lead from one category to a similar category in another data source or to a product in a related category. The degree of similarity or relatedness is not postulated in the original data but is approximated using some presumably intelligent technique.

Our e-commerce portal has no own features which allow purchasing products. It has no shopping cart and no payment system. Instead, we refer users to the websites from which the product descriptions come, so that they can make their purchase there.

The EC-Fuice data warehouse serves as an exhaustive data store for multiple purposes:

- Analysis of the product data using OLAP tools.
- Analysis of the web usage data from the web portal using OLAP tools.
- Automatic generation of the web usage based web recommendations

The database structure of the EC-Fuice data warehouse is tailored for analytical use by both humans and automated tools. The analytical (OLAP) interface to the data warehouse allows the manifold analysis of the competition. For example, it allows the comparison of individual products, price niveau comparison in different categories, analysis of the price trends over time and comparative analysis of the product spectrum's breadth with respect to price. We have communicated the results of our analysis to the company which operates the website http://www.softunity.com. The results of the analysis were assessed by the company's specialists and some price adjustments were made to the company's product assortment based on these results.

10.2 Data Integration in EC-Fuice

Essential parts of the e-commerce data are the product data and the product categories. In order to implement the navigation between the data sources, we have to match these data and establish mappings. To achieve this, we are using iFuice as the data integration platform and COMA++ as the tool for ontology matching. In this section we give a short description of both systems, sufficient for understanding of their application in our prototype. For more detailed information, please refer to the corresponding papers. iFuice is described in the paper [RTA+05], COMA in paper [DR02]. COMA++ is an extension of COMA described in [ADMR05] and [Do06] which features substantial improvements over its predecessor. One of these improvements is the ability of COMA++ to perform ontology matching. In this section we also discuss the collaboration between iFuice and COMA++ within the EC-Fuice framework.

10.2.1 iFuice

iFuice is a software platform for information integration and fusion which has been developed by the Database Group at the University of Leipzig. It has already been successfully applied in several projects. It was used for example for the comparative analysis of the bibliographical data from the leading database-related conferences and journals [RT05]. It was also used to implement the integration of the bioinformatics-related data. The goal of the application of iFuice in the field of bioinformatics was the consolidation of the data related to different genes and proteins, available from different public and private data sources [KR05].

iFuice is based on peer-to-peer executable mappings between data sources. The peer-to-peer architecture allows easy addition of new data sources. Executable mappings can be established between objects in the same data source or between objects coming from different data sources. The execution of mappings and the handling of the mapping results are controlled by the iFuice component called "mediator". The iFuice mediator is domain-independent, i.e. the same mediator is used for all problem domains. The mappings themselves are specific to the given problem domain. The executable mappings can be plugged into the mediator using several interfaces:

- as a Web Service. For the Web Service based data sources used in EC-Fuice we use Apache Axis library[20] to connect to web services.

- as a relational database. The relational database data sources used in EC-Fuice are connected using the respective JDBC libraries of the respective relational database servers.

- as an XML database or an XML file. In EC-Fuice, we use Exist as an XML[21] Database . For XML Files, we use Xerces[22] as XML parser and Saxon[23] as XQuery processor.

- as a plain text file

- using a custom Java object. An example of a custom Java object can be an HTML parser which extracts information from HTML pages of the websites.

---

[20] http://ws.apache.org/axis/
[21] http://exist.sourceforge.net/
[22] http://xerces.apache.org/xerces-j/
[23] http://saxon.sourceforge.net/

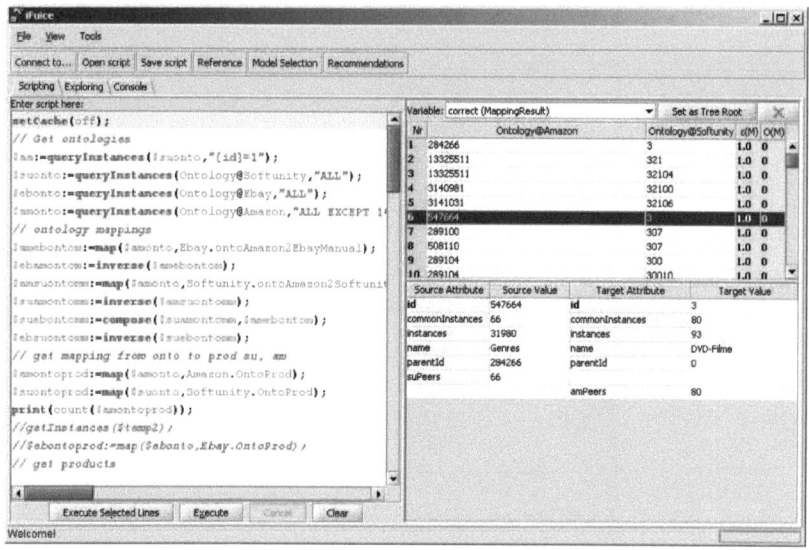

Figure 3.2. Screenshot of the iFuice GUI

For creating HTML parsers in EC-Fuice we use the Java HTMLParser library[24].

In contrast to the many other methods for information integration, iFuice doesn't require the creation of a global schema. The absence of a global schema leads to a decrease in the implementation effort, since it is known that creation of the global schema requires much effort but the quality of integration on the instance level nevertheless cannot be guaranteed. Instead, iFuice relies on a domain model which is of higher conceptual level than a global schema and reflects the semantic relations within the problem domain. A domain model is less detailed than a global schema and is easier to create and maintain. An iFuice domain model incorporates the objects types which exist in the given domain (for example publications, authors, venues for the bibliographic domain or genes, proteins and sequences for the bioinformatics domain) and the mapping types which exist between these object types (for example same publication, authors of a publication, etc.). Different data sources can provide objects of the same type. iFuice distinguishes "physical data sources" and "logical data sources". A physical data source is the a "real-world" data source, which can provide objects of different types. A physical data source encapsulates one or more Logical Data Sources (LDS). Each logical data source provides objects of one type. iFuice does not require the specification of all attributes of an object type in the domain model.

---

[24] http://htmlparser.sourceforge.net/

10 Architecture of EC-Fuice

However, the key attribute, also called *object id*, must be specified. The value of the object id must be present in all objects and unique for the given LDS. The mapping types represent semantic relations between object types. Every mapping type can have several mapping implementations which are specific to the data sources. For example, mapping type "author of publication" can have the implementation "return object of type 'author' from the data source B which corresponds to the object of type 'publication' from the data source A".

The iFuice mediator supports two methods for executing iFuice mappings. One method is navigational, in which the user navigates from one object to another in iFuice GUI using mappings between them. This method is useful for users wishing to explore the data in the data sources.

Another method is based on the iFuice scripting language, which allows creating of the scripts able to perform more complex data integration tasks. The scripts can be executed either by calling the iFuice mediator from a program written in a programming language or by specifying the script to be executed in iFuice GUI. The screenshot of the iFuice GUI is shown in Figure 3.2. The screen in Figure 3.2 is divided in several areas. The area on the right contains the text of the script which is used to integrate and manipulate the data. The right side shows the data in different variables which contain input and output data for the script, as described later on. The upper part of this area shows the list of objects or object pairs, the lower part shows the attributes of the respective objects.

The iFuice scripting language is based on a powerful set of operators which perform various operations and optionally assign the results of these operation to variables.

Variables can hold values of the following common data types: Integer, Float, and String. In addition to these common data types there are also iFuice-specific data types: ObjectInstances, MappingResult, AggregatedObjects, and AggregatedMappingResult. The data type ObjectInstances, as the name suggests, contains a set of object instances. The data type MappingResult describes a set of object correspondences, i.e. a set of object instance pairs. Each correspondence in a MappingResult has an associated quality metric. The quality metric is a value of type Float in the range [0..1]. The quality metric is set by the iFuice mapping during its execution. The set of all object instances on the left side of each correspondence in a MappingResult is called the domain of the MappingResult. The set of all object instances on the right side of each correspondence in a MappingResult is called the range of the MappingResult.

The type AggregatedObjects describes a set of aggregated objects. An aggregated object is a set of semantically equal object instances from different data sources. An AggregatedMappingResult is a set of correspondences between aggregated objects. We do not use AggregatedObjects and AggregatedMappingResult in EC-Fuice.

The iFuice variables are not strictly typed, i.e. each variable can hold values of any supported type. By convention of the iFuice scripting language the variables are denoted by identifiers prefixed by "$". In some cases, when an operation requires a reference to the variable rather than the value held by the variable, the variable name needs to be prefixed by the symbol "&".

The data types Integer and Float types support the basic arithmetic operations "+","-","*","/". String data type supports the concatenation operation "+".

The iFuice operators which we have utilized for implementing EC-Fuice are summarized in Table 3.1 and described further in this section. Description of the other operators can be found in the paper [RTA+05]. There are also some new useful operators which have been introduced to iFuice after the paper [RTA+05] was published. We utilized these operators in EC-Fuice and describe these operators here as well. For each operator in Table 3.1 we also show a possible set of input parameters. For example, $MR denotes that the operator expects a variable containing a MappingResult as input parameter. $O denotes a variable containing ObjectInstances. The notation $variable shows that the operator can handle variables containing different data types. Sometimes there is more than one way to invoke an operator. So, for example, the operator queryInstances can be used to query a data source or to query a variable of type ObjectIstances. In such cases, we show one of the invocation variants in the table and describe other invocation variants further in text.

Operator	Short description
queryInstances(DataSource, "query")	Query instances from a data source
queryMapResult($MR,"query")	Query a variable which contains a MappingResult
getInstances($O)	Get all attributes for objects instances
map($O,Mapping)	Execute mapping Mapping using $variable as input and return MappingResult
traverse($O,Mapping)	Execute mapping Mapping using $variable as input and return ObjectInstances
compose($MR1,$MR2)	Find all equivalent object instances in the range of $MR1 and the domain of MR2. Return a MappingResult consisting of the domain ObjectInstance from $MR1and the range ObjectInstance from $MR2 for all such equivalent object instances.
union($variable,$variable)	Perform the set operation ∪ on the sets of object instances or correspondences in the input variables
intersect($variable,$variable)	Perform the set operation ∩ on the sets of object instances or correspondences in the input variables
diff($variable,$variable)	Perform the set subtraction operation on the sets of object instances or correspondences in the input variables
attrMatch($O1,$O2,MatchMethod, Attribute,Attribute,Threshold)	Perform generic attribute-based matching sets of object instances in the input variables using one of the match methods provided by iFuice
match(($O1,$O2,Matcher)	Perform matching sets of object instances in the input variables using a custom matcher

domain($MR)	Return the set of object instances from the domain or MappingResult
range($MR)	Return the set of object instances from the range or MappingResult
inverse($MR)	Switch the domain and the range of a MappingResult, i.e. mapping result $O1->$O2 becomes $O2->$O1
print($variable)	Output the contents of a variable to the console
if \<condition\> then \<operators\> end	Execute operators if a condition is true
while \<condition\> do \<operators\> end	Repeat operators while condition is true

Table 3.1. iFuice operators used in EC-Fuice

One of the essential iFuice operators is the operator "map". This operator executes a mapping, taking a variable of the type ObjectInstances and the name of the iFuice mapping to be executed as input parameters. The operator "map" returns data of the type MappingResult. An example of executing the operator "map" using the iFuice scripting syntax is given below:

$SoftunityToAmazonMappingResult:=map($SoftunityProducts,Softunity.Softunity2Amazon);

Here *$SoftunityProducts* is a variable which contains data of type ObjectInstances. Such variable can be obtained for example using the operator queryInstances, which is discussed later on. ":=" stands for the assignment operation. "*Softunity.Softunity2Amazon*" is the name of the iFuice mapping. According to the EC-Fuice naming convention, the names of the mappings have a form of

"*\<DatasourceName\>.\<NameOfTheMappingProper\>*"

where "DatasourceName" denotes the first of the data sources for which the iFuice mapping is applicable. This naming pattern is however only a convention and not an iFuice requirement.

There are several kinds of iFuice mappings. The kinds of mappings can be classified along different perspectives. With respect to the kind of the input data, we discern query mappings and id mappings. The id mappings establish correspondences between the objects from two data sources or within the same data source. Internally iFuice represents such mappings as a set of correspondences between object ids. Query mappings differ from the id mappings in that they do not map objects from data sources to each other, but rather map a special object of the type "query" to a set of output objects. They allow getting objects based on given criteria from a data source. The query is formulated in the query language which is native to the data source. For example, it can be SQL for the relational database source, XQuery for an XML data source, a special proprietary language for a web service or just a set of keywords for an HTML data source. Below are some examples of executing a query mapping using the iFuice scripting syntax:

$SoftunityProduct:=queryInstances(Product@Softunity,"title like 'Harry%'");
$AmazonOntology:=queryInstances(Ontology@Amazon,"Software,Video,Games EXCEPT Software/Specials,Games/Specials,Video/For Rent");
$eBayProducts:= queryInstances(Product@eBay,"keyword");

The operator queryInstances may also be applied to iFuice variables which contain data of the type ObjectInstances. In this case, a special iFuice query language is used, which is similar to the syntax of SQL "WHERE" clause. The only additional requirement compared to SQL is that attribute names must be surrounded by square brackets:

$SoftunityProduct1:=queryInstances($SoftunityProduct,"[title] like '%Potter%'");

A similar operator queryMapResult is provided for querying variables of the type "MappingResult". To distinguish between the attributes of the two object instances which constitute a correspondence, the attribute names are prefixed with respectively "domain." and "range.". A special attribute "_confidence" is available for access to the quality metric of the correspondence. An example of the usage of the operator queryMapResult is shown below:

SoftunityToAmazonMappingResult1:=queryMapResult(SoftunityToAmazonMappingResult, "[domain.title] like 'Harry%' and [range.title] like '%Potter%' and [_confidence]>0.5");

With respect to the semantics of the executable mappings iFuice differentiates between "same"-mappings and association mappings. "Same"-mappings establish correspondences between the objects which represent the same "real-world" object, i.e. are semantically equivalent. It should be noted, that "same" mappings in practice do not guarantee the full identity of the object instances, i.e. recall and precision values of 100%. Such mappings may contain errors, which should of course be minimized in order for these mappings to be practically useful. Association mapping represent types of semantic relations other then equivalence. The particular semantics of the association mappings are specific to the problem domain.

Many real-world domains, including the domain of e-commerce, are characterized by the large volume of available data and therefore impose high memory requirements on the data integration applications. Because of that, iFuice allows mappings which require only sets of object ids as input and output data. This way, the storing of the complete object with all attributes in memory can be avoided. Every LDS must provide a special routine, which allows getting all attributes of the object with a given id. These routines are utilized by the iFuice operator getInstances. An example of the executing the operator "getInstances" is given below:

$eBayProducts:=getInstances($eBayProductIds);

The variable $eBayProductIds contains data of type ObjectInstances. In every object instance, however, only the id attribute is present. The operator getInstances determines the LDS from which the object instances contained in the parameter originate and executes the appropriate "getInstances"-implementation. After execution, the result variable $eBayProducts contains object instances with all attributes.

iFuice makes a distinction between "single mappings" and "bulk mappings". This notation characterizes the handling of data inside of the implementation of the iFuice mapping and the interface between mapping and the iFuice mediator. In case of a single mapping the iFuice mediator iterates over the set of input instances and performs one call to the executable mapping for every instance. Such executable mappings are relatively easy to implement and are more easily comprehensible, since the programmer needs to implement only the matching of a single instance. Bulk mappings on the contrary are called one time for the entire input dataset and not once per instance. They require more implementation effort but allow speeding up the execution of the mapping, especially in the case of large input sets. Bulk mappings also offer additional possibilities of utilizing the relations which exist within the input dataset. Such bulk mappings are especially suitable for the ontology mapping, since they receive the entire ontology in one input set with all nodes and edges and can use this information while computing the mapping.

The iFuice mediator also allows traversing executable mappings and composing mapping results. Traversing mappings means executing a sequence of mappings. Thereby the output of the previous mapping becomes the input of the next mapping. The result of the traversing is a MappingResult which contains correspondences between the input data of the first mapping and the output data of the last mapping. Composing is analogous to traversing, with the difference that it is done not over a sequence of executable mappings but over a sequence of MappingResult variables. Operators such as union and diff can be applied to the data of the types ObjectInstances and MappingResult. The execution flow in the iFuice scripts can be managed using flow control operators similar to the ones found in the modern programming languages. Examples of operators which perform these operations are shown below (the code does not constitute a continuous program but rather a collection of fragments from different programs):

$SoftunityToeBayProductsMappingResult:= traverse($SoftunityProducts,
{Softunity.Softunity2Amazon, Amazon.Amazon2eBay});
$SoftunityToeBayProductsMappingResult:=compose(
$SoftunityToAmazonProductsMappingResult,
$AmazonToeBayProductsMappingResult);
$eBayProducts:=union($eBaySoftware,$eBayGames);
$CommonProducts:=intersect($SoftwareProducts,$GameProducts);
$OnlySoftwareProducts:=diff($SoftwareProducts,$GameProducts);

// Example of a "while" loop construct
$j:=0;
while $j<=9 do

print ("[id] like '"+ $j+"%'");
if $j>3 then
$ebprodtemp:=queryInstances($ebprod,"[id] like '"+$j+"%'");
else
getInstances($ebprodtemp);
end
$j:=$j + 1;
end

The lines in the iFuice scripts which begin with the symbols "//" are considered comments and not further interpreted by the iFuice mediator. We will use comments for explaining the details of the scripts later on.

iFuice also has the concept of a "matcher". Matchers operate on the data of the type MappingResult and adjust the value of the quality metric basing on some algorithm. Matchers can be for example applied to improve recall and precision of "same"-mappings based on some additional information.

iFuice provides several standard matcher algorithms, including trigram string attribute similarity and affix string attribute similarity. Below is an example of using standard trigram attribute matcher:

$SoftunityToAmazonMappingResultRefined:=
attrMatch($SoftunityToAmazonMappingResult, "[title]", "[title]",MATCHER_TRIGRAM, 0.3)

Here, *$SoftunityToAmazonMappingResult* holds the initial MappingResult which will be refined by the matcher. *$SoftunityToAmazonMappingResultRefined* is the variable which will hold the resulting MappingResult after the execution of the matcher. Parameters with value "[title]" give the name of the attributes which will be used by the attribute matcher. MATCHER_TRIGRAM sets the name of the matching algorithm to be executed. The last, optional parameter value 0.3 sets the similarity threshold for the attribute matcher.

It is also possible to implement and use own matchers. Below are the examples of using custom matchers:

$SoftunityToAmazonMappingResultRefined:=match($SoftunityToAmazonMappingResult,
Softunity.CategoryMatcher)

Here, *$SoftunityToAmazonMappingResult* contains the input MappingResult and *$SoftunityToAmazonMappingResultRefined* contains the output mapping result. "Softunity.CategoryMatcher" is the name of the custom matcher.

Adding new data sources, executable mappings and custom matchers to iFuice requires relatively little effort. They are configured using XML configuration files, an example of which is shown in Appendix. The domain model, i.e. object types, mapping types and relations between them are also stored in the XML files.

In general, iFuice is a highly customizable integration platform featuring several highlights, which are especially important for building modern e-commerce applications:

- Absence of the global schema
- Peer-to-peer-like paradigm
- XML-based configuration
- Implementation in Java programming language, for which a large number of adapters for diverse data sources already exists or can be easily created
- Executable mappings which allow implementing highly complex data transformations
- Rich possibilities for composing executable mappings and manipulating data and mapping results

These distinctive features make iFuice a good choice as a platform for integrating data in the e-commerce domain.

10.2.2 COMA and COMA++

COMA is a platform for schema matching developed by the Database Group at the University of Leipzig [DR02]. COMA++ described in [ADMR05] and [Do06] is an extended version of COMA which has a significant number of additional features compared to its predecessor. The novel feature of COMA++ which is particularly important for the topic of our research is its ability to match ontologies. COMA++ encompasses the full functionality of COMA. Because of this, henceforth we will be speaking only of COMA++.

The task of schema and ontology matching is to obtain semantic mappings between input schemas or ontologies. Such mappings consist of the correspondences between the elements of the schemas or ontologies. The correspondences between the real-world concepts which are represented as schema or ontology elements are characterized by high diversity and semantic richness. Such correspondences may have different cardinality, i.e. be 1:1, 1:n or n:m correspondences and have specific direction. For schemas, the correspondences often have associated "mapping expressions", which specify how the instances of one schema can be transformed into instances in another schema. In general case, however, it is not practically feasible to produce mappings encompassing the entire complexity of such real-world correspondences with an automatic tool. Therefore, COMA++ uses a simplified representation of a mapping. All the correspondences in a COMA++ mapping correspondences have cardinality 1:1 and type "similarity". Each correspondence also has an attached value from 0 to 1 denoting the degree of similarity, where 0 stand for no similarity and 1 for equality. The interpretation of the domain-specific meaning of the similarity values is left to the application which uses the results of the mapping. The correspondences with cardinalities 1:n and n:m are represented through multiple 1:1 correspondences. The COMA++ correspondences are non-directed. It is however possible to configure the matching process in such a way that only the correspondences having a specified direction are included in the resulting mapping.

COMA++ is based on a generic data model which allows supporting input schemas and ontologies expressed in different languages, such as Structured Query Language (SQL), W3C XML Schema Definition (XSD), Resource Description Framework (RDF), Web Ontology Language (OWL), and XML Data Reduced (XDR). COMA++ translates the input schemas and ontologies into the internal format based on rooted directed acyclic graphs. The rooted acyclic graphs are stored in the COMA++ repository implemented using the relational database technology. The repository is also used to store the resulting mappings between schemas and ontologies.

COMA++ consists of the following components:

- parsers/importers for the input data
- schema pool and mapping pool
- repository

- match customizer, which is in turn comprised of:
  - a library of matching algorithms (or shortly matchers)
  - mapping refinement strategies
  - execution engine
  - exporters
- graphical user interface (ComaGUI)

The parsers and importers are responsible for reading the schema, ontology and mapping data in the various supported input formats and for loading these data into the schema pool and mapping pool. The schema pool and mapping pool contain the schemas, ontologies and mappings in the main memory which can be immediately used for matching. The schemas in the schema pool can be subjected to preprocessing, aimed for example to transform complex data types into simple ones or recognize shared element which are declared inline at multiple places[Do06]. The preprocessing techniques of COMA++ are focused in the first places on preprocessing of schemas rather than ontologies. We do not use these techniques in this work and therefore omit the description of the schema preprocessing in COMA++.

The repository provides a persistent storage for schemas, ontologies and mappings which can be used later. The relational database server MySQL is used to implement the repository.

The match customizer allows specification of parameters which influence the matching process. The parameters which can be configured by the match customizer are:

- the choice of the matchers from the matcher library
- configuration of the combined matchers, constructed from the matchers in the matcher library
- mapping refinement strategy
- combination of the similarity values and selection of match candidates based on the calculated combined similarity

To match the schemas and ontologies, COMA++ provides an expandable matcher library. Below we discuss the matching algorithms provided by COMA++ and the parameters of these algorithms, focusing on the algorithms and parameters which are important for understanding of the experiments described later in this thesis. The built-in matching algorithms (or simply matchers) fall in two categories[25]:

---

[25] In the original COMA and COMA++ papers [DR02][ADMR05] the hybrid matchers were called simple matchers and combined matchers were called hybrid matchers. The naming of the matcher types which is used here originates from [Do06]. Such naming better reveals the nature of the matchers. So, in a hybrid matcher the combination the algorithms which constitute the matcher is hard-coded. This applies also in the case when only a single algorithm is used. In the combined matchers the interaction of the algorithms of which the matcher is comprised can be flexibly configured.

- hybrid matchers
- combined matchers

The following hybrid matchers are available:

- **Affix:** matches affixes, i.e. prefixes and suffixes of a string.
- **N-gram:** (bigram, trigram, etc.): matches all common n-letter substrings of a string.
- **EditDistance:** calculates the string similarity based on the number of edit operations needed to transform one string into another, so called Levenshtein metric[Lev66]
- **Soundex:** calculates the phonetic similarity of the strings based on soundex algorithm.
- **Synonyms:** calculates string similarity based on the synonym table, provided by user.
- **Data types:** calculates the similarity of the fields in database schema, based on their data types.
- **UserFeedback:** based on the matches and mismatches specified interactively by user.
- **ReuseSchema:** this matcher uses the results of previously matched schemas or ontologies which are stored in the repository. The intuition behind this matcher is that some schemas which need to be matched may be similar to the schemas already matched. This is an extension of the idea of a Synonym matcher, with the difference that in Synonym matcher the synonyms need to be entered manually, whereas the reuse matcher tries to determine the semantic similarity based on previous experience.
- **ReuseFragment:** analogous to the ReuseSchema matcher, however operates not on results of matching the entire schemas but on fragments of previously matched schemas.
- **Taxonomy:** this matcher calculates the similarity of the elements based on their distance to each other in the taxonomy provided by user.

At the time when we conducted our experiments COMA++ provided no instance-based matchers. Currently, COMA++ has implemented constraint-based and content-based instance matchers [EM07]. This work is discussed in Section 13.2 in more detail.

Some of the hybrid matchers, for example affix, n-gram, and EditDistance can operate on different input data. The possible types of input data include node names, paths from the root of the internal graph, data types, descriptions or other additional data. To enrich the input data additional types of input data can be obtained from original data using preprocessing. These generated input data can be constituents of the properties of the input elements, for example individual lexical terms which constitute the element name or description, deciphered abbreviations etc. Another type of the generated input data is obtained by considering the structural context of the matched elements. Such input data are manifold. Following are the types of the element data which can be generated by COMA++ and supplied to the matchers:

- **Parents, Siblings, Children**: the elements of the schema/ontology which appear respectively as parents, siblings or children of the node in the internal directed graph. The original relations need not necessarily have "child-parent" semantic.

- **Leaves**: the children of the element in the internal directed graph which have no further children.

- **Ascendants, Descendants**: ascendants and descendants of the element in the internal directed graph.

- **AscPaths, DescPaths**: paths from the root of the internal graph respectively to the ascendants and the descendants of the element.

The type of input data can be configured for every matcher invocation. In the course of matching the same matcher can be applied several times on different input data.

The built-in combined matchers are pre-configured combinations of the hybrid matchers, determined empirically and known to be successful for some often encountered matching tasks. COMA++ also provides flexible possibilities for combining the hybrid and combined matchers into more complex combined matchers in order to achieve higher quality of the resulting mapping.

Another technique COMA++ provides in order to increase the quality of the resulting mappings is the ability to do iterative refinement of the mappings. The process of matching is executed iteratively. Depending on the strategy chosen in the match customizer, one or several iterations are executed. The mappings obtained in one iteration can be used as input data for the next iteration. COMA++ provides several strategies for refinement of the mappings such as context-dependent matching, fragment-based matching and reuse-oriented matching. Context-dependent matching refines the mapping based on the intuition that similar elements usually have similar neighborhoods. These neighborhoods are called "contexts". COMA++ provides two strategies for performing context-dependent matching: AllContext and FilteredContext. In case of the AllContext strategy all found contexts are matched, in case of the FilteredContext strategy only the contexts whose cumulative similarity is higher than the given threshold are matched.

Fragment-based matching is useful for large schemas, which are likely to have relatively small matching portions. The conventional approach of matching all elements of one schema to all elements of other schema may lead to performance degradation as well as deterioration of the quality of the resulting mapping [Do06]. In this case, it makes sense first to determine the portions of the schemas which have significant similarity and then match the elements contained in these portions. Reuse-oriented matching is a matching strategy which uses mappings in the repository and works in collaboration with the reuse matchers. There's also a special ontology matching strategy specific to the COMA++ version which collaborates with the taxonomy matcher and is using a shared taxonomy.

It has been widely recognized that fully automatic schema and ontology matching does not achieve practically acceptable quality in general case and that human intervention is usually necessary. COMA++ takes this into account and provides several ways of allowing human assistance to the automatic matching. COMA++ allows fully automatic matching with posterior manual adjustment and also and iterative semi-automatic approach where human intervention happens after every match iteration of the matching process.

The matching process itself is carried out by the execution engine according to the parameters specified in the match customizer. Every iteration consists of several basic steps. The basic steps of the match iteration are component identification, matcher execution and similarity combination. During the component identification step COMA++ generates the input data for matchers basing on the internal graphs of the source and target ontologies. The matchers are then executed independently from each other. Every combined matcher is executed in a manner similar to the entire matching process. In the similarity combination step the similarity values returned by the individual matchers are combined and the match candidates are selected. The combination and selection process in its turn consists of three substeps, with an optional fourth:

Aggregation: in this substep the similarity values computed by different matchers are aggregated, so that for each pair of elements exactly one similarity value is obtained.

Ranking: in this substep we rank the elements of one schema with respect to the other schema according to the similarity values obtained in the previous step. The direction of the ranking (i.e. elements of which schema are ranked) is set by the parameter Direction as described later in this Section.

Selection: in this substep the best match candidates are selected from the ranked elements.

At the end of the last iteration an additional substep of may be performed, which combines the similarity values of the individual mappings to a single value which denotes the cumulative similarity value of the matched schemas or ontologies. This substep is required for combined matchers.

The following parameters of the steps can be adjusted using match customizer to control how each step is being executed:

Aggregation: aggregation strategies can be selected among max, min, weighted and average. Here, max and min denote that respectively maximal and minimal values are chosen among all similarity values returned by matchers. In case of weighted strategy the similarity value is calculated according to the formula:

$$\text{WeightedSim}(s_1, s_2) = \sum_{m \in M} w_m * \text{sim}(s_1, s_2, m) \text{ with } \sum_{m \in M} w_m = 1$$

[Do06], where s_1, s_2 are the elements in the matched schemas, similarity between which is being calculated, M – set of matchers which provided similarity values for correspondence between s_1 and s_2, sim(s_1,s_2,m) – similarity value provided for correspondence between s_1 and s_2 by the matcher m $\in$M. *Average* is a special case of the *weighted* strategy, where all the weights w_m are equal.

Direction: for the ranking step, the following direction settings are available: *LargeSmall, SmallLarge, Both*. As the names suggest, direction can be specified with respect to the size of the schemas being matched. In case when the setting *Both* is selected, the correspondences appear in the resulting mapping only when they are identified as correspondences in both directions. In our experiments we use only the setting *Both,* since we are only interested in bidirectional mappings.

Selection. For selection, several parameters can be specified: *MaxN, MaxDelta, Threshold*. The parameter MaxN takes an integer value which specifies how many top-ranking correspondence candidates will appear in the resulting mapping. The parameter MaxDelta takes a floating-point value which specifies that all correspondence candidates whose similarity value differs no more than MaxDelta from the highest ranking correspondence candidate are taken over to the resulting mapping. MaxDelta can be specified as absolute value or relative to the value of the highest ranking correspondence candidate. Threshold is a floating-point value which specifies that no correspondence candidate with similarity value less than threshold should appear in the resulting mapping. Unlike previous steps, the parameters in this step can be combined. This is often useful, since each parameter used alone has some drawbacks. So, MaxN and MaxDelta may return correspondences with too low similarity value, while Threshold may return too few correspondences. A reasonable configuration is using MaxN or MaxDelta combined with relatively low value of the Threshold parameter to cut off the admittedly low-quality correspondences.

Combination. Two strategies are available for combination of the similarities of the multiple correspondence candidates to obtain one cumulative similarity value: *average* and *Dice*. *Average*, as the name suggests, is obtained by dividing the sum of all similarity values through the total number of elements in the schemas or ontologies being matched. *Dice* is based on the Dice coefficient [CAFP98] and is the ratio of the elements which can be matched to the total number of elements in the input ontologies or schemas. Dice coefficient is not influenced by the individual similarity values of the correspondence candidates.

COMA++ allows exporting schemas, ontologies and mappings in a proprietary text-based format. The mappings can be exported as OWL/RDF as well. We have also implemented a wrapper for the COMA++ repository, which allows exposing of the

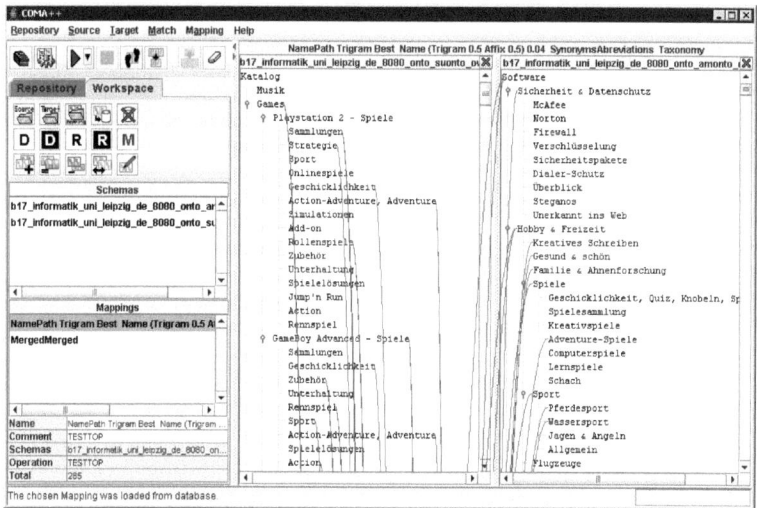

Figure 3.3. COMA++ graphical user interface

ontology mappings created by COMA++ to iFuice as iFuice mappings. Using this wrapper, COMA++ and iFuice can transparently exchange data between each other.

COMA++ features a powerful graphical user interface shown in Figure 3.3 which can be used to:

- import schemas, ontologies and mappings into the schema pool and mapping pool
- persist selected schemas, ontologies and mappings into repository, load or delete them from the repository
- configure the parameters of the match customizer
- manually edit mappings, specify fragments for fragment-based matching.

The COMA++ GUI also allows operations on schemas and ontologies, such as:

Domain: given two schemas/ontologies and a mapping between them, return the matching part of the source schema/ontology.

InvertDomain: given two schemas/ontologies and a mapping between them, return the non-matching part of the source schema/ontology.

Range: given two schemas/ontologies and a mapping between them, return the matching part of the target schema/ontology.

InvertRange: given two schemas/ontologies and a mapping between them, return the non-matching part of the target schema/ontology.

The COMA ++ GUI also provides access to the following operations on mappings:

Merge: merge two mappings into one, which contains all correspondences present in at least one of the original mappings.

Diff: return all correspondences from one mapping which are not contained in another mapping

Intersect: return all correspondences from one mapping, which are also contained in another mapping

Compare: COMA ++ also supports comparative evaluation of different matchers and strategies. The COMA++ GUI allows selecting a mapping as a base for comparison and comparing it either to another mapping or to all available mappings with identical source and target schemas/ontologies. For each pair of mapping, COMA++ calculates the values of recall and precision, which are widely known measures in the field of information retrieval. Also COMA++ calculates the values of the combined metrics F-Measure [Rijs79] and Overall, which has been introduced in [MGR02] under the name Accuracy.

In general, COMA++ is a versatile platform which has proven to be successfully applicable to schemas and ontologies from many problem domains. We use COMA++ to create mappings between E-commerce ontologies, based on the structural and lexical information contained in the ontologies. The instance data are not taken into consideration for generating COMA++-based mappings.

10.2.3 Integration of Web Data using iFuice and COMA++

The iFuice platform plays a central part in our architecture for web data integration. iFuice acts as a base framework for data extraction, transformation and integration operations. It also provides the temporary working storage for both product instance and product category data and performs the loading of data into the web portal operational database.

The process of the integration of the e-commerce data in iFuice utilizing COMA++ is schematically shown in Figure 3.4. For clarity, we show only two data sources in Figure 3.4. In case when more data sources need to be integrated, they are integrated pair-wise. The data shown in the picture are limited to product instances and product categories, i.e. here we do not show any additional information which may be provided by a data source. In iFuice, the products and product categories are handled uniformly as object instances of different object types. The products are handled as object instances of type "Product", the product categories – as object instances of type "Ontology". COMA++ is used as a tool to implement iFuice mappings for the object instances of type "Ontology".

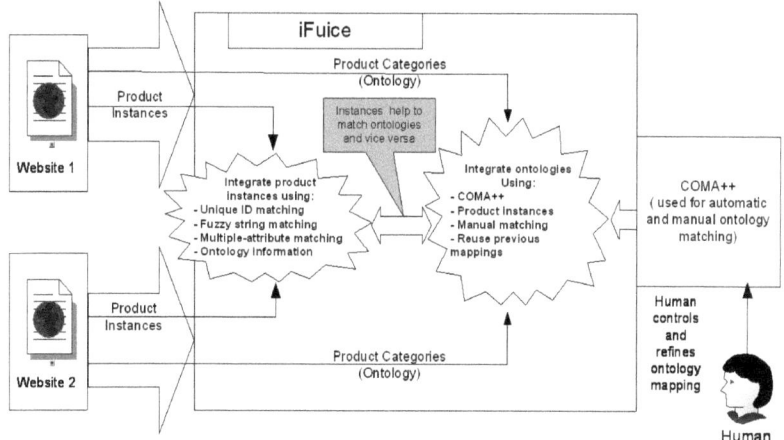

Figure 3.4. Integrating e-commerce data in iFuice.

As shown in Figure 3.4, the data from the data sources are imported into iFuice. To enable the data import, the data source usually provides several executable mappings. At least two executable mappings are mandatory. One of the executable mappings should be a mapping which allows obtaining either all products or all product categories. The other executable mapping should map the products to product categories or vice versa, depending on what type of data is provided by the first executable mapping.

Normally, however, the data sources provide more than two executable mappings. This allows more convenience and more flexibility for the iFuice scripts and may also provide additional data useful for matching. A typical set of executable mappings usually includes query mappings for both products and product categories and at least one of the mappings between the products and product categories within one data source. The inverse mapping for a given executable mapping can be obtained by applying the iFuice operation *inverse*()[26] on the materialized results of the original executable mapping. This is very important for the cases when due to the nature of the data source the mapping in one direction can be implemented more easily than in the other direction. In such cases, it is sufficient to implement only the easier executable mapping. By convention, in our executable mappings between products and categories every product which belongs to a certain product category also belongs to all parent categories of that category (i.e. we use "is-a" relations for products in the ontologies). In the mapping results produced by our executable mappings, if a product has an explicit correspondence to a category, there are also explicit correspondences to all parents of this category. The relations between categories in the ontology are however "child-of" (i.e. a category only has an explicit

---

[26] See Table 3.1 for the description of the operator *inverse*()

correspondence to its parent and not to the parent's parent). This convention is consistent with the way Softunity, Amazon and eBay assign products to the categories in the ontology. Product ontologies from other data sources can be converted to this convention using special executable mappings. Such convention is not an obligatory requirement. However, this greatly simplifies the iFuice scripts used to control the data integration process.

The integration process is managed by custom iFuice scripts, which allow tight fitting of the integration process to the particularities of the e-commerce data. The goal of our integration system is to provide automatic integration of the data sources which are specified in the design of the website.

The toothed clouds in Figure 3.4 represent the matching of the object instances of the same object type coming from different data sources to each other. The thick arrows in Figure 3.4 show the cooperation between the process of matching of different object types made possible by the compound COMA++/iFuice framework. The exact sequence of operations which are executed in the course of the matching process can be flexibly configured using iFuice scripts. For example, it is possible to first match the product data using fuzzy string matching and then refine the resulting matching using multiple-attribute matching. Further the results of the product data matching can be refined using the results of the ontology matching. Such flexibility is made possible by the fact that all the needed data are available in the iFuice cache. The result of the integration process shown in Figure 3.4 consists of two mappings between the participating data sources. One of the mappings contains correspondences between the products, the other mapping the correspondences between the ontologies of the respective data sources.

The process of exporting of the resulting data is not shown in Figure 3.4. The export of the integrated data into Web Portal Operational Database and EC-Fuice data warehouse is implemented using the executable mappings, which return pre-defined values "successful" or "not successful" as mapping result.

The data integration process is best illustrated using an example. The iFuice script shown below performs the data integration process which is graphically presented in Figure 3.4. The script is simplified for better demonstrativeness:

// Import
$suonto:=queryInstances(Ontology@Softunity,\"ALL\");
$suontoprod:=map($suonto,Softunity.OntoProd);
$suprodonto:=inverse($suontoprod);
$suprod:=range($suontoprod);

//Matching Section
//matching products
$suamprod:=map($suprod,Softunity.SoftunityProduct2AmazonProduct_TitleEquals)
//matching ontology without COMA++
$suamonto:=map($suprod,Softunity.SoftunityProduct2AmazonOntology_TitleEquals)
//matching ontology using COMA++ in automatic mode

$suamontoComa:=map($suprod,COMA.ComaAutomatic)

//Export
$ExportStatus:=map($suprod,ECFuice.ExportProducts)
$ExportStatus:=map($suprod,ECFuice.ExportOntology)

In this simple script the products and ontologies are mapped in the simple (but not the best possible) way based on the string equality title attribute of the products and product categories. Other ways of mapping the data are described in the later sections. A part of the script which prepares the data for loading into the EC-Fuice operating database is shown in Appendix 3.

The following simple ways of matching are provided: unique id matching, fuzzy string matching, multiple-attribute matching, ontology-based. In the next chapter we will show that these simple techniques are not working very well alone and present other approaches which combine these simple techniques to achieve better quality of the generated mappings. The combined techniques are implemented by amending the iFuice scripts.

Building of such an integration script is one of the core tasks for creating an integrated website based on the EC-Fuice architecture. The E-commerce data, as well as many other types of data typically found on the web, change frequently. Therefore, the data integration process should be designed to allow repeated execution when the data in the data sources change.

The data integration process should be also tailored to the requirements of the application and the characteristics of the input data. Ideally, the design of such integration data process should be carried out similarly to the AHP (Analytic Hierarchy Process) method as suggested for ontology matching in [KW04a]. AHP is a systematic approach developed to structure expectance, intuition and heuristics-based decision making into a well-defined methodology on the basis of sound mathematical principles [BR04][27]. Such a structured approach however requires that a sufficient body of expert knowledge about how different matching techniques and their combinations perform for different data is accumulated. In the AHP approach, the decisions about using specific matchers are then made basing comparing the application requirements against the characteristics of the matchers in the expert knowledge base.

However, at the moment we have only a limited understanding of how the different matching techniques and particularly their combinations behave in different situations. Therefore, we apply an iterative process to design the data integration script and to select the best matchers. In every iteration we make assumptions about the performance of the matchers based on the knowledge about how they operate. Then we test the matchers with different parameters, select the best ones and make assumptions about further

---

[27] It is important to note, that AHP is not a computer algorithm, but rather a methodology to be applied by humans while designing computer algorihtms which contain a heuristic component.

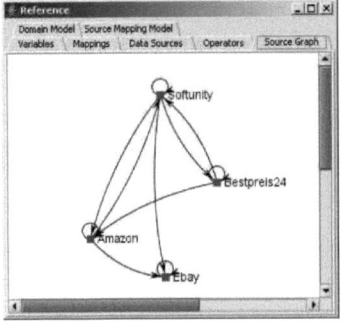 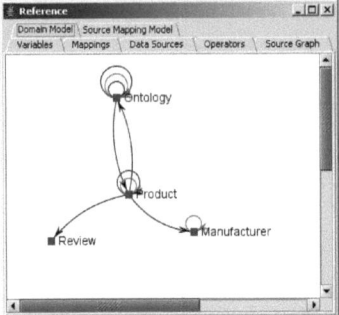

Figure 3.5. Source graph	Figure 3.6. Domain model

improvements by combining the current matchers with additional matchers. We will illustrate this iterative process by presenting examples of it in Sections 11.1 and 11.2.

The matching of the product data can be used to facilitate the matching of the ontologies and vice versa. One of the approaches to matching ontologies is by using the techniques provided by COMA++. COMA++ has automatic matchers and also a GUI, using which the human editor can control and refine the ontology mapping. COMA++ can be called from iFuice in automatic or interactive mode. In interactive mode, a human editor

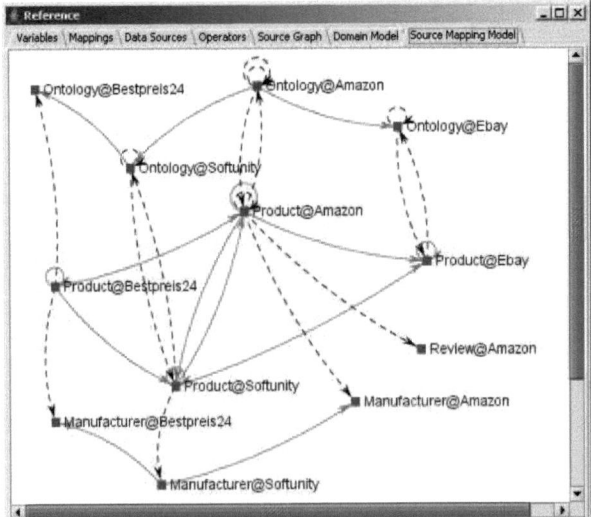

Figure 3.7. Source-mapping model

can control and refine the ontology mappings.

The four data sources used in our prototype are shown on the graph in Figure 3.5. The arrows in Figure 3.5 denote the existence of mappings between the data sources, irrespectively of the types of the mappings or the types of objects which are mapped. The mappings of the objects within one data source are shown with closed arrows. Figure 3.6 shows the domain model, i.e. the object types and the types of mappings between the different objects types. The object types that we are already familiar with are Product and Ontology. There are also two additional object types – Review and Manufacturer. These object types represent data which are instrumental for the generation of recommendations. In Figure 3.6, arrows denote the existence of the mappings of a certain mapping type from one object type to another irrespectively of the data sources from which the objects come.

Figure 3.7 shows the graph of the source-mapping model. In this graph, every vertex represents one LDS, i.e. object type provided by a particular data source. Every edge in the graph shown in Figure 3.7 is one mapping. "Same"-mappings are represented with solid lines. Association mappings, i.e. all mappings which represent relations other than equality are represented with dashed lines.

The results of the mapping execution are stored in the cache. The data in the cache are updated from the data sources at regular intervals of time. The time intervals are set specifically for every data source. So, Amazon, Softunity and Bestpreis24 are updated once a week. The eBay data due to its nature changes more often. Therefore, the eBay data is updated every three days. Although the data on the eBay website change more frequently than every three days, it is not possible to update eBay data more frequently, since the average duration of the query which retrieves all needed eBay data is 48 hours. The update of the data is done in the following way: the iFuice cache is cleared of all objects coming from the specific data source. Then, the entire iFuice integration script is executed. The data from the data sources which are absent from the cache are re-fetched from the sources, otherwise the data is taken from the cache.

11. INTEGRATING DATA: EXPERIMENTS AND RESULTS

In this chapter we describe the experiments on matching product data and product categories and present experimental results. We used Softunity and Amazon as sources of data for our experiments. These two data sources were chosen for our experiments because of the existence of an unambiguous mapping between the products of Softunity and Amazon. This unambiguous mapping serves us as the baseline for comparison of different matching methods. The amount of data used in the experiments is illustrated in Table 3.2.

	Nr. of product categories	Nr. of products	Nr. of categories with product instances
Amazon	1930 (manually pruned)	42942	1753
Softunity	466	2711	204

Table 3.2. Number of products and product categories in the data sources used in the experiments.

The goal of the experiments was to explore the quality of mappings which can be achieved by matching instances and ontologies separately with existing tools and to analyze the improvements which can be brought by combining these mappings. As shown in Table 3.2, not all categories on the product ontologies have associated product instances. The reason for this is that the product assortment changes more often than the ontology structure, therefore at different times some product categories may or may not have associated product instances. If a product category does not have associated product instances, it is not shown on the website, but it can still be queried using a direct access to the website database (Softunity) or using a web service API (Amazon).

The e-commerce ontologies which we used in our experiments have a number of characteristics typical for this kind of ontologies. These ontologies do not exhibit a rich palette of semantic features. So, only one type of concept is used – product category, i.e. class. Only one type of relation is used – all relations between the classes are specialization relations. According to the classification in [KW04], our e-commerce ontologies exhibit taxonomical structure, i.e. based on specialization relations as opposed to mereologic structure based on the subsumption relations. The ontology nodes have no attributes apart from names. The ontologies are organized as trees. It is however possible for the product instances to belong to several categories in different ontology subtrees simultaneously. The top of the ontologies is comprised of the three areas which we have selected for experiments: "Software", "Games", "DVD" or "Video". The classes below are for the most part aligned along the thematic axis, i.e. they represent the classification of the product's content with respect to genres, using commonly accepted genre denominations. For example[28]:

"Games->Action"; "Games->Adventure";"Games->Strategy"

or

"DVD->Documentary"; "DVD->Comedy"; "DVD->Western"

However, some of the ontology branches are orthogonal to this axis. This is particularly characteristic for the Amazon ontology.

The following branches are the examples of orthogonal ontology branches: "Amazon->Software->Specials", "Amazon->Games->Specials", "Amazon->Video->For Rent". These branches represent "crosscuts" of product instances belonging to other branches based on some criteria. For example, the "Specials" branches contain product instances which are (usually temporarily) put on special sales conditions by Amazon. "For Rent" is a category containing the subset of the video products which Amazon allows to be rented. There are also some ontology nodes which represent the same concept as their parent nodes but denote a root of an orthogonal sub-ontology, for example "Amazon->DVD->By genre", "Amazon->DVD->By year" and "Amazon->DVD->By author". Since the extracted ontologies do not provide a mechanism to distinguish between these relations, these orthogonal branches cannot be filtered out automatically. We had to exclude some branches, for example ""Amazon->DVD->By year" and "Amazon->DVD->By author" from the extracted Amazon ontology manually, because these branches were clearly orthogonal to the rest of the ontology. The categorizations by year and by author are not found in other ontologies we used in our system, therefore they could adversely affect the results of both COMA++-based and instance-based matching. We do not provide complete listing of the used ontologies in this thesis because of the large amount of data which would break the format of this document. These ontologies are available for browsing online at the respective websites http://www.softunity.de/, http://www.amazon.de/ and http://www.ebay.de. In this thesis, we show only relevant portions of the ontologies to illustrate some of their characteristics and issues arising during the integration process.

Both product mappings and ontology mappings are used to create browsing structure of the website as well as to generate the recommendations. Browsing and recommendations impose different requirements onto the mappings. Browsing requires mappings with strictly defined types of correspondences, usually only one type per mapping. For example, browsing between the versions of the same product coming from different data sources requires that the utilized mapping contains only the correspondences between strictly equal products. The mappings which are used for recommendations are

---

[28] The notation A->B means, that the concept B is a child of the concept A in the given ontology. The notation can be repeated (A->B->C). Sometimes we also use the name of ontology as the first element in such notation to denote the ontology to which the concepts belong.

not subject to such strict requirements. They can also make use of correspondences between products and ontology nodes which are similar or related in some way.

We have conducted the following series of experiments:

- Match Softunity products to Amazon products with iFuice. Recall and precision are determined using unambiguous EAN mapping.
- Match Softunity ontology to Amazon Ontology with COMA++. Recall and precision are calculated with respect to the manual mapping.
- Combine matching ontology with matching products; evaluate how recall/precision is affected.

11.1 Integrating Product Data

In this chapter we discuss the product matching, i.e. establishing the mappings between the products of different data sources. Our architecture provides rich possibilities for creating such mappings. In this chapter we illustrate how the manifold possibilities provided by iFuice can be instrumental in creating and improving the product mappings. We use a helpful fact that between the products of two data sources which we use in our system, Softunity and Amazon, exists an unambiguous mapping using EAN. The abbreviation EAN stands for European Article Number which is a unique product number. It is commonly known as "barcode" number. Since 2005 EAN has also become standard in the North America and de facto worldwide. Other data sources do not have such unambiguous mappings. So, for example, the product data available from ebay.de do not include EAN numbers. Such data must be matched using algorithms which do not guarantee 100% recall/precision. To find the best ways to match the products, we have tested different matching techniques on the products from the two data sources we have an

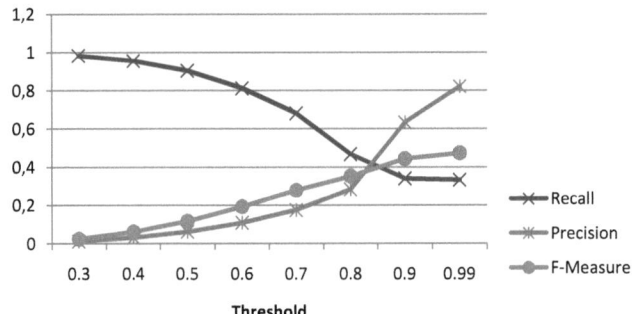

Figure 3.8. Recall, precision and f-measure for trigram-based similarity

unambiguous mapping for and then analyzed the results using the recall and precision calculated with respect to the unambiguous mapping. The characteristic excerpts from results of the matching of products between Softunity and Amazon using different matching algorithms are shown in Tables 3.3 and 3.4. These tables show the name of the applied algorithm, the value of the threshold parameter in case the given algorithm requires it, the total number of correspondences returned by the algorithm, the number of correct correspondences, the values of recall and precision and the value of F-Measure[Rijs79] which combines recall and precision in a single metric. The first line of the Table 3.3 shows the results of the unambiguous product matching based on EAN number. These results act as a comparison baseline for other methods of matching.

Line Nr	Matching methods	Threshold	Total	Correct	Recall	Precision	F-Measure
1	EAN		1981	1981	1	1	1
2	Title equivalence		803	660	0,333	0,821	0,474
3	Trigram	0.3	157564	1951	0,984	0,012	0,024
4	Trigram	0.4	58943	1894	0,956	0,032	0,062
5	Trigram	0.5	28566	1793	0,905	0,062	0,117
6	Trigram	0.6	14703	1611	0,813	0,109	0,193
7	Trigram	0.7	7682	1350	0,681	0,175	0,279
8	Trigram	0.8	3262	928	0,468	0,284	0,353
9	Trigram	0.9	1067	677	0,341	0,634	0,444
10	Trigram	0.99	804	661	0,333	0,822	0,474

Table 3.3. Matching Softunity and Amazon products using EAN, title equality and trigram similarity with different threshold values.

The second line in Table 3.3 shows the results of the matching based on the equality of the product title attribute which is the most simple and obvious way of matching products. The recall and precision values are symptomatic here. Although 1981 products are in fact identical, as the EAN mapping guarantees, only ~33,3% of them have identical titles. Also, of the products with identical titles only ~82.1% are identical, i.e. have the same EANs.

This illustrates the severity of the data cleaning problem in the real-world data, since the company which operates Softunity also acts as a supplier to Amazon, i.e. a subset of the product assortment of Softunity is sold via the Amazon website. The product information concerning this subset of products is regularly exported by Softunity and imported by Amazon. Amazon then formats the product information according to its presentation requirements. As our results show, within only one step of import/export of data between different organizations the product titles diverge substantially.

Human analysis of the input product data shows, that many of the discrepancies in the titles of the products which are exported from Softunity and imported by Amazon result from slight variations of the title, for example from addition of some information or from permutation of the words ("The King of Queens" -> "The King of Queens (4DVDs)" or "The King of Queens"->"King of Queens, The").

To be able to match such titles, we need a matching algorithm which tolerates variations in the spelling. We have investigated the following algorithms: trigram matching [MS99], affix matching, edit distance matching, MSSQL Fuzzy Lookup. The trigram string matching is based on calculating the number of identical trigrams in the input strings. A trigram is any three-character substring of the given string. Affix matching is based on the longest common prefix or suffix of the input strings. Edit distance matching is based on the so called Levenshtein metric [Lev66]. Fuzzy Lookup algorithm provided by Microsoft SQL 2005 Integration Services is based on a combined string similarity score. This combined score depends on the following factors:

- Number of matching tokens in the input strings

- Number of matching n-grams in the input strings. N-gram is a substring of the input string with the length n. Only a probabilistically chosen subset of all present n-grams is used for the matching.

- Edit distance, i.e. number of token or character insertions, deletions, substitutions and re-orderings which need to be made to transform one string to another.

- Inverse token frequency in the entire corpus of strings being matched. The more frequent the token is, the less information about the quality of the match is it considered to convey. The rare tokens are considered to be more important for the discovery of the potential matches.

The MS SQL Fuzzy Lookup algorithm is described in more detail in [CGGM05] and [CGGM03]

All the above algorithms are supplied with two input sets of products and a threshold value parameter. They calculate the similarity scores for the products in the input data sets and return the correspondences with similarity score equal or greater than the supplied threshold value. For every returned correspondence the value of the similarity score is returned as well and can be used further. The value of the similarity score is a floating-point number in the range [0..1], where 0 stands for no similarity and 1 for equality. The trigram matcher, affix matcher and edit distance matcher are the standard attribute matchers provided by iFuice in the operator *attrMatch*. In addition to the two input parameters containing object instances of the type Product and the threshold value, this operator takes the name of the matching algorithm (TRIGRAM, AFFIX, EDITDIST) and the names of the attributes to be matched, in our case "title", as input. The MSSQL Fuzzy Lookup algorithm is implemented as an executable iFuice mapping. This mapping loads the input data into temporary tables on a separate instance of Microsoft SQL Server

2005 and makes a call to the MSSQL Integration Services which perform Fuzzy Lookup. The results of the Fuzzy Lookup execution are then returned to iFuice.

The level of the tolerance to the variations in spelling is based on the threshold value. We have tried all variation-tolerant matching algorithms with threshold values from 0.3 to 0.9 with step 0.1 and additionally the threshold value 0.99. However, for the sake of brevity we do not show the results for all combinations here. Instead, in Table 3.3 we illustrate how the results produced by the trigram matcher change when changing the value of the threshold parameter. For demonstrativeness, in Figure 3.8 we show the results from the Table 3.3 (lines 3 to 10) in graphical form. As shown in Table 3.3 and in Figure 3.8, lower threshold values result in increased recall. However the variation tolerance of the trigram matching leads to the decrease of precision, making the threshold of 0.5 and below practically useless. One can see that in case of the threshold 0.99 the results are almost identical with exact matching and share a common disadvantage of having low recall and few correspondences, i.e. low coverage. This is especially disadvantageous for our purpose of creating navigation between products from different data sources. If such mapping having low coverage is used for implementing navigation between products, a large fraction of the products would have no counterparts to navigate to. Other matching algorithms not shown in Table 3.3 react in a similar way to changes of the value of the threshold parameter. As one can see, in case of the low threshold such as 0.3 the trigram algorithm is able to find ~98% of the correct correspondences at a cost of finding a very large number of incorrect correspondences. Thus, we can take the match results produced by this algorithm as a basis for further refinement. We apply additional matching algorithms to these results in order to filter out the incorrect correspondences.

One such additional matching algorithm can be designed after investigating the values of the title attribute in the input data. Since the products contained in the input data are mostly software and games, they usually have a version number after the title. Often there are several versions of the same product line. The titles of such products differ only through one or few digits which constitute the version number. The variation-tolerant string matching algorithms consider this a very minor difference, while in fact it is a major one. In iFuice, we implemented a special "version number" matcher, which is able to detect the version numbers using the commonly used version number format (i.e. version number is usually one or more digits at the end of the title, possibly with a dot in between). Before applying this matcher, the title attribute is cleaned of comments which are usually also located at the end of the title and enclosed in parenthesis.

Another additional matching algorithm is based on the product ontology information which is available in our iFuice environment. Large fraction of the products common to Softunity and Amazon is comprised of games, which have different versions for different platforms, such as PC, Sony Playstation, Microsoft Xbox, Nintendo DS, etc. However, there is no attribute in the product information which denotes the intended platform. The title attributes of these products are identical for Amazon products. Softunity products usually have the indication of the platform at the end of the title in parenthesis. This way, the matching algorithms with low variation tolerance are unable to find correspondences for these products. The matching algorithms with higher variation tolerance are able to find these correspondences, however they also erroneously identify other products from the same product line as correspondences, even if these products are intended for a different platform. To solve this problem, we can use the fact that the products intended for different platforms belong to different categories in the respective product ontologies. To use this for refining the mapping, we need the following information: the mapping from the products to the ontology in the same data source and mapping between the ontologies of the two data sources. The mappings between products and ontologies are supplied by the data sources. The mapping between the ontologies is created using COMA++. We use a simple matcher which matches the ontology nodes basing on their names and then refine the obtained result manually using COMA++ GUI. The checking of whether the instances belong to the corresponding categories is easy to implement due to the convention that when an instance belongs to a category, it also belongs to all its parent categories. Therefore, no costly operation of traversing the ontology tree is needed.

Series	Matcher algorithms	Threshold	Total correspondences	Correct correspondences	Recall	Precision	F-Measure
1	EAN		1981	1981	1	1	1
2	Title eq		803	660	0,333	0,821	0,474
3	Any of: Trigram, EditDist, Affix	0.99	804	661	0,333	0,822	0,474
4	MSSQL Fuzzy Lookup	0.99	804	661	0,333	0,822	0,474
5	Trigram with version number matcher	0.99	804	661	0,333	0,822	0,474
6	Affix with version number matcher	0.99	804	661	0,333	0,822	0,474
7	EditDist with version number matcher	0.99	804	661	0,333	0,822	0,474
8	MSSQL Fuzzy Lookup with version number matcher	0.99	804	661	0,333	0,822	0,474
9	Affix with version number matcher	0.9	815	664	0,335	0,814	0,475
10	MSSQL Fuzzy Lookup	0.9	2995	1229	0,620	0,410	0,494
11	Affix with ontology matcher and version number matcher	0.8	1014	750	0,378	0,739	0,500
12	Affix with ontology matcher and version number matcher	0.6	2290	1079	0,544	0,471	0,505
13	Trigram with ontology matcher and version number matcher	0.7	3139	1305	0,658	0,415	0,509
14	MSSQL Fuzzy Lookup with ontology matcher and version number matcher	0.6	3954	1524	0,769	0,385	0,513

15	MSSQL Fuzzy Lookup with version number matcher	0.9	2633	1215	0,613	0,461	0,526
16	Affix with ontology matcher and version number matcher	0.7	1498	925	0,466	0,617	0,531
17	MSSQL Fuzzy Lookup with ontology matcher and version number matcher	0.7	3027	1439	0,726	0,475	0,574
18	MSSQL Fuzzy Lookup with version number matcher	0.8	3750	1739	0,877	0,463	0,606
19	MSSQL Fuzzy Lookup with ontology matcher and version number matcher	0.8	2312	1367	0,690	0,591	0,636
20	MSSQL Fuzzy Lookup with ontology matcher and version number matcher	0.9	1643	1204	0,607	0,732	0,664

Table 3.4. Matching Softunity and Amazon products. Only the results of the algorithms with F-Measure greater than that of title equality matching are shown.

In Table 3.4 we show only the algorithm/threshold combinations which achieved higher F-Measure than the algorithm based on the equality of the title. We have investigated all base algorithms and also their combinations with the version number matcher and both version number matcher and ontology matcher. The results of the variation-tolerant algorithms are sorted by the value of F-Measure. The same results are also presented graphically in Figure 3.9.

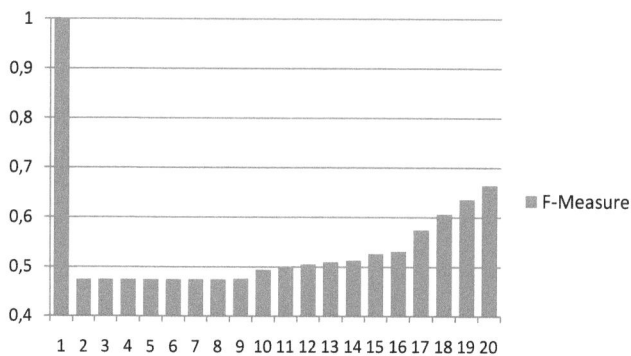

Experiment Series Number (description in Table 3.4)
Figure 3.9. Matching Softunity and Amazon products: F-Measure for different experiment series

Looking at the results of the comparison of the matching algorithms, we can see that the relative complexity of the MS SQL Fuzzy Lookup algorithm pays off and results in better matching results compared to the more simple Trigram, EditDist and Affix algorithms.

Another benefit of the Microsoft SQL Fuzzy Lookup which is not reflected in Table 3.4 is that it performs the matching task considerably faster than the matching algorithm supplied by iFuice, since it uses a special index structure called ETI (error tolerance index)[CGGM03], which contains all pre-computed tokens and n-grams used for matching. The three basic algorithms supplied by iFuice have achieved better F-Measure values then the title equality matcher only with the most restrictive threshold of 0.99, which can be intuitively understood. Indeed, although by lowering the threshold we are able to find more correct matches than the title equality matcher, this also results in a significantly lower precision which brings F-Measure down as well. The MS SQL Fuzzy Lookup alone also performs better with higher thresholds of 0.99 and 0.9.

Looking at the results of MS Fuzzy Lookup algorithm with threshold 0.9, we can see how the results of the matching are improved by applying additional matchers. MS Fuzzy Lookup with threshold 0.9 without additional matchers achieves F-Measure value of 0.494. Applying the version number matcher increases this value to 0.526. Applying both version number matcher and ontology matcher increases F-Measure to 0.664.

We have also investigated other matching methods not shown in Table 3.4, for example the possibility of using attributes *price*, *manufacturer* and *description* in addition to the title attribute. However we discovered that due to errors in the web service interface provided by Amazon it is not possible to use these data. For example, Amazon web service tends to return the offer prices for used products instead of its own prices. These offer prices have large deviance to the product list prices and therefore cannot be used for matching. The manufacturer attribute for Amazon products which come from Softunity is set to the value "Koch Media" (the company which operates Softunity website). The description attribute is returned only for a small fraction of the products.

The evaluation results presented here can be improved further by applying the knowledge of the input data. So, for example, the version matcher can be extended to recognize not only the numerical versions, but also special suffixes like 'Pro', 'Professional', 'Update', or different language versions which are also usually specified at the end of the title attribute. We do not investigate such improvements here, however, since the implementation would be straightforward and the obtained results rely on very data-specific knowledge.

Here, we merely intend to illustrate how the rich possibilities provided by the iFuice environment can be used in combination with the domain knowledge to build and improve the reusable executable mappings between products.

To create the product mapping between other data sources we used the techniques similar to the described above. We do not present the experimental results for these mappings here since we have no means of assessing the quality of these mappings due to absence of the unambiguous EAN mapping.

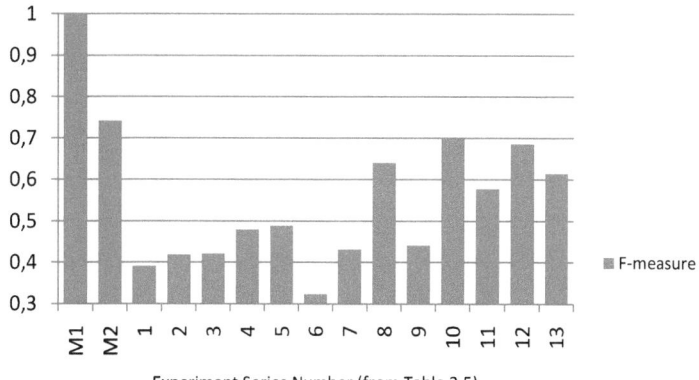

Figure 3.10. Matching Softunity and Amazon ontologies:
F-Measure for different experiment series

11.2 Integrating Ontologies

In this section we explore the possibilities which our architecture provides for matching ontologies. Using COMA++ we can match ontologies based on lexical and structural similarity of the nodes in the ontology. We will also use the results of the instance matching presented in the previous section. As described in Section 10.2.2, COMA++ has a large number of matchers and rich possibilities for their combination with a large number of input parameters. We do not possess the complete knowledge of the behavior of the different matchers and parameter combinations in different situation. Due to the overwhelmingly large number of possible combinations, the complete analysis and comparison of all these combinations is practically impossible. Therefore, we make some assumptions based on the human analysis of the ontology data to achieve a good initial configuration. After the initial configuration is determined, we try to improve the matching strategy iteratively, gradually optimizing the results.

Some of the COMA++ features are not applicable to the ontologies in general, for example the matchers using data type and context-based strategies. Context-based strategies are important only for shared elements. Since we have no shared elements in our ontologies, all the context-based strategies are equivalent. Some matchers are not applicable to our specific input ontologies. For example, matchers which use descriptions cannot be utilized since our ontologies do not contain node descriptions other than the node labels.

For the experiments, we used COMA++ only in the automatic mode (with the exception of the manual mappings used as a base for comparison). The execution of

COMA++ in automatic mode is performed from iFuice. The calls to COMA++ are implemented as calls to iFuice matchers:

$suamontoCOMA:=match($suonto,$amonto,SU_AM_COMA_MATCHER);

Table 3.5 shows the results of matching Softunity and Amazon product ontologies using COMA++ matchers. We performed several series of experiments with COMA++ matchers. After each series the results of matching were analyzed based on the domain knowledge and the available knowledge about the behavior and characteristics of the COMA++ matchers. This way the possibilities for further improvement were determined. In Table 3.5, only the best algorithms in each series of experiments are shown. In Figure 3.10, the same results are presented in graphical form. In the following subsections we discuss the series of the experiments and the matching results in more detail. The manual matching results (M1 and M2 in Table 3.5) are presented in subsection 11.2.1. The COMA++-based experiments (series 1 to 7 in Table 3.5) are discussed in 11.2.2. The instance-based matching results (series 8 and 9 in Table 3.5) and the the results of combined matching (COMA++ and instance-based, series 10 to 13 in Table 3.5) are presented in 11.2.3.

Series	Best algorithm and parameter combination in series	Total	Correct	Recall	Precision	F-measure
M1	Manual	346	346	1	1	1
M2	Manual based on lexical/structural similarity only	204	204	0,589	1,00000	0,741
1	NamePath Trigram MaxN=0,MaxDelta=0.08,Threshold=0.3	212	109	0,315	0,514	0,390
2	NamePath Trigram + Name Trigram 0.04	218	118	0,341	0,541	0,418
3	NamePath Trigram + Name (Trigram 0.5 +Affix 0.5) 0.04	220	119	0,343	0,540	0,420
4	NamePath Trigram + Name (Trigram 0.5 +Affix 0.5) 0.04 + Synonyms/Abreviations	284	151	0,436	0,531	0,479
5	NamePath Trigram + Name (Trigram 0.5 +Affix 0.5) 0.04 + Synonyms/Abreviations + Taxonomy	285	154	0,445	0,540	0,488
6	COMA++ Default combined matcher	111	74	0,213	0,666	0,323
7	COMA++ Default with synonyms	156	108	0,312	0,692	0,430
8	Instance-based EAN Dice>= 0.5	285	202	0,583	0,708	0,640
9	Instance-based MSSQL Dice>= 0.5	280	138	0,398	0,492	0,440
10	COMA + Instance-based EAN Dice>=0.5	505	297	0,858	0,588	0,698
11	COMA + Instance-based MSSQL Dice>=0.5	518	249	0,721	0,48	0,576
12	COMA + Instance-based EAN	464	278	0,803	0,599	0,686

	Dice>=0.5 (excluding Ncorresp=1)					
	COMA + Instance-based MSSQL					
13	Dice>=0.5 (excluding Ncorresp=1)	425	237	0,684	0,557	0,614

Table 3.5. Matching of the Softunity and Amazon ontologies using COMA++

11.2.1 Manual Ontology Mappings

The baseline for the comparison of the matching quality of the different match algorithms is the manual mapping shown in the first line of Table 3.5. The manual mapping was created using the mapping editor provided by the COMA++ user interface. The input ontologies were designed for the practical purpose of website navigation and do not grasp the complete formal knowledge about the domain. Because of that, human domain-specific knowledge about both product categories and product instances was used to create the manual mapping. It is important to note, that the manual mappings are inherently subjective. This subjectivity needs to be taken into account when reviewing the values of recall, precision and F-measure in Table 3.5, since they are calculated with respect to the manual mappings.

An important issue which needs clarification before creating the manual mapping is how to handle the different types of relations. Although only one type of relation – "specialization" – exists in our input ontologies, there are several types of relations which may exist between the nodes of different input ontologies, for example:

Equivalence: the concepts represented by the nodes in two ontologies are semantically equivalent. The equivalence of the concepts can however rarely be stated with full confidence. Much more often one can speak of approximate equivalence. Even the seemingly obvious equivalency correspondences like "Amazon->Games" <-> "Softunity->Games"[29] is not a complete equivalence, because for example the Amazon category includes additional subcategories for game consoles "Sega Saturn" and "Gizmondo" which do not exist in the Softunity ontology. On the other hand, category "Softunity->Games" includes subcategory "Game solution books" which is absent in Amazon. There are also equivalences which are not visible at first glance but can be recognized using background domain knowledge. So, for example, the categories "Softunity->DVD->Western" and "Amazon->DVD->Classic Western" are not equivalent at first glance, since the notion "Western" is broader than just "Classic Western". However, since the DVD assortment of the Softunity shop consists in general only of the digitally re-mastered classical movies, the categories are equivalent in this given case.

Specialization: the nodes in one ontology can be mapped to nodes in another ontology as children. Sometimes this can be based on the equivalence of the parent of the given node to a node in another ontology, sometimes there is no equivalent parent, for

---

[29] We use the notation A<->B to denote the correspondence between the concept A in one ontology and the concept B in another ontology.

example when child-parent relation is expressed in the node name: "Comedy" <-> "Comedy, Satire, Slapstick", "Science Fiction"<->"Science Fiction & Fantasy". Sometimes it is hard to determine whether we are dealing with equivalency or specialization, for example: "Thriller" <->"Psychothriller". We consider only immediate specialization and not specialization over several nodes, because these distant specialization relations can be deducted from the immediate specialization relations.

There can be other, less common types of relations, for example partially overlapping concepts: "Amazon->Games->Computer games->Action & Adventure"<->"Softunity->Games->PC-Games->Adventure & Role games".

Although multiple types of relations may exist between the nodes of different input ontologies, the correspondences in our mappings are all of the same type "similarity".

Taking this information about the creation of the manual ontology mappings into account, we can assume that several "correct" manual ontology mappings may exist, depending on which human knowledge is available and which types of relations are considered as "legitimate" correspondences in the resulting mapping.

In the manual mapping which we used as a baseline for our experiments we chose the criteria of the selection of the correspondences in accordance with our goal of creating website navigation. The following criteria were applied to select the correspondences:

- The equality relations are always considered "legitimate" correspondences.

- The specialization in general is not considered "legitimate" correspondence when it can be deducted from the existing equivalence-based correspondence. This is done to eliminate redundant correspondences, because taking all specialization relations into account would generate additional correspondences for every child of a node which participates in an equivalence-based correspondence, thus leading to an explosion of the number of correspondences which do not add any new information. So, for example, given that the category "Amazon->Software" has 10 children, the category "Softunity->Software" would have at least 11 correspondences to the Amazon ontology, one to "Amazon->Software" and 10 to its children. Although redundant correspondences are not wrong, they can be confusing to the user if used for navigation on a website. We do consider specialization in the cases where no equivalency exists between the node parent in one ontology and a node in another ontology. In special cases we also allow correspondences when a node in one ontology corresponds simultaneously to a node and its child in another ontology. Such special cases occur when the concept represented by the child node is almost as broad as its parent's concept, for example "Softunity->Games->Accessories"<->"Amazon->Games->Accessories->More Accessories". It occurs also when the child node is a root of an orthogonal sub-ontology, for example "Softunity->DVD" <-> "Amazon->DVD->By production land" and "Amazon->DVD->By format".

- Nodes which exhibit partial semantic overlap are considered "legitimate" correspondences in absence of equality correspondences between their children, for example: "Amazon->Games->Computer games->Action & Adventure"<->"Softunity->Games->PC-Games->Adventure & Role games".

Since COMA++ matchers consider only information about product categories, we have also created another manual mapping (Table 3.5, second line). This mapping is a subset of the previous mapping and is based only on the structural/lexical information contained in the product ontologies. The correspondences which cannot be determined without utilizing the background domain knowledge not contained in the nodes and their relations in the input ontologies are excluded in this mapping. This way we approximate the upper limit which can theoretically be achieved by COMA++ without utilizing the instance information.

The number of correspondences given in Table 3.5 shows the number of 1:1 correspondences in the mappings. Some of these correspondences in fact represent 1:n correspondences. Although the size of the Amazon ontology is ~4.1 times larger than the size of the Softunity ontology, the bias of 1:n correspondences with respect to Amazon ontology is not large. There are 38 1:2 correspondences with two elements on the Amazon side and 45 1:2 correspondences with two elements on Softunity side. For 1:3 mappings however, there are 20 correspondences with three elements on the Amazon side and only 2 with three elements on the Softunity side. The cardinality 1:4 appears 5 times, 1:5 and 1:6 one time each, in all cases with n elements on the Amazon side. All other correspondences are 1:1 correspondences. It is important to note, that Amazon ontology and Softunity have only a partial, although significant, overlap. Because of this, even the manual matching can match only some concepts in the ontologies and not all concepts.

11.2.2 Ontology Mappings Created Using COMA++

The most important source of information about the identity of the nodes in the ontologies is the names of the nodes. In fact, our nodes have no attribute other than the name attribute. However, the names of the individual nodes can be confusing, since in our ontologies many different nodes have the same name. Since our ontologies are represented as trees, the path to a node from the root uniquely identifies this node. So we may have two nodes with name "Action", one being "Games->Playstation 2->Action" and another "Games->Xbox->Action". Due to these peculiarities of the input data, we start with the COMA++ matcher "NamePath" as our basic matcher. This matcher is a combined matcher which takes the paths from the respective ontology roots to the input elements and computes string similarity between them. Several algorithms for computing the string similarity, among them Trigram, Affix and EditDistance, can be configured. Before computing the string similarity, the input strings are tokenized, i.e. single terms are extracted. Similarity values are then computed for every term and stored in a similarity cube. The maximal similarity values for every term are then averaged to return a single similarity value.

It is also possible to configure a combination of similarity scores computed by several string similarity algorithms. In our 1st series of experiments, we have compared the matching quality of these three string similarity algorithms. As described in Section 10.2.2 of this chapter, COMA++ provides several parameters for selection of the matching candidates. In addition to specifying an absolute threshold value for the similarity score, one can also specify so called MaxDelta and MaxN values. We have explored the combinations of the parameters with each of the three string similarity algorithms to find the best algorithms and combinations. We have iterated the value of Threshold from 0 to 1 with step 0.1 and the value of MaxN from 1 to 10 with step 1. We have iterated the value of MaxDelta from 0 to 1 with step 0.1. After we have determined that the best values are achieved with MaxDelta of 0.1 and that the quality of the matching decreases as MaxDelta increases, we have additionally iterated MaxDelta from 0 to 0.2 with Step 0.01. We have determined that the best matching results are achieved using the Trigram string similarity algorithm with MaxN=0, MaxDelta=0.08, Threshold=0.3. The matching in this series of experiments and in all subsequent experiments was performed using bidirectional mode of COMA++ (Direction=BOTH). In this mode, the matching is performed two times, from larger ontology to the smaller and from smaller to larger. The intersection of the two unidirectional results serves as the final result of the matching.

After examination of the results of the matching produced in the 1st series of the experiments and the differences between the manual mapping and the mapping obtained using the NamePath matcher it became clear that some of the false correspondences found by the NamePath matcher and some of the missed correspondences can be attributed to the fact that in the paths of the nodes serving as input for the NamePath matcher all components of the path are considered equally significant for determining the similarity. This may lead to the calculated similarity value being too high, especially in the not infrequent cases when the node name is much shorter than the full path to the node. In the 2nd series of experiments, we have investigated how the aggregation of the NamePath matcher with the Name matcher, which matches only the name attributes of the nodes, can improve the matching quality. Similar to the NamePath matcher, the Name matcher allows using several string similarity algorithms such as Trigram, Affix, EditDistance. The similarity scores returned by the Name and NamePath matchers were aggregated using the weighted aggregation strategy provided by COMA++. We have explored how the values of the aggregation weights influence the quality of the matching. We have tried the three string similarity algorithms and iterated each of them with aggregation weight for the Name matcher W from 0 to 1 with step 0.1. The aggregation weight for NamePath matcher was set respectively to 1-W on each iteration. The best performing string similarity algorithm was the Trigram Algorithm, the best values are achieved around W=0.1. We have then iterated the value of W from 0 to 0.2 with step 0.01 to find out more precise value of the optimal W, which appeared to be 0.04. The values of the parameters MaxN, MaxDelta, Threshold stayed unchanged. Through aggregation of the Name matcher with the NamePath matcher we were able to obtain additional correct correspondences in the resulting ontology mapping. For example, "Software->Betriebssysteme" is now correctly matched to "Software->Tools & Utilities->Betriebssysteme" and "Software->Sound->Sampler" to "Software->Musik->Sampler".

After assessing the mappings produced in the 2nd series of experiments, we have found that although the Affix string similarity algorithm performed in general worse than the trigram matching algorithm, it had better results for a certain pattern of correspondences. This pattern was characterized by the names of the top product categories added to the names of the lower product categories, for example "Games->Game Boy Advanced Games -> Sport Games" vs. "Spiele->Game Boy Advanced->Sport". Thus, in the 3rd series of the experiments we have investigated the aggregation of the Trigram and Affix string matchers in the Name matcher. It is not reasonable to use the Affix matcher in the NamePath matcher, since the paths to different nodes often have common prefixes. We have iterated the value of the aggregation weight Wt of the Trigram matcher from 0 to 1 with step 0.1. The aggregation weight for Affix matcher was set respectively to 1-Wt on each iteration. The best results were achieved when the weights of the Trigram and Affix matchers were equal.

Many of the words used in the input data are lexically different but have the same meaning, i.e. are synonyms. In our German e-commerce ontologies this is especially the case, since for many notions in the areas of Software and Games both German and English equivalents exist which are used interchangeably. The use of abbreviations is also common. COMA++ contains a special matcher which allows users to specify a set of synonyms and abbreviations. We made a set of 6 synonyms (for example "Game"<->"Spiel", "Business"<->"Geschäft") and one abbreviation ("PSP"->"Playstation Portable") and activated synonym matching in both NamePath and Name matcher, which resulted in significant increase in the matching quality. The synonym matcher returns high similarity values when a synonymy exists and 0 otherwise. The synonym matcher was aggregated with the Trigram matcher using Max aggregation strategy. Thus the synonym matcher has no influence on the similarity score when no synonymy exists.

Further extension of the synonym matcher is the taxonomy matcher. It also uses the data supplied by user, but the relation between terms are expressed not as a set as equivalent terms, but as a taxonomy. The similarity between the terms is determined by the distance between them in the taxonomy. We have created a small taxonomy with three nodes: "Filme"(the root of the taxonomy),"DVD" and "VHS" (children of the root). In the 5th series of the experiments we have tested the ontology matching using the taxonomy matcher along with the synonym matcher for both Name and NamePath matchers. The taxonomy matcher was aggregated with the Name and NamePath matchers similarly to the synonym matcher. Although in our experiments the results of the taxonomy-based matcher were only marginally better than the results of the synonym-based matcher (three additional correct correspondences), the use of taxonomy-based matcher seems to be promising. Similarly to synonyms, taxonomies allow introducing additional domain knowledge into the matching process. However, taxonomies also provide richer semantics compared to synonyms, since not only equivalence of the terms but also less strict relations can be specified. Our taxonomy is a very simple one; intuitively, specifying more elaborate taxonomy would increase the quality of the matching result (assuming the taxonomy to be relevant and of high quality), however this would also increase the amount of manual work. One possible way to decrease the manual effort is to use a ready taxonomy provided by some external source[30]. However such taxonomy was not available for our problem domain.

In addition to the matchers we described here we have also tried combinations of the NamePath Matcher other matchers provided by COMA++, such as Leaves, Children, Siblings and Parents. However, these matchers were unable to improve the matching performance. In case of the Leaves, Children and Siblings matchers the results contained many false positives. The reason for this is that many subcategories with the same names are located in different subcategories in the same ontology. For example, both categories "Games->Playstation 2" and "Games->Nintendo DS" contain subcategories "Action", "Strategie" and "Sport". Thus, the assumption that nodes having similar children, leaves or siblings should be similar is not pertinent for our ontologies. The Parents matcher was not able to improve the matching results, since the information about the parent node is already taken into account by the NamePath matcher.

Comparison of the matching results to the results of the manual mapping based on the lexical and structural similarity shows that the recall values of the COMA++ mappings are gradually approaching the recall values of the manual mapping. The precision values are however remarkably lower.

The COMA++ matching results presented in the experiment series 1 to 5 have required a significant amount of human analysis and experimenting. In the next two series of experiments we have investigated what results can be obtained with the default configuration of COMA++, i.e. without additional effort. In series 6 we used COMA++ default matcher with no default parameter values. The matcher configuration in series 7 is the same as in series 6 but with the synonyms and abbreviations as used in experiment series 5. The results of using the default COMA++ matcher are significantly worse than in our custom matcher configurations. Using synonym and abbreviation tables however remarkably improves the matching quality.

Our custom combined COMA++ matchers are fitted to the specific type of input data and are not suitable as generic matchers. This complies with our intent to create a specific matcher, which would grasp the particularities of our ontology data without being dependant on the concrete data. Although the concrete ontology data will be changing with time (i.e. some nodes may be added to or removed from the ontology, the names of some nodes may be altered), we anticipate the general characteristics grasped by our matchers to be preserved.

11.2.3 Instance-based and Combined Mappings

So far we have not used the instance information to match the ontologies. In this section we explore how the information about products instances can be instrumental in matching product categories. The method we use in matching ontologies to determine the

---
[30] For example http://www.schemaweb.info/

similarity of any two categories is using Dice coefficient[31]. For this, we use the mappings between product instances and ontology nodes within each data source and a mapping between the product instances of the different data sources. The Dice coefficient for categories a and b is defined as

$$Dice(a,b) = 2*|Cab| / (|Sa| + |Sb|),$$

where C is the set of correspondences between products which belong to a and b, Sa, Sb set of products which belong respectively to the categories a and b.

In the 8th and 9th series of experiments we have investigated the quality of the ontology mappings produced using only the instance information. The instance-based matching of the Softunity and Amazon ontologies is implemented using the following iFuice script[32]:

1: $amontosuprod:=compose($amontoprod,inverse($suamprod));
2: $suontosuprod:=compose(compose($suontoprod,$suamprod), inverse($suamprod));

3: groupAttr(&amontosuprod,"nInstances","count(*)");
4: groupAttr(&suontosuprod,"nInstances","count(*)");

5: $suamontoINSTANCE:=match($suontosuprod, $amontosuprod, SU_AM_ONTO_INSTANCE_DICE);

6: $suamontoINSTANCE_DICE01:=queryMapResult($suamontoINSTANCE, "[_confidence]>=0.1");

In this script we first establish the mappings $amontosuprod and $suontosuprod (lines 1 and 2). These mappings map the nodes of both Softunity and Amazon ontologies to the set of Softunity product instances. Here we use only those Softunity products which have counterparts on Amazon. The mapping from Amazon ontology to Softunity products (variable $amontosuprod) is created by composing the mapping from Amazon ontology to Amazon products with the mapping from Amazon products to Softunity products stored in the variable $suamprod. This instance mapping can be created using one of the methods described in the previous section. In the 8th series we have used the unambiguous EAN-based mapping between product instances. In the 9th series we have used the product mapping based on MSSQL Fuzzy Lookup combined with ontology and version number matchers which appeared to be the best among the instance mappings investigated in Section 11.1 with the exception of the unambiguous EAN mapping. The mapping $suontosuprod is created from the mapping $suontoprod which maps Softunity ontology to

---

[31] The later work [MR08] has investigated using instance-based similarity measures other than Dice. However, the Dice coefficient has achieved the best results in the experiments. [MR08] is described in the Section 13.2 in more detail.
[32] The line numbers are not part of the iFuice scripting language syntax and are added for better readability.

Softunity products by filtering it to contain only those Softunity products which have corresponding Amazon products.

To perform the filtering, we compose the mapping $suontoprod with the mapping $suamprod twice, first in the forward direction and then in the inverse direction. After creating the mappings $amontosuprod and $suontosuprod we create auxiliary attribute nInstances in every node in the ontologies (lines 3 and 4). The attribute is created using iFuice operator groupAttr which can be applied to the variable of type Mappingresult. For every object instance in the domain of the mapping the operator groupAttr calculates the value of the specified SQL aggregate function on the object instances in the range of the mapping and assigns the calculated value to a new attribute in the domain object instance. The attribute nInstances which contains the number of instances in every ontology node is utilized to calculate the Dice coefficient later on.

The generation of the instance-based ontology mapping is performed by a call to the user-defined matcher SU_AM_ONTO_INSTANCE_DICE (line 5). This matcher returns correspondences between all nodes in the Softunity and Amazon ontologies which have at least one common product instance and calculates the Dice coefficient for every correspondence. For our experiments we have filtered the correspondences having Dice>=T, where T is a threshold value. To filter the mappings by the Dice coefficient value we used iFuice operator queryMapResult with T=0.1 (line 6 in the sample script). In both 8th and 9th series of the experiments we have iterated the value of T from 0 to 1 with step 0.1. The best F-measure values were achieved with Dice>=0.5. As one can see in Table 3.5, the quality of the ontology matching based on the unambiguous EAN product mapping surpasses the quality of the best COMA++-based mapping. Such unambiguous mappings are however rarely available in practice. The ontology mapping based on the fuzzy string matching in the series 9 achieves however only the quality comparable with the default COMA++ matching without any data-specific enhancements (series 7).

The sets of correspondences in instance-based mappings contain a significant number of correspondences not found in the COMA++ mappings. The reason for this is that although some product categories are semantically similar, which results in the large number of instance correspondences, their lexical similarity may be small. Analogously, many of the correspondences found by COMA++ cannot be found in the instance mappings. In cases when the product assortment changes frequently, some categories may contain no instances at some points of time. Such categories cannot be matched using the instance matcher. Another reason for this may be the dispersion of the instances of a product category in one data source between multiple categories in the other data source. So, in the COMA++ mapping produced in the 5th series of experiments only ~16% of the correspondences are also found in the instance-based mapping from the 9th series. In the instance-based mapping these common correspondences constitute ~17% of all correspondences.

Therefore, it can be beneficial to merge the COMA++ mapping and the instance-based mapping to one mapping. This can be accomplished using the following iFuice script:

$suamontoMERGED:=union($suamontoCOMA,$suamontoINSTANCE);$

In this script, variables $suamontoCOMA and $suamontoINSTANCE represent respectively the results of the matching Softunity and Amazon ontologies using COMA++ and instance mapping. The united mapping is stored in the variable $suamontoMERGED, the duplicate correspondences are eliminated. Apart from the possibility for combining the mappings using the operator *union* as presented in the above script, iFuice also provides other possibilities for accomplishing this. So, the iFuice operator *union* can take third parameter, which controls how the weights of the correspondences in the different mappings can be combined. Functions such as *Max, Min, Average* and others are available for combining the weights. The resulting weights can be used to further filter the merged mapping. The default value for this parameter is *Average*, i.e. the weights in the merged mapping are obtained by calculating arithmetic average of the weights in the source mapping. In our experiments, however, the merged mapping is not further filtered and the value of the third parameter is therefore of no consequence. Another possibility to combine the mapping is by using the iFuice operator *intersect*. This operator performs the set operation ∩ on the sets of correspondences in the source mappings to obtain the resulting mapping. However, as mentioned above, the overlap between the instance-based mappings and COMA++ mappings is very small. As a result of this, the mappings obtained by using the operator *intersect* contain too few correspondences to be used for our purpose of creating navigation on a website.

We have tried the combination of COMA++ mapping and instance-based mapping in the 10th and 11th series of experiments. As COMA++ mapping we took the mapping produced in the 5th series of experiments. In the 10th series of experiments we combined it with the instance-based mapping utilizing EAN product correspondences. In the 11th series of experiments we tested the combination of the COMA++ mapping with the instance mapping based on the product correspondences determined using MSSQL Fuzzy Lookup and additional instance matchers as described in Table 3.4 (series 20). For both instance-based mappings we have repeated the merging process for every threshold value used in the experiment series 8 and 9. The values of recall, precision and F-measure for the best mappings obtained by merging COMA++ and instance-based mappings are shown in Table 3.5, experiment series 10 and 11.

Further, we have noticed that some category correspondences with very high Dice value produced by the instance-based matcher are based on very few instance correspondences. Since the low number of correspondences can be attributed to "noise" in the input data, we have filtered out the category correspondences having less than or exactly N instance correspondences. We have repeated the experiments for values of N in the range [1..5] in the experiment series 12 and 13. The input data were the same as in respectively series 10 and series 11.The best results were achieved in cases when only the category correspondences having exactly one instance correspondence were filtered out. In the case when EAN-based instance mapping were used, the result obtained by applying the "noise reduction" was worse than without it. In case of MSSQL-based instance mapping the "noise reduction" leads to increase in the mapping quality.

11.2.4 Problems Discovered in the Process of Ontology Matching and Possibilities for Improvement

We have investigated the possibilities for matching ontologies using our framework on example of the Softunity and Amazon ontologies. We have been able to obtain mappings which can be used as a basis for creating the navigation on the integrated website. As mentioned earlier, we apply the ontology mapping for two purposes– creation of the browsing structure and generation of the recommendations. The correspondences in our automatically produced ontology mappings may represent different types of relations between the nodes in the input ontologies, which makes them not immediately suitable for creating the browsing structure. However, our automatically produced ontology mappings are suitable for generating recommendations, since all the correspondences represent nodes that are somehow related to each other. To create web browsing structure, the automatically produced ontology mappings need to be manually refined. The refinement of the automatically produced ontology mappings can be carried out using COMA++ mapping editor. Such refinement of the existing mapping requires considerably less effort than creating a manual ontology mapping from scratch. The obtained refined mapping can be than used for creating the browsing structure on the integrated website.

While analyzing the results of the automatic ontology mapping we have become aware of several problems which cannot be solved by the combination of COMA++ and instance matchers but require extensions to the entire architecture.

Many of these problems result from using **untyped correspondences** in both COMA++ and iFuice, i.e correspondences which do not have sufficient semantic expressiveness. As discussed in the previous section, there can be many possible types of relations between the nodes in the different input ontologies. Our automatic matching algorithms are aimed in the first place at finding the equivalence relations. However, since the specialization relations frequently exhibit distinguishing features which are also characteristic to the equivalence relations (such as lexical similarity and large number of common instances), significant number of specialization-based correspondences also appear in the matching results. Since we have defined our manual mapping to include specialization-based correspondences only in special rare cases, the majority of these correspondences are wrong with respect to our manual mapping. If we had redefined our manual mapping to include all specialization-based correspondences, the automatic mapping would still be of poor quality with respect to the manual mapping since it is able to determine only a fraction of the specialization-based correspondences. To improve the quality of the automatic matching by better handling the specialization-based correspondences, one of the following techniques can be proposed:

- remove all specialization-based correspondences from the automatic mapping.
- add all specialization-based correspondences to both automatic mapping and manual mapping.

- partially prune specialization-based correspondences from the automatic mapping based on the rules similar to the ones we used for manual mapping, i.e. all the specialization-based correspondences are removed except for those which cannot be deducted from the equivalence correspondences.

To implement any of these techniques, we need to be able to assign different relation types (i.e. "equivalence" or "specialization") to correspondences. We also need to implement special matchers which would be able to determine the relation type for a correspondence by looking at the lexical and structural information provided by the ontology and also at the instance data.

One such problem is caused by the fact that 1:N and N:M correspondences are represented as multiple 1:1 correspondences in our system. So, for example, category "Softunity->Filme" is mapped to a union of "Amazon->DVD" and "Amazon->VHS"(i.e. cardinality 1:N, Figure 3.11). Category "Softunity->Spiele" for example is mapped to "Amazon-DVD->Spiele" with cardinality 1:1. Since in both cases the relation is represented by 1:1 correspondences, we are not able to distinguish between the first and the second case. Possible solutions for this problem are addressed in [TKR07]. The authors propose using set correspondences to overcome the limitations of 1:1 correspondences. They study of how this improves the mapping needs yet to be done. In this section we refer to some of the improvements proposed in [TKR07] when appropriate.

Figure 3.11. Concept in one ontology mapped to a union of concepts in another ontology.

Another problem which is not addressed by our approach yet is the problem of **structure violations**. (Figure 3.12) The problem of structure violations could be best illustrated by example: let the ontology class a1 in the ontology A be the parent of the class a2 and the class b1 in the ontology B accordingly the parent of the class b2. It is possible that in the mapping between the ontologies A and B both the correspondence a1->b2 and b1->a2 exist. Since we use untyped correspondences to represent several types of relations, we cannot distinguish whether there is a contradiction

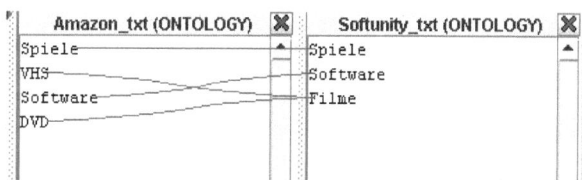

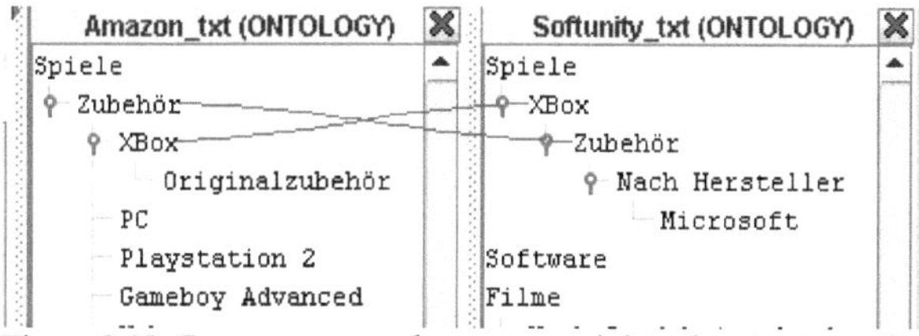

Figure 3.12. Some correspondences may violate the structure of the ontologies

in this setting. If one of the underlying relations is of type parent-child and the other of the type child-parent, than both correspondences are legitimate. If however both relations are of type parent-child, then a **structure violation**

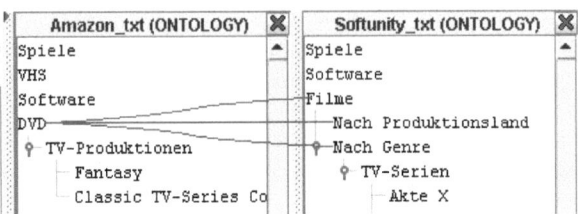

Figure 3.13. Orthogonal subontologies

exists in the ontology mapping. Whether such structure violation is problematic, depends on the intended use of the ontology mapping. It can be argued that correspondences which violate the ontology structure can still be useful as recommendations.

Severe problems are caused by **orthogonal subontologies** (Figure 3.13) which are frequent in the Amazon product ontology. These problems are especially stepping forward in connection with the instance mapping. Because of the orthogonal subontologies, the category „Filme->Kinder- und Jugendfilm->Zeichentrick" (Movies->Movies for Children->Animation movie) is instance-mapped to „Filme->By production land->Japan" (Figure 3.14) and the category „DVD->Classic Western Collection" to „Filme->By production land->Italy". These correspondences are not unfounded because an overwhelming number of animation films are produced in Japan and a large number of classic "western" movies are "Italo-westerns" produced in Italy. Such correspondences can in fact be used as interesting recommendations. However, they are clearly erroneous if we are looking for the equivalency-based correspondences.

Orthogonal subontologies can be removed by preprocessing the input ontologies. We have manually pruned some of the larger orthogonal subontologies from the ontologies we use in our system. However there is a large number of smaller orthogonal subontologies which require much effort to be pruned manually. Some automatic or semi-automatic preprocessing techniques for removing orthogonal subontologies may be required to improve the quality of the ontology mappings.

An improvement to the instance-based ontology matching techniques used here was proposed in [TKR07]. The key idea of the improvement proposal is to use SimMin similarity measure instead of Dice similarity measure used here. The SimMin similarity measure between two ontology concepts is calculated according to the following formula:

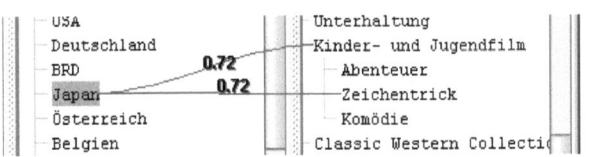

Figure 3.14. Correpondences in orthogonal subontologies found by instance matching

$SimMin(a,b) = |C_{ab}| / min(|S_a|, |S_b|)$,

where C_{ab} is the set of correspondences

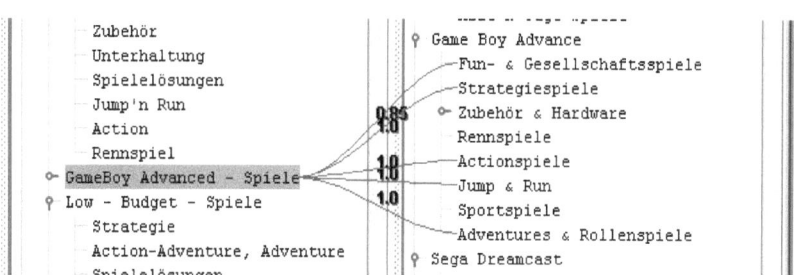

Figure 3.15. Additional child-parent correspondences found by instance matchning with SimMin coefficient

between instances which belong to a and b, S_a, S_b set of instances which belong respectively to the concepts a and b.

The authors of [TKR07] also used the e-commerce ontologies from www.softunity.com and www.amazon.de in their work. The ontologies were restricted to the areas Software and Games. Since in our experiments we used the data from the areas Software, Games and Video, our results are not directly comparable to the results provided in [TKR07]. We have implemented an algorithm analogous to the algorithm described in [TKR07]. In our experiments, we have not been able to notice direct improvements in the recall and precision with respect to our manual mapping. The human analysis of the resulting mapping in COMA++ GUI shows that the algorithm described in [TKR07] is able to find larger number of correspondences which are correct from the point of view of the distribution of instances. However, these correspondences do not comply with the guidelines we set for our manual ontology mapping, i.e. that the equality relations are preferred, and other relations are considered redundant if they can be inferred from the equality relations. In particular, for every equality correspondence found by the algorithm based on Dice similarity measure the algorithm described in [TKR07] tends to produce additional correspondences for child-parent relations. For example, for the concept "Softunity->Games->Game Boy Advanced" the instance-based matching with threshold Dice>=0.5 produces one correspondence to the concept "Amazon->Games->Game Boy Advanced". The instance-based matching with SimMin coefficient produces for the same Softunity concept 5 correspondences to the children of "Amazon->Games->Game Boy Advanced", such as "Amazon->Games->Game Boy Advanced->Strategy", "Amazon->Games->Game Boy Advanced->Jump & Run" etc., as shown in Figure 3.15. The value of the SimMin measure equals to 1.0 for four of these correspondences, therefore it is not possible to filter these correspondences out using a threshold value.

Although it appears that the replacement of the Dice similarity measure through SimMin similarity measure alone does not improve recall and precision, the method based on the SimMin provides better coverage, i.e. it produces more promising correspondence candidates which in combination with methods for post-processing of the ontology mapping proposed earlier in this section can lead to improvement in the quality of the ontology mapping.

The work in [TKR07] also studies the use of direct references from the products to nodes in the product hierarchy vs. indirect references. The direct references are those when the products are explicitly assigned to the nodes in the product hierarchy. The indirect references are those which are explicitly assigned either to the nodes or to their descendents in the hierarchy. In the work presented in this thesis we study only the indirect references, since during the data extraction process all indirect references are transformed into explicit, i.e. direct references.

Additional improvement of the ontology mappings can be achieved by using matchers which establish correspondences based on the neighborhood of the given pair of objects as described in [TR07].

11.2.5 Evolution of data, ontologies and mappings

Both product instance data and the ontologies provided by our data sources change over time. This poses a problem of maintaining the instance and ontology mappings up-to-date with the changing data. In particular, one of the incentives for implementing automatic ontology matching algorithms was that such algorithms can be designed once according to the characteristics of the input data and then be continually used with the changing input data. The naïve method for keeping the mappings up-to-date is by simply repeating the automatic matching when the data change. As we have determined, however, our automatically produced ontology mappings are not suitable for creating the browsing structure for a website without manual post-processing. Of course, we can repeat the automatic matching and post-process it manually each time the data change. Although manual post-processing of the automatically produced mapping requires less effort than the creation of the manual mapping from scratch, it still becomes quite laborious if we need to repeat it many times.

A special research area called *ontology evolution* or *schema evolution* investigates different problems of handling changes in ontologies. These problems include change capturing, propagating of changes from one ontology to another, ontology versioning etc. A detailed overview and bibliography for this research field can be found in [HS04][RB06][33]. The particular problem of maintaining up-to-date mappings that we are facing in our system is called mapping evolution [HS04]. In particular the system ToMAS [VMP03][VMP04][VMPM04] is specially designed for handling the problem of mapping evolution. This system allows sophisticated handling of structural changes such as moving an element from one position to another but does not handle the additions of the new elements. In fact, it is not possible to handle element additions by using a pure evolution-support system. This task requires the cooperation of an evolution-support system and an ontology-matching system in order to find the correspondences for the newly added elements. In our system, however, additions are of great interest, because according to our

---

[33] Online bibliography is located at http://se-pubs.dbs.uni-leipzig.de

experience additions constitute the majority of all changes occurring in e-commerce ontologies.

To solve the problem of maintaining up-to-date ontology mappings in our system, we take the following approach:

After the initial generation of the automatic ontology mapping and its manual refinement, we generate two additional ontology mappings: auxiliary negative mapping and auxiliary positive mapping. Both auxiliary mappings are created using iFuice scripts. The original automatically generated mapping and the manually refined mapping serve as input data for the scripts. The auxiliary negative mapping contains the erroneous correspondences which were contained in the automatic mapping and removed by the manual post-processing. The auxiliary negative mapping is created with the following script:

$auxiliaryNegativeMapping:=diff($automaticMapping,$manuallyRefinedMapping);

Auxiliary positive mapping contains the correspondences which were not found by the automatic mapping and added during manual refinement. It is created with the following iFuice script:

$auxiliaryPositiveMapping:=diff($manuallyRefinedMapping,$automaticMapping);

When the ontologies are updated from the data sources, the ontology mapping is generated in the following way: First the automatic matching process employing COMA++ and instance matchers is run. Then the auxiliary positive mapping is added to the results of the mapping to provide for missing correspondences and the auxiliary negative mapping is subtracted from it to remove the known errors:

$updatedMapping:=diff(union($newAutomaticMapping,$auxiliaryPositiveMapping), $auxiliaryNegativeMapping)

This way only the correspondences which are relevant to the newly added nodes are added to the mapping. The new correspondences may be correct or incorrect with the expectation of our automatic mapping. The old manually refined correspondences persist. Our approach does not solve the problem completely: the mapping quality will still deteriorate due to the imperfectness of the automatic matching and the mapping will eventually need a new manual revision after certain number of changes in the input ontologies. However, according to our experience, the changes in our input ontologies are infrequent and the amount of changes is small with respect to the size of ontology. Therefore, the time between the manual revisions can be kept large without significant deterioration of the quality of the mapping.

In contrast to the system ToMAS [VMP03][VMP04][VMPM04], our approach does not specially handle re-structuring of the ontology without removing or adding elements. This functionality is a subject of further research. In our current architecture, correct propagation of such restructuring to the mapping depends on whether the automatic matching algorithms can correctly recognize the correspondences for the relocated elements in the new locations. Manual adjustment of correspondences is of course also possible.

COMA++ has special Reuse matchers which can be generally useful in the situations similar to the described above. Indeed, in our experiments these matchers have been able to find many additional correct correspondences in the changed ontologies. However, these matchers have also generated a large number of false positives. This is due to a peculiarity of our ontologies: our ontologies have a large number of homonymous nodes in different subtrees. Because of this homonymy, the reuse matchers generate a large number of 1:n correspondences where only one of the n elements is usually correct. We have been able to somewhat alleviate this effect by combining Reuse matcher with NamePath matcher, in order to take the current subtree into account. The number of false positives however remained too high for practical use.

We have also implemented an approach to handle the evolution of the instance data with respect to the mappings. This approach is analogous to the iFuice-based approach with auxiliary mappings described above. We manually create auxiliary mappings which contain the correspondences typically overlooked by the automatic matching and the correspondences which are false positives. The former are added to the mapping created automatically, the latter are subtracted from this mapping using the corresponding iFuice operators.

11.3 Integrating Data: Summary

In this chapter we investigated the data integration approaches which can be used for creating an integrated e-commerce website within our framework EC-Fuice.

We concentrated on two main types of input data for creating the integrated website – product instances and product ontologies. For both input data types, mappings can be generated for two purposes – browsing and recommendations. Since there can be several types of browsing and several types of recommendations, several mappings may need to be created for each purpose. The incentive for our work was to create a set of integration routines, which can be repeatedly used during the lifetime of the integrated website to update and maintain the integrated data and settings.

We performed several series of experiments for both instance matching and ontology matching. The product instance and product category data for the experiments were taken from Softunity and Amazon data sources, since unambiguous product instance mapping exists between these data sources which can be used to assess the quality of the various methods for instance matching.

We investigated the following methods for matching of the product instances

- several simple matchers based on well-known string similarity algorithms.
- a more complicated fuzzy string matcher provided by the Microsoft SQL Server which combines multiple string similarity algorithms.

- combination of the string matching algorithms with the ontology data available in the EC-Fuice framework.
- We have also investigated using additional attributes for matching, however with no success due to the specifics of the input data.

For matching product ontologies, we have investigated the following possibilities:

- matching using COMA++ matchers
- matching based on the product instance mapping and on the information on which product instance belongs to which product category
- combination of the mapping produced with COMA++ and the instance mapping.

We have recognized that while our automatically produced ontology mappings can be used as recommendations, they are not suitable for creating browsing structure without further manual refinement. Subsequently, we have proposed a technique which allows minimizing the manual effort when the data change.

Many researches point out that the mapping of ontologies is a challenging task [MR08][ELTV04][KW04]. This pertains also to the task of matching product ontologies of the e-commerce websites, with an additional difficulty of product ontologies containing deliberately incomplete information about the domain. We have identified a number of problems which arise during the matching of e-commerce product ontologies and proposed several ways to further improve their matching.

12. EC-FUICE IMPLEMENTATION

12.1 Database Structure

In this section we review the structure of the relational databases which we use in the EC-Fuice platform. We highlight the structural specifics of these databases which are targeted to optimize the usage and performance of the databases for their respective tasks.

12.1.1 iFuice Database

The iFuice relational database is used internally by the iFuice platform to hold the information about the problem domain, the mappings, the objects with attributes and the variables. Our iFuice implementation uses MySQL Server to store and manage the relational database.

The structure of the iFuice database is shown in Figure 3.16. The iFuice database has a generic, domain-independent structure, designed to deal with various objects without the need to specify the attributes of the objects in advance. If we were to change our problem domain from e-commerce to some other domain, we wouldn't need to change the structure of the iFuice database. The database structure can be logically divided into three parts: "domain model", "source-mapping model", "objects and variables". The "domain model" is a very generic part. It consists of two tables which contain types of object which are present in the domain and mapping types, i.e. types of relations between objects. The second part of the schema is the "source-mapping model", which contains information about data sources and mappings. The table "datasources" contains the descriptions of the physical data sources connected to iFuice, for example "Amazon", "eBay" etc. The table "Ids" contains so called "logical data sources", i.e. object types coming from a given data source, for example "Product@Amazon", "Review@Amazon".

The content of the tables in the domain model and source-mapping model are loaded from XML configuration file. The information for the mapping mediator on how to execute the mappings is also loaded from the XML configuration file. The information contained in the domain model and source-mapping model is used by the mapping mediator for executing iFuice scripts. The iFuice scripts may return results which are stored in variables. The variables are stored in tables displayed in the third part of the schema in Figure 3.16 "Objects and variables". We have three types of scalar variables: float, integer, string. The values of the scalar variables are stored directly in the corresponding tables. We also have variables of type ObjectsInstances and Mapping Result which can correspondingly contain a collection of object ids and a collection of correspondences between object ids. The collections are stored in separate tables. The objects which are referenced by the object ids are stored in the table "object". The attributes of the objects are stored in the table "attribute".

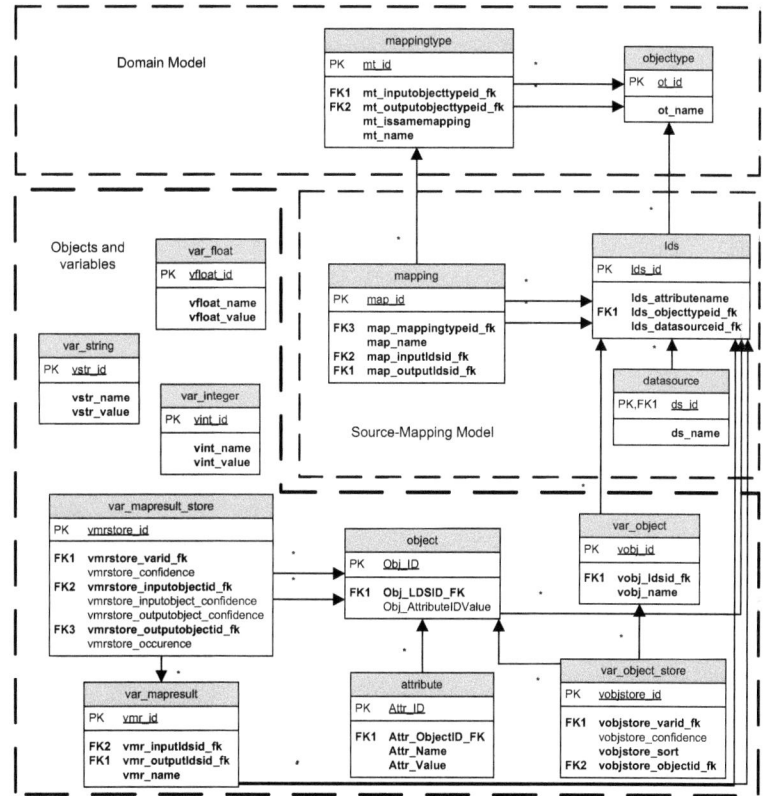

Figure 3.16. Structure of the iFuice database

For sake of brevity, we have omitted the tables which contain variables of types AggregatedObjects and AggregatedMappingResult, since they are not used in our system.

As can be seen from Figure 3.16, the database schema places few restrictions as to types of objects, mappings, number of attributes etc. However such generic schema has a trade-off in complexity of the queries which are needed to perform common tasks. For example a query which returns a list of objects with multiple attributes which can be used on the website to display a product listing would require either a large number of queries or a complicated query with multiple subqueries. The database schema in Figure 3.16 already has one feature which is able to simplify the queries commonly used by iFuice, namely the value of the attribute "ID" which is commonly referenced by iFuice queries is stored with

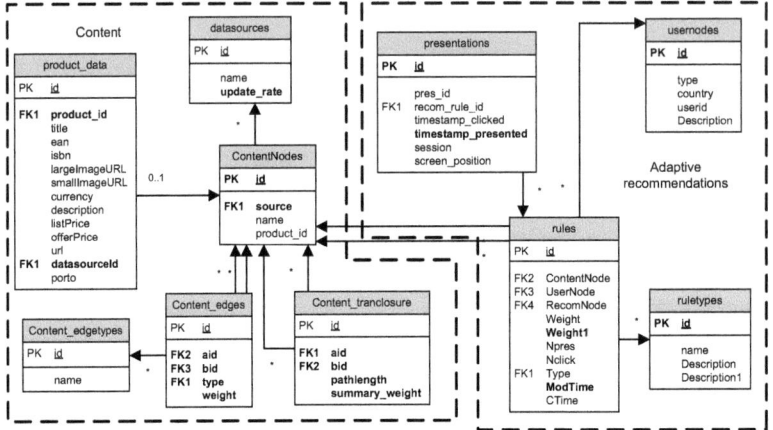

Figure 3.17. Schema of the web portal operational database

the object, as opposed to other attributes which are stored in the table "attribute". However, this is still not sufficient to efficiently execute the queries required by the EC-Fuice web portal. Therefore, we use iFuice directly only for integrating the data and for special "live" recommendations which are discussed in Section 12.3. After the integration, we use a special iFuice mapping to transfer the data into the Web Portal Operational Database which is discussed in the next section.

12.1.2 Web Portal Operational Database

The schema of the web portal operational database is shown in Figure 3.17. The web portal database is designed to immediately provide the data to the web application which visualizes the integrated data to the web user as HTML pages. The web portal operational database is implemented using MySQL database server. The structure of the web portal database is designed to provide high performance when executing queries which typically come from the web application. This structure is not only domain specific, but also specific to the tasks and queries pertinent to the web interface functions. This is why the database design exhibits some redundancy in tables: we have both the table containing individual ontology edges and the table containing the transitive closure of the ontology, i.e. the minimal paths between all nodes in graph. We need the first table to find out the types of the individual edges and the second one to quickly find all connected nodes. The mappings between nodes originally coming from different input ontologies are also saved as ontology edges.

The database schema in Figure 3.17 can be compared to the schema of recommendation database in Part II, Section 4.4.1. The schema in Figure 3.17 is logically divided into two parts. The right part of the schema deals with adaptive web recommendations and bears significant similarity to the schema presented in Part II. Compared to the schema in Part II, this schema is simplified – the parts which are not utilized in our portal are removed. So, the table TimeNodes and the fields which reference the table TimeNodes are removed, since we do not provide time-specific recommendations in EC-Fuice web portal. The part of the schema related to the table "UserNodes" is simplified from a graph-like structure to a single table with the individual user nodes. The table Rules has been amended with fields which show modification time and creation time. The part which is responsible for the content has been expanded in comparison to the schema in Part II. It is shown in the left part of Figure 3.17. The table "ContentNodes" is similar to the one used in Part II. The content nodes stored in this table are the ontology nodes belonging to the product hierarchies as well as product instance nodes. Every product instance node corresponds to an individual product in the table "product_data". Ontology nodes have no corresponding entries in the table "product_data". The table "presentations" contains the presentations which have been presented in the current web sessions on the website.

When a session ends, the information about the presentations is removed from the table "Presentations" and pushed into the EC-Fuice data warehouse by the ETL application which is discussed in the next session. Since we do not have an explicit logout function in our website, the user sessions end automatically after a pre-defined period of inactivity. The timeout for a session is defined in the configuration of the application server. The common value for the session timeout is 30 minutes.

The access to the web portal operational database by the web portal is implemented using the ORM (Object-Relational Mapping) technology. ORM technology enables the developer to declaratively describe the object-relational mapping between Java classes and tables in a relational database. Afterwards, the developer can use the instances of the OR-mapped classes as if they were resident in memory. The storing and retrieving of the class instances in the relational database is handled transparently by the ORM library. We use the ORM library Hibernate[34] which supports multiple levels of caching to increase the performance. The data structure of the web portal operational database is optimized for use with an ORM library.

12.1.3 EC-Fuice Data Warehouse

The EC-Fuice Data Warehouse is implemented using Microsoft SQL Server 2005[35]. Microsoft SQL Server 2005 is a newer version of Microsoft SQL Server 2000 which was used to implement Web Data Warehouse in Part II of this thesis. Compared to the functionality of its predecessor described in Section 4.4.2, SQL Server 2005 features a

---

[34] http://www.hibernate.org/
[35] http://www.microsoft.com/sql/

new ETL tool called **Microsoft Data Integration Services** which contains features such as Fuzzy Lookup which we use to perform matching of the instance data in EC-Fuice.

The relational database schema of the EC-Fuice data warehouse is shown in Figure 3.18. The structure of the EC-Fuice data warehouse is largely similar to the structure of Web Data Warehouse as shown in Figure 2.37 in Section 4.4.2. The differences are stipulated by the fact that EC-Fuice data warehouse contains data from multiple data sources. The tables Product and ContentNodes are amended with a field denoting the source of the information. This field serves as a foreign key for the new table Datasource which contains the list of available data sources.

To import the product data into EC-Fuice Data Warehouse we use an ETL tool created using the Microsoft Data Integration Services toolkit. The ETL tool for importing the product data is executed periodically. For web usage data we use a specially developed real-time ETL tool using a server application written in Java. The ETL application transforms the data into the format suitable for loading into the warehouse tables. The ETL application's being real-time means that every pageview in the EC-Fuice web portal generates a set of input data which is immediately forwarded into the data warehouse. It should be noted that the rate at which the EC-Fuice portal is able to serve pages to web users is much greater than the rate at which the ETL application is able to transform the data and load it into the warehouse.

However, the load placed by the web users on the EC-Fuice portal is distributed unevenly. The EC-Fuice portal has peak times when pages must be served quickly but most of the time it experiences little load. To evenly distribute the load placed on the ETL application, we use buffering inside the ETL application. The ETL application consists of two concurrently working asynchronous processes. The first process gets the usage data from the EC-Fuice portal and puts them into the queue. The second process takes the data from the queue, transforms them and loads into the data warehouse.

The OLAP interface to the EC-Fuice data warehouse is implemented using Microsoft Analysis Services[36]. The OLAP interface is leveraged both programmatically and by human users. Programmatically the OLAP interface is used for the generation of the web recommendations, for example the web recommendations based on web usage history. The human users of the OLAP interface are not the end customers as in the case of the web portal, but the business users, i.e. business analysts. The human interface for OLAP can be realized either using special OLAP tools or with help of Microsoft Excel's OLAP features such as PivotTable and PivotChart.

We have created the OLAP-Cubes Session, Pageview, Presentation and Product based on the EC-Fuice data warehouse. The composition and usage of these cubes are similar to the respective cubes based on Web Data Warehouse as described in Part II, Section 4.4.2.

---

[36] http://www.microsoft.com/sql/solutions/bi/default.mspx

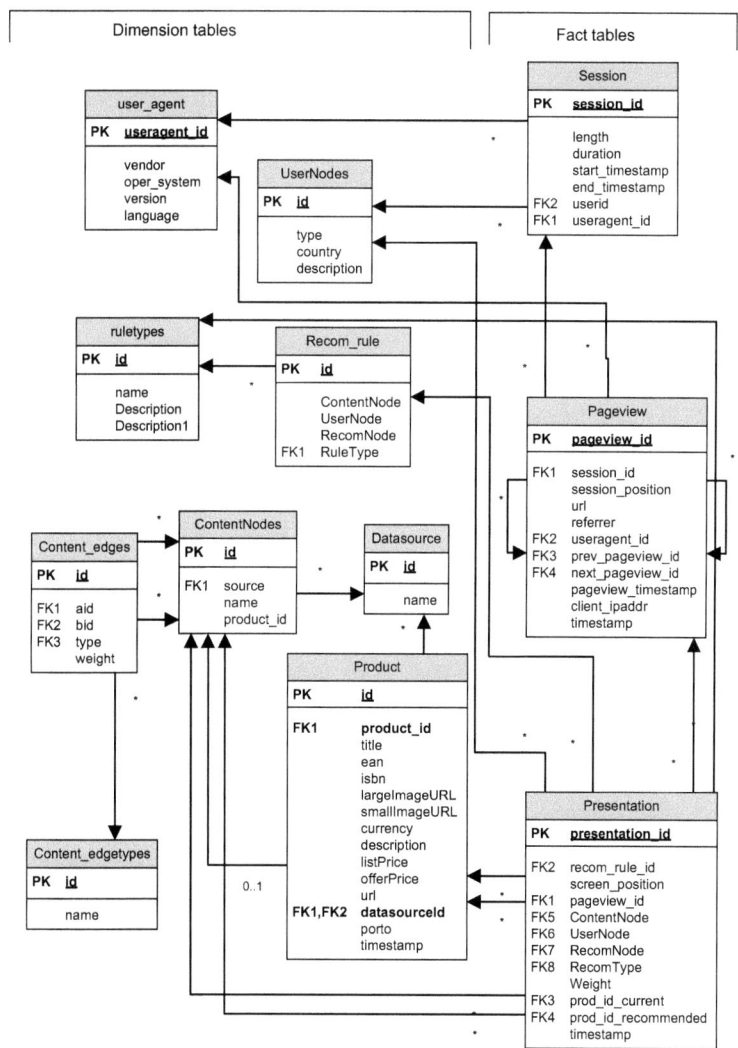

Figure 3.18. Database structure of the EC-Fuice data warehouse

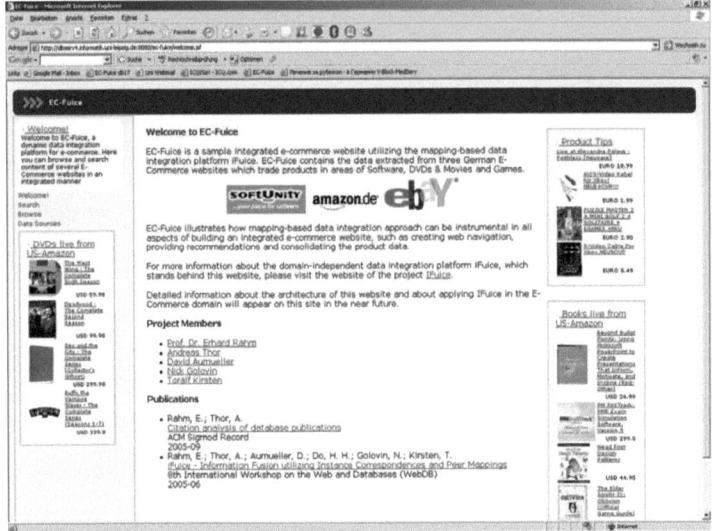

Figure 3.19. EC-Fuice web portal welcome screen

12.2 EC-Fuice Web Portal Interface

12.2.1 Overview of the Web Interface

The interface of the EC-Fuice web portal is designed to facilitate user navigation in the large amount of e-commerce data. EC-Fuice web portal provides user with two types of navigation. The first type of navigation is browsing of the integrated website structure which is constructed from the browsing structure of the original data sources. This type of navigation is based on the relations which already exist in the original data sources. It includes the navigation between the categories in the same data source and the navigation from a category to a product. The second type of navigation is generated by the EC-Fuice framework and is based on relations calculated using iFuice mappings. This second type of navigation is presented chiefly in form of web recommendations.

The snapshot of the welcome screen of the EC-Fuice web portal is shown in Figure 3.19. The main content panel is shown in the middle of the screen. The navigation menu is located on the left side. The web recommendations are presented on both left and right sides. The navigation menu and web recommendation panels are present in every EC-Fuice page view. We will describe the recommendations in more detail in the next subsection. In this subsection we omit the recommendations from the subsequent screenshots for brevity.

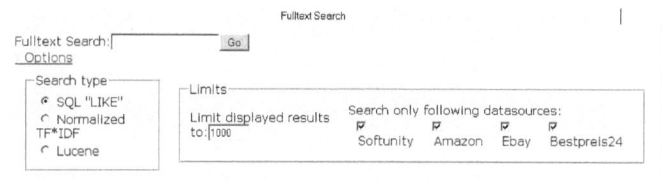

Figure 3.20. EC-Fuice web portal: search form.

The navigation menu on the left side contains four options: "Welcome", "Search", "Browse", "Data sources". The menu option "Welcome" returns the user to the welcome page. The menu options "Search" and "Browse" are the two principal ways to proceed from the main screen to the product data. These are the traditional navigation options for e-commerce websites. The menu "Data sources" provides the information about the data sources connected to the system, in particular the number of products and ontology nodes.

Clicking on the menu option "Search" takes user to the search form shown in Figure 3.20. The user is prompted to enter the search keywords. Clicking on the link Options extends the panel which shows additional options for the full-text search. Here the user can choose the algorithm used for searching. Three search algorithms are available: substring search using simple SQL operator LIKE, search using normalized TF*IDF algorithm as implemented in the MySQL server[37] and search using open-source full-text search library Lucene[38]. The user also has the possibility the change the limit for displayed results and select data sources which should be included to or excluded from the search.

After the user clicks the button "Go", the list of products matching the search criteria is presented (Figure 3.21). For each product, we show picture, title, price and shipping costs if specified. Some products present on the Amazon website are in fact not sold by Amazon. They are stubs which serve as an anchor for sellers of used products. Such products have no Amazon price, as shown in the second line of the search results in Figure 3.21. For every product in the result list we also show a list of categories to which the product belongs. If a product exists in several data sources, each entry is shown separately in the list. The data source from which the product comes is shown with an icon preceding the product title. If same-mapping from this product to products in other data sources exist, we show the icons of the respective data sources after the title.

---

[37] http://dev.mysql.com/doc/internals/en/full-text-search.html
[38] http://lucene.apache.org

Clicking on a product name in the search result list brings the user to the product view which is described later in this section. Another way to get to the product view is by browsing the product categories. After the user selects the option "Browse" in the main menu, the product category view is presented (Figure 3.22). The product categories of each data source are presented separately. At any given time, only the product categories of one source are presented. The user can however switch between them in several ways. It is possible to change the currently shown product ontology by selecting the data source in the root of the product category tree. It is also possible to use the links located next to the category names. These links are shown if one or several categories in other data sources match to the given category in the current data source. Clicking on such link brings the user to the product ontology of the respective data source. The categories matching to the original category are highlighted.

The user can also choose, whether all available categories are shown in the product category tree or only those which have associated products.

Clicking on the name of a product category displays the product list for this category. The product list for a category is similar to the list of search results shown in Figure 3.21. Additionally, the user can select whether to see the list of products which belong only to the selected category from the same data source or also from other data sources in case when they have categories which map to the current one.

The presentation of a product on the website is shown in Figure 3.23. We show the characteristics of the product, such as categories it belongs to, title, id, price, picture. We also present a URL which leads to the page at the original website where this product can be found. If we have a same-mapping from this product to products in other data sources.

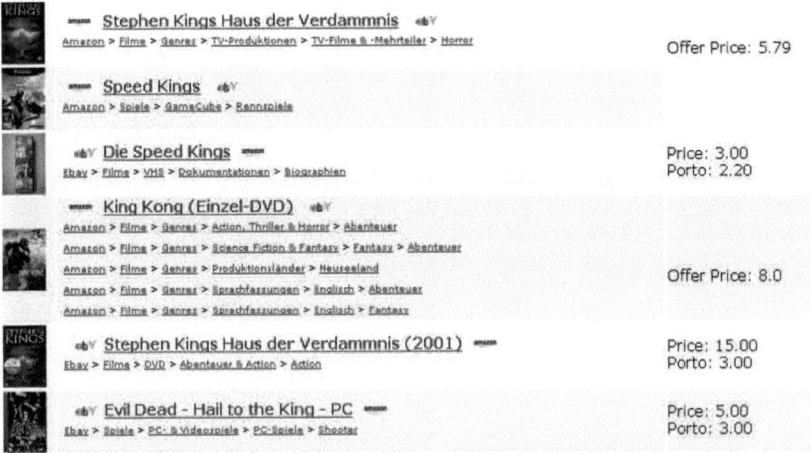

Figure 3.21. EC-Fuice web portal: search result list (search term is "King").

We do not fuse the attributes of the products. In our experiments, it has proven to be not feasible to fuse the attributes of products with satisfactory quality. One of the reasons for this is because eBay often has more than one matching product with different price and description. Thus, it is unclear which of the matching products should participate in the fusion.

The web portal is implemented in Java using the J2EE[39] (Java 2 Enterprise Edition) framework and is a presentation-oriented multi-tier web application. The presentation layer of the application is implemented using the JSF[40] (Java Server Faces) technology.

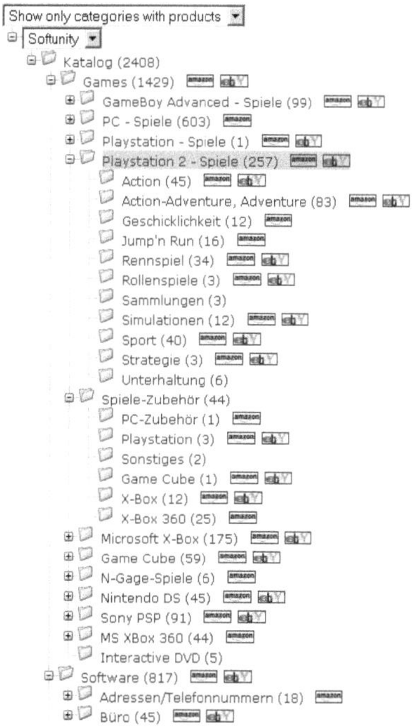

12.3 Web Recommendations

In Section 12.3.1 we present the types of recommendations which can be used in the integrated data environment. In Section 12.3.2 we show examples of different types of recommendations used in EC-Fuice web portal.

Figure 3.22. EC-Fuice web portal: browsing the product category tree.

12.3.1 Types of recommendations

As mentioned earlier, web recommendations constitute a significant part of the navigation in the EC-Fuice web portal, especially for the navigation between different data sources. The types of web recommendations which can be used in the integrated data environment are manifold.

The web recommendations in EC-Fuice web portal can be classified based on several criteria. The web recommendations can be classified in the following way with respect to the point of time when they are generated:

- Live – these recommendations are calculated immediately before they are presented.

---

[39] http://java.sun.com/javaee/
[40] http://java.sun.com/javaee/javaserverfaces/

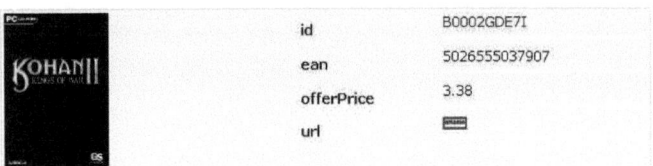

Figure 3.23. EC-Fuice web portal: Product view.

- Pre-calculated – these generations are pre-generated at regular intervals of time and stored in the database for quick access.

Whether a recommendation should be pre-calculated depends on the time needed to generate it. Calculating live recommendations may slow the presentation of the web page. Therefore, in most cases it is advisable to pre-calculate the recommendations. In cases when such pre-calculation is not possible, the presentations delays can be avoided by using asynchronous loading discussed later in this section.

The recommendations can be non-adaptive or adaptive. After being generated by the recommenders, the non-adaptive recommendations stay unchanged throughout their lifetime. The adaptive recommendations are adjusted according to the web users' navigational behavior. The adaptation can happen on the level of a single recommendation or the level of the recommender. The recommendations adaptive on the level of single recommendation need to be pre-calculated, so that they can be stored in the database and later adjusted. Different techniques for creating adaptive web recommendations were discussed in the Part II of this thesis.

In the integrated data environment the web recommendations can be classified by the utilization of the data sources:

- Recommendations from the same data source -- the recommended content comes from the same data source as the presented content.
- Recommendations from other data sources integrated in the EC-Fuice Operational database.
- Recommendations based on external data sources. The recommended content is not integrated in the EC-Fuice Operational database and is obtained by directly calling an iFuice mapping which serves as recommender. The recommender obtains the recommendations in some recommender-specific way, for example by sending an HTTP request to an external website or calling a web service.

By the type of loading into the web page the web recommendations can be divided into the following categories:

- Static recommendations are shown in the web page as usual parts of the content. The place on the web page where they appear is defined by the page layout.
- Asynchronously loaded recommendations use so-called AJAX (asynchronous JavaScript and XML) technology. These recommendations are usually also shown at pre-defined places on the web page. However, they are not loaded simultaneously with the rest of the web page. Instead, the web page contains a small script which is executed in the user's browser after the web page is loaded. This script requests additional content from the server. As soon as the requested content becomes available, it is inserted into the website at pre-defined places.
- Event-based recommendations are shown, when a certain event occurs in the browser, for example when the user holds the mouse pointer over a certain HTML element or text on the web page. The event-based recommendations can be either shown at the places pre-defined by the layout or the position of the recommendations can be calculated dynamically relative to the HTML element which triggered the event. Although the recommendations can be loaded together with the web page in the hidden state and then visualized at the needed moment, it is advisable to load such recommendations asynchronously using the AJAX technology to decrease the size of the initially loaded web page.

The recommendations are usually shown on the web page in blocks. Each such block contains several recommendations. By selection of recommendations which are shown in one recommendations block the recommendations can be classified as single-recommender or mixed. In case of single-recommender recommendations all

recommendations in the block are generated by the same algorithm. In case of mixed recommendations the recommendations in one block may come from different algorithms. It has been observed, that users have more trust in recommendations when they see an explanation of how the recommendations were generated. In case of single-recommender recommendations the recommender-specific description can be shown in the title of the recommendation block. In the mixed case, the explanation can be shown either for every recommendation(to save the space on the page, the explanation can be shown as so-called "tooltip", i.e. it becomes shown when user holds the mouse pointer over the recommendation), or a generic explanation can be shown for the entire block.

Figure 3.24. Screenshot of the EC-Fuice web portal during loading of the asynchronous recommendations.

Figure 3.25. Screenshot of the EC-Fuice web portal after the asynchronous recommendations are loaded.

All the recommendations we discuss here are context-dependent. The notion of context was discussed in detail in Part II. In this Part the notion of the context with respect to content has been adjusted. Here the content part of the context can be not only the currently presented content as a whole, but also a specific content element which is focused or highlighted on the web page. Whether a recommendation depends on the content of the entire web page or on the state of some specific element on the page is a further criterion for classifying the web recommendations.

There are other thinkable criteria for classifying the web recommendations, for example based on the position on the page, presentation design etc. However these types of classification are less relevant for our project and we therefore do not discuss them here. The classification of the recommendation types should be distinguished from the classification of the recommendation generators, i.e. algorithms used to generate the recommendations which have been presented in the Part II of this thesis.

12.3.2 Recommendations used in EC-Fuice web portal

In this section we illustrate how the different types of recommendations discussed in the previous section are used in EC-Fuice web portal. Figures 3.241 and 3.25 show the right side content pane of the web page where some of our web recommendations are shown. The pane contains three blocks of recommendations. We will describe these recommendations with respect to the classification criteria listed in the previous section.

The first from above recommendation block shown in Figures 3.24 and 3.25 contains pre-calculated adaptive recommendations. The adaptation is done on the level of single recommendation and implemented using the reinforcement learning based algorithm described in Part II. The recommendations are mixed, i.e. can come from different recommenders. We use the following recommenders to generate recommendations shown here: product similarity, sequential association rules, item-to-item collaborative filtering, and manual recommendations. The recommended products can come from any of the data sources connected to iFuice. The recommendations links lead user to the respective product pages in the EC-Fuice web portal. External data sources are not used here. We use a generic explanation "Product Tips" for this recommendation block.

The second recommendation block presents live recommendations based on data from external data source – the eBay website. Although we have information about products from eBay in EC-Fuice operational database as well, we do not use it here for two reasons. The first reason is that we have limited the eBay products stored in EC-Fuice operational database to those products which have a "Buy now" price ("Sofort kaufen"). The second reason is that the eBay data in EC-Fuice operational database are updated at regular intervals of time. That means that the information in the EC-Fuice operational database is not the latest information available. This is acceptable for products which have a fixed price, is however not acceptable for auctions where the price can change every second. The recommendations in the second block are loaded asynchronously using AJAX technology and present last second auctions from eBay. Figures 3.24 and 3.25 illustrate the process of asynchronous loading using the AJAX technology. Figure 3.24 shows the recommendation blocks immediately after the web page is loaded. At this moment, an additional request is sent to the server in order to obtain the recommendations. Until the response for this request is obtained, the placeholder string "Getting recommendations from eBay" is shown in the recommendation block instead of the recommendations. As soon as the response is obtained, the recommendations are presented to the user as shown in Figure 3.25. The position of the recommendation block is set statically in the layout of the website. All recommendations shown in the block come from a single recommender. In order to obtain the recommendations the recommender sends an HTTP request with the keywords describing the current context on the EC-Fuice web portal to the search engine of the website http://www.ebay.de/. The obtained search results are formatted and returned to the web user as recommendations. The explanation "Last-Second eBay" is shown in the header of the recommendation block. The recommendations in this block are not adaptive. The recommendation links lead user directly to the eBay website.

The third recommendation block is similar to the second recommendation block. The data source which provides the recommendations is the books assortment on the website http://www.amazon.com. We do not have the contents of this data source in EC-Fuice operational database (there we have integrated the German version of the website, http://www.amazon.de, which has its own product assortment and its own prices). Therefore an external call to the keyword search web service of the US Amazon is made. As soon as the data is returned, it is formatted as recommendations and presented to the user. The keywords for the request are extracted from the content-related part of the current context of the EC-Fuice website. It should be noted that the content context of the EC-Fuice website is in German language, the web service provided by US-Amazon however expects keywords in English language as input parameters. Initially, we have implemented the translation of the keywords in the recommender before sending them to Amazon web service. The translation was implemented using the free of charge web service provided by the company Linguatec (http://www.linguatec.de/). However, after some time this free web service has become unavailable. We have not found any other web service providing the similar service. At the moment, we send the German keywords to the Amazon web service. We have discovered, that due to the large number of English and international keywords in the names of product categories and titles and descriptions of the products this recommender is in many cases still able to provide good quality recommendations without keyword translation. The recommendation links shown in this recommendation block lead to the website http://www.amazon.com.

Apart from the three recommendation blocks on the right side, we also show one recommendation block on the left side of the web page. This recommendation block presents DVD products from US-Amazon and operates similarly to the recommender showing Book products from US-Amazon.

The main content panel, the panels containing the navigation menu and the four recommendations panels take all the space of the web page which is available in the browser window without the need for extensive scrolling. It is known that the areas of the website available only via scrolling tend to get less user attention. Therefore, in addition to the recommendations positioned statically in the web page layout we also use "floating" recommendations. The floating recommendations are used in the category browsing view, product list view and individual product view. Figure 3.26 shows the presentation of the floating recommendations in the category browsing view. The recommendations used for the floating presentation are pre-calculated and adaptive on the level of recommenders. The recommendations use multiple data source connected to iFuice framework. The floating recommendations are event-based. They appear when the user holds the mouse pointer over some element on the web page for the time which is sufficient to assume that this element has attracted the user's attention. The elements which represent product

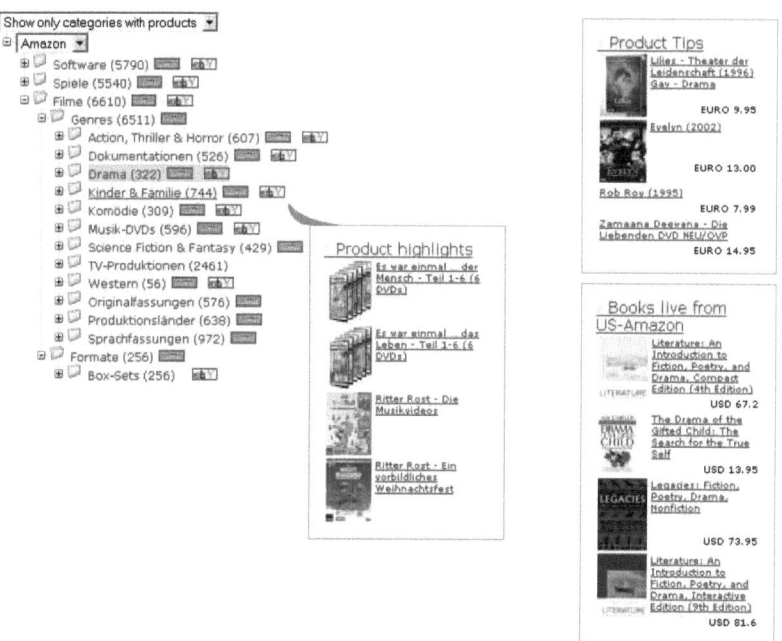

Figure 3.26. Floating recommendations shown during category browsing.

categories or individual products can be used to trigger the floating recommendations. In the EC-Fuice web portal we set the time interval after which the request is sent to the server to show the recommendations to 2.5 seconds. The recommendations are presented to the user after the response from the server is received. The floating web recommendations are shown near the element which has triggered them. They can overlay the other content on the website. To hide the floating recommendations and thus reveal the content overlaid by the recommendations, the web user can move the mouse pointer away from the highlighted element and either click on the empty space on the web page or hold the mouse pointer over the empty space for some time.

The blocks of floating recommendations show recommendations coming from the same recommender. The utilized recommenders however can be different, based on the analysis of the web usage data in the EC-Fuice data warehouse similar to the adaptive recommender selection process discussed in Part II. We use the following recommenders for floating recommendations in the EC-Fuice portal:

For the recommendations to the categories presented in the category browsing view:
- new products in the category
- most viewed products in the category (product highlights)
- related categories from other data sources

For the recommendations to the products presented in the product view:
- similar products from the same categories to which the product belongs
- related categories from other data sources

It is possible to use other recommenders as well.

13. RELATED WORK AND DISCUSSION

The presented work borders on two large research fields: data integration and ontology matching. In this section we present the related projects in these two research fields and discuss some highlights which differentiate the work presented in this thesis from other work or liken it to other work to in the respective research fields. In Section 13.1 we discuss the distinctive features of our approach and present the related work in the field of data integration. In Section 13.2 the related ontology matching projects are presented.

13.1 Related Work in the Field of Data Integration

To the author's knowledge, there are no works that claim to provide a complete or nearly complete survey of approaches to the data integration problem. Two works provide an overview of the data integration research field in general. The work by A. Halevy and others [HRO06] presents a short but broad overview onto the field, whereas the work by M. Lenzerini [Lenz02] takes a theoretical perspective. The latter work formally defines a data integration framework, and explores different problems of global schema modeling and declarative query processing. In fact, much of the discussion in the field of data integration is devoted to the issues dealing with the way the data sources are described with respect to the global schema (local-as-view, global-as-view, global-local-as-view, respectively LAV, GAV, GLAV) and with the optimization and execution of the declarative queries over the integrated data. Although the work presented here corresponds to the formal theoretical definition of the data integration framework given in [Lenz02], it uses neither global schema nor declarative queries. Because of that, a significant part of the discussion in the field of data integration research is not directly relevant for our architecture. In the following subsections we discuss several of the relevant projects individually. During the discussion of the individual projects we also elaborate on the features of EC-Fuice which are similar or different from the comparable features in the discussed projects. Before discussing the individual projects, we would like to highlight some issues which distinguish out approach from many or all projects listed below. These common differences result from our architecture responding to the practice-relevant issues which arise in the field of integrated e-commerce sites. These issues common to the data integration in e-commerce were summarized in the invited talk of A. Gupta (Amazon.com) at the EDBT2000 [Gupt00]. Mr. Gupta has led research in the field of virtual database technology at Junglee Corp. before it was acquired by Amazon. Listed below are some of the relevant issues from [Gupt00]:

Objects, not relations. Unclear separation of schema and instance. The needs of e-commerce applications with respect to storing and accessing the data are not well served by the relational database model. So, the attributes of the objects may change often. Multivalued attributes, such as different sizes and colors for a t-shirt, are possible. The data often needs to be stored and accessed in a hierarchical way as opposed to the flat way suggested by the relational model.

Query, not transaction. Queries pose a greater challenge to e-commerce websites than transactions. Data to be queried, such as product information, is often separate from transaction data, such as shopping cart and payment data. According to the data from Amazon.com, their website processes 50 times more queries than orders. Being focused on the query answering is a common feature for many heterogeneous data integration systems as opposed to multi-database systems. According to [Gupt00], query response times are much more critical than the transaction response times.

Limited queries, not ad-hoc queries. Tightly integrated keyword searching. The e-commerce applications usually provide limited possibilities for querying the data: usually they are restricted to keyword search and simple attribute search. According to [Gupt00], the majority of customers are unsophisticated and do need rich possibilities for querying data. Such customers are best served with the keyword search. On the other hand, the few structured queries which are used by the e-commerce applications internally need to be optimized a-priori. In our e-commerce system we do not address answering declarative structured queries on the multiple data sources. Instead, we use iFuice scripts which can be viewed as manually optimized query execution plans. However, it is still possible to declaratively query the materialized data in EC-Fuice using SQL query language.

Incomplete query results. The users do not necessarily need to see all query results. Usually, however, they are interested in getting the first results quickly. We address this issue by using paging in the keyword search results. The first page of the result list is shown to the user immediately when it becomes available. Further results are shown when the user chooses to view the subsequent pages.

Inexact matches. The users seldom know what exactly they are looking for. Therefore, it is important to provide them not only with the exact results for their query but also some related results. We address this issue by providing web recommendations in the search results. Two of the three keyword search algorithms we provide also support returning additional query results. So, the Lucene full-text search library provides the possibility to include all variants of keyword flexion and declination into the search query. MySQL full-text search supports so-called "query expansion"[41]. Query expansion means that the full-text search is performed twice. In the first run the query engine determines all keywords which frequently co-occur with the user-specified keywords. In the second run, the keywords determined in the first run are used together with the user-specified keywords to perform keyword search and return the results to the user.

Caching and materialized views. E-commerce applications are expected to provide sub-second response times. It has been our experience that even well established

---
[41] http://dev.mysql.com/doc/refman/5.0/en/fulltext-query-expansion.html

industrial-strength relational database systems such as IBM DB2, Microsoft SQL Server or MySQL can provide sub-second response times on heavily loaded websites only with additional caching on the level of the web application, i.e. in the main memory. To provide sub-second response in EC-Fuice web portal, we have used massive data materialization, optimized the relational database structure and implemented the asynchronous loading of those portions of web page content which are based on the non-materialized data. We know of no comparative study of the response times for the other data integrations projects. Several other projects address the query answering performance issues of the data integration systems. For example, the project Tukwila [ILW+00] discusses the issues related to performance and techniques for adaptive query processing.

Availability, not consistency. E-commerce applications stress availability, not consistency. Less consistent data may still be sufficient to persuade the user to buy a product.

Data cleaning. As we have illustrated in Chapter 11, e-commerce applications require extensive data cleaning. Not all of the projects described below address data cleaning. Some of the systems assume that the data coming from different data sources is either homogeneous in format or homogeneous in both format and value representation.

Information Manifold

The influential project Informaton Manifold from the authors of the overview paper [HRO06] is described in [LRO96]. Information Manifold is the first project to use "Local as view" concept to describe the data sources. The authors describe the system as source independent and query independent. In comparison to EC-Fuice, Information Manifold integrates a much larger number of data sources (~100 sources). We have not experimentally investigated the scalability of EC-Fuice with respect to the number of the data sources. However, since EC-Fuice does not contain components such as query planner, the performance of which could drastically depend on the number on sources, we can assume that EC-Fuice system is sufficiently scalable with respect to the performance given a large number of data sources. However, EC-Fuice may exhibit scalability problems with respect to the amount of implementation work which is needed to integrate an additional data source into EC-Fuice. Indeed, although it is sufficient to implement only one mapping to integrate a new data source into EC-Fuice, for better efficiency it is advisable to implement the mappings to as many other data sources as possible, since composing mappings may lead to an increased error rate in the resulting mapping. This may lead to the explosive growth of the total number of mappings in case when new data sources are added.

The authors of the Information Manifold emphasize the combination of AI approach with database techniques in their system. AI techniques are used to solve the tasks of query optimization, query reformulation and query execution. The underlying data model is relational with object-oriented features. The data model supports a class hierarchy with inheritance and is significantly more complex than the domain model we use in

EC-Fuice. Information Manifold is designed for answering ad-hoc declarative queries on the data from heterogeneous data sources. That distinguishes Information Manifold from our approach, where the data is queried using scripts which utilize the executable mappings. Information Manifold needs to establish a query plan in order to execute a query, whereas an iFuice script represents a ready query execution plan. The approach with scripts and executable mapping is especially useful for building web applications, which rely not on ad-hoc structured queries but on full-text search and pre-defined navigation. The disadvantage of the script-based approach is that more knowledge about what data is provided by which data source is needed to build such a script than to pose a declarative query.

TSIMMIS

TSIMMIS [CGH+94] is one of the first data integration projects which targets the heterogeneous, diverse and semi-structured data, such as the data found on the web. TSIMMIS stands for "The Stanford-IBM Manager of Multiple Information Sources". TSIMMIS's data model is built around the special data exchange language OEM (object exchange model), which includes many of the features found in later XML and RDF/XML languages. However, the information need not be stored as OEM inside the TSIMMIS system, as opposed to some XML-based systems where XML is also used to store the data. Similar to XML, OEM allows nesting objects. In EC-Fuice nesting of objects is not supported explicitly. Nesting in EC-Fuice can however be expressed as a mapping between objects. TSIMMIS also provides a special OEM-QL language for querying data stored as OEM. The authors claim that they use no global database schema. The later surveys classify their approach as GAV. A distinctive feature of TSIMMIS is the ability to have several mediators which can interact with each other. In EC-Fuice, another integrated website can act as a data source. Other ways of cooperation between several EC-Fuice instances are not addressed in the design of the EC-Fuice system. Similar to EC-Fuice, the TSIMMIS mediator does not need to understand all the data it handles [CGH+94]. Special attention in the design of the TSIMMIS system is given to the constraints on the integrated data. TSIMMIS also allows browsing and exploring the integrated data. TSIMMIS provides a web interface called MOBIE (which can be sees as the counterpart to the EC-Fuice web portal). The web user obtains access to the data integrated by TSIMMIS by starting with entering a query on the website and then browsing the returned results. The authors also mention the possibility to present the user with the results of the "frequently asked queries", which can be viewed as a move towards web recommendations.

Ariadne, SIMS

The project Ariadne is described in [KMA+01] and the project SIMS in [AKS96]. Ariadne is an extension of the SIMS mediator architecture. The SIMS mediator comprises the core of the system and performs answering queries to the distributed heterogeneous data sources. Ariadne concentrates on web data sources, information from which is obtained using HTML-scraping. Ariadne and SIMS support declarative queries and are based on the domain model which is represented using Loom knowledge representation language[MB87]. SIMS data model describes classes with relations and inheritance As opposed to EC-Fuice/iFuice, the data model is more detailed and contains attributes. SIMS is able to answer declarative queries using the query planner. SIMS supports mappings on the instance level, either as an executable mapping or as a mapping table, analogous to respectively a mapping and a MappingResult in iFuice. The system allows using combined methods for instance mapping. For example, SIMS can combine textual similarity with machine learning which learns the abbreviations. The authors propose an active learning system where the system asks the user whether the rules according to which the mappings are created are good or not. In our system, these rules (i.e. iFuice scripts) are pre-defined. The Ariadne architecture includes possibilities for selective materialization based on the analysis of the user query distribution. The authors mention that they have integrated online electronic catalogs with products including pricing, availability, manufacturer etc. They have however not indicated whether the hierarchical structure of the catalogs was also integrated.

The authors point out that one shortcoming of their architecture is the inability to execute recursive query plans. This is addressed in the next projects of the same working group – data integration system Prometheus [TAK03] and query execution engine Theseus [BDKM00].

Prometheus, Theseus

In the projects Prometheus[TAK03] and Theseus[BDKM00], the workgroup which has previously created the projects Ariadne and SIMS has addressed the following issues: execution of recursive integration plans, view integration technique with dynamic service composition, support for geo-spacial data types, record linkage and object consolidation. The integrated web project BulidingFinder[MAK+04] based on Prometheus and Theseus allows users to search for building information and satellite images based on the information from several data sources. Similarly to Ariadne and SIMS, Prometheus is based on domain model. In the project BuildingFinder the mediator supports the RDQL query language. The query is then translated into Datalog query which is executed by the Theseus query execution engine. The query results can be returned as RDF.

VISPO

The project Vispo is described in [CFP+02], [BA04]. The project is explicitly focused on e-commerce applications. In the motivating scenario, several enterprises organize a virtual marketplace nicknamed "virtual district" in order to cooperate on the web. XML is used as data exchange format in the "virtual district". To overcome the semantic heterogeneity, the authors propose the use of common ontology. The handling of ontologies in Vispo is different from EC-Fuice. In EC-Fuice, we treat ontologies as a kind of data: we store in them the same data storage where the instance data are stored and process them using the same operators. In VISPO the ontologies are treated as metadata and are clearly separated from the instance data. Vispo features a three-layer domain ontology which is constructed from the input XMLS data. The classes extracted from the input XML are clustered. Ontological concepts and semantic relations between them are generated from the clusters. The generated ontological concepts are then associated with categories in one of the available standard taxonomies.

The 5-level UNSPSC (United Nations Standard Products and Services Code)[42] is proposed as a possible standard taxonomy. We do not make use of UNSPSC in EC-Fuice, since it doesn't contain detailed hierarchy levels for the products which we have in our system.

MOMIS

The application of the system MOMIS [BB04][BBB+04][BBB+02] to an e-commerce environment is described in [BGV02]. MOMIS allows integrating data from heterogeneous data sources, such as relational databases, object-oriented databases, XML. MOMIS is based on a global virtual schema. The global virtual schema is generated from the source descriptions. The global virtual schema used in MOMIS is more sophisticated than the domain model used in EC-Fuice. The global virtual schema contains attributes and data types. In the extension of the system described in [BBB+06] the global virtual schema also contains a list of "relevant values" for the individual attributes. MOMIS uses several lexical techniques to generate the global virtual schema, for example a generated common thesaurus. Instance-based mappings are not used to generate the global schema. In the paper [BGV02] special attention is given to matching hierarchical product catalogs. Three standard hierarchical product classification systems are taken as an example: the aforementioned UNSPSC, NAICS (North American Industry Classification system)[43], Ecl@ss (European classification system)[44]. With respect to the possible use in EC-Fuice, all these product classification systems share a common shortcoming of being not detailed enough for the assortment of the products processed by EC-Fuice. In contrast to EC-Fuice, in MOMIS the classification hierarchies are incorporated into the global virtual schema, i.e. are considered by the system as metadata rather than data.

The classification hierarchies are matched to each other using the MOMIS system based on the following (the description is based on the classification in [RB01]): schema-level information, different matching granularity is possible, language-derived, considering auxiliary information. The correspondences can be generated in three ways: schema-derived, lexicon-derived, human-supplied. As opposite to the EC-Fuice approach, the instance-level information is not used to match the classification hierarchies.

---

[42] http://www.unspsc.org/
[43] http://www.naics.com/
[44] http://www.eclass.de/

To describe the mappings between the classes, more sophisticated system than in EC-Fuice is used: the mappings can be of several types, namely: synonymy (i.e. equality), broader term/narrower term (subclass/superclass), related (loose relationship). Similarly to the use of COMA++ GUI in EC-Fuice, the mappings between classification hierarchies in MOMIS are generated in a semi-automatic way. The human engineer can refine and amend the mappings using the graphical tool "Source Integration Designer". The classification hierarchies are then merged with help of the tool ARTEMIS[CAC01].

ActiveXML

Active XML [ABM+04] is a peer-to-peer based framework developed at INRIA, France, which allows declarative data integration. The Active XML approach is based on XML and web services. ActiveXML takes a novel approach with respect to the input data and data source descriptions, namely: it blends the difference between the data and the information on how to obtain these data. The core idea of ActiveXML lies in augmenting the usual XML data with calls to web services. The ActiveXML documents are normal XML documents from the point of view of a conventional XML parser. The difference lies in how these documents are processed by the peers participating in the data integration. Some tags in ActiveXML documents are treated as calls to web services, which can be either conventional web services or ActiveXML peers. ActiveXML positions itself not as a data integration system but as a "language and system to facilitate data integration" [TAXT03]. Therefore, ActiveXML is not designed to address many of the issues addressed by other projects listed here. However, there are some contact points between ActiveXML and our research. To some extent, we also combine data with service calls (calls to iFuice mappings to provide live recommendations) for the presentation in the EC-Fuice web portal using the combination of Java, JavaScript and HTML languages. We also utilize iFuice scripts written in iFuice script language to control the execution of mappings and processing the mapping results. ActiveXML is an interesting generic approach, which could potentially help perform both these tasks within the same language framework.

OntoWebber

OntoWebber[JDW01] is a project which deals with building a semantic web portal from different data sources. The data sources are required to comply with the Semantic Web requirements (RDF, UML/XMI, HTML). The architecture of the OntoWebber system is based on a domain ontology. In OntoWebber, ontologies are handled as data. The ontologies are extracted from the data sources and then combined into one reference ontology. The focus of the OntoWebber lies in formalization and modeling of the creation of an ontology-based web portal. OntoWebber formalizes the four layers of an integrated web portal: the integration layer, the articulation layer, the composition layer and the generation layer. The authors specifically mention the modeling of the website personalization. The authors make provisions for the following models: maintenance model, personalization model, content model, presentation model, domain model and multiple navigation models. OntoWebber expects the input data either to be in RDF format or to be easily expressed as RDF. For the generation layer, [JDW01]discusses several types of generation of the website from models with respect to the performance of the resulting website, ranked from most performant and least flexible to least performant and most flexible: pre-generation of static HTML pages, generation of JSP pages, or direct interpretation of the models. OntoWebber does not discuss the problems of data extraction, data cleaning, ontology matching and ontology integration in detail. Instead, it refers to other projects such as TSIMMIS[CGH+94], InterDataWorking[MD00] and ONION[MWK00] for the detailed discussion of these issues. An important difference between the concepts of OntoWebber and EC-Fuice is that that OntoWebber relies on a centralized authority which is responsible for creating and maintaining the reference ontology, whereas EC-Fuice takes a more decentralized, peer-to-peer like approach without a reference ontology.

Online Citation Service (OCS)

The works [RTA07][TAR07] propose a data integration framework for mashups based on iFuice platform. The term "mashup" denotes a new type of interactive website which combines data and services from different web sources [RTA07]. iFuice is used to provide the created mashups with sophisticated data integration functionality. The authors discuss the capabilities of their framework using the example mashup site "Online Citation Service" (OCS)[45], which was implemented using the presented framework. In comparison to EC-Fuice, the interactive aspect of web data integration is significantly more developed in the framework presented in [RTA07][TAR07]. In EC-Fuice most of the data integration work is performed by iFuice scripts in offline mode, although we also use live recommendations which are generated by iFuice in online mode. In OCS, iFuice scripts are executed online in response to the user navigation on the site. Since some of these scripts can take longer to complete, the authors also use asynchronous execution mode implemented using AJAX technology. This way, the web user can see first partial results in relatively short time; missing data are added to the web page as soon as they become available. Another improvement in comparison to EC-Fuice is the use of the special operator *fuse*. This operator fuses different versions of the same real-life entity into one object. In EC-Fuice different versions of the same real-life entities are linked together but not fused into one object. In general, the presented framework allows web developers to define complex mashup websites using a high level script language. The focus of the work is being placed on the rich data integration capabilities, which are not present in other currently available mashup frameworks.

---

[45] http://dbs.uni-leipzig.de:8080/OCS/Index.html

SEAL, Ontobroker

SEAL[MSS+01] is an approach for creating semantic portals (SEAL stands for Semantic portAL) based on the Ontobroker[DEFS99] architecture. Although the usage of different data sources is implied in the SEAL architecture, it is not discussed and no explicit support for heterogeneous data sources is offered. The authors focus on the AI techniques for creating semantic portals. The SEAL architecture is based on a knowledge warehouse and the Ontobroker inferencing system. One of the ideas of the authors is that data contained in the ontologies themselves is not sufficient to integrate the semantics. This is consistent with our experience that for example thesauri and abbreviation dictionaries can be very helpful in bringing the concepts from different ontologies together. SEAL supports semantic personalization. Explicitly described is the manual personalization, but the authors also mention semantic logfiles which can be analyzed to perform automatic personalization and optimization of the web portal.

Omelayenko and Fensel

A series of works by Omelayenko and Fensel [OF01][OF01a][OF01b] specifically deals with integration of product catalog integration in B2B e-commerce. The system described by the authors works on XML basis and uses transformation rules expressed in XSLT. The architecture is based on the assumption that input data are expressed in XML. The authors propose to use RDF for internal representations of the data sources and models. The work adopts the layered structure proposed in [MD00]. Due to the architecture's being focused on XML and XSLT, some problems are not addressed, in particular the data integration from heterogeneous data sources. Also, the (semi)automatic generation of the transformation rules is not addressed. It is arguable that all transformations which may need to be performed in the heterogeneous data environment can be adequately expressed with XSLT and that the use of transformations written in a full programming language such as Java can be given up.

13.2 Related Work in the Field of Ontology Matching

There is a large body of published work devoted to the ontology matching (also known as ontology alignment). We will not try to give a complete overview of the research in this field here. Instead, we refer to the publications [Noy04], [NS05] and [KS05]. The first two publications contain a rather concise informal overview of the research in the field, whereas the last one presents a more thorough survey. An even more extensive work on the state of art in ontology matching is presented in the KnowledgeWeb deliverables [KW04] and [KW04a]. Many researchers which analyze the field of ontology matching research point out that the major works in the field come from two communities: the AI community and the database community. The interest on the ontology matching in the database community has evolved from the interest on matching of database schemas.

The survey of work on schema matching is presented in [RB01]. The work presented in this thesis has an affiliation to the work provided by the database community, since the COMA++ platform which we utilize is an extension of the schema matching platform COMA. Since our work concerns not the ontology matching in general but rather a specific technique of combining the instance-based ontology matching with other mapping techniques, in the following subsections we will describe some of the relevant ontology matching projects which also use instance-based matching.

Instance Matching in COMA++

The COMA++ architecture is described in Section 3.2 in detail. Here, we discuss the instance-based matchers in COMA++ which were not available at the time when we conducted our experiments. The instance-based matchers integrated into COMA++ are introduced in [EM07]. The additional instance-based COMA++ matchers which are described in [EM07] target in the first place schema matching. In the later paper [MR08] they have been extended for matching ontologies, in particular web directories. The following instance-based matchers are presented in [EM07]:

Constraint-based matchers. This type of matcher checks whether the instances of the ontologies satisfy a pre-defined set of constraints. The constraints can be for example defined as a string pattern, numeric range, containment of a substring etc.

Content-based matchers. This type of matcher determines the similarity of two elements by executing a pair-wise comparison of instance values using a similarity function [EM07]. Any of the several string similarity functions implemented in COMA++ can be used to calculate the instance similarity. The list of the string similarity functions is provided in Section 3.2. The matching of ontologies in COMA++ using content-based matchers is similar to the work presented in this thesis. Since our approach uses iFuice mappings to determine the instance similarity, we are not limited to the string similarity functions provided by COMA++ and can use complex combined mappings. However, in our architecture the matching of ontologies using instance information requires two systems (iFuice and COMA++), whereas in the approach described in [EM07] such matching is implemented within one system.

Similarity propagation. Since the instances in the ontology may often be sparse, i.e. not all ontology concepts may have associated instances, it may be promising to propagate the similarity values to parents of the concepts which have associated instances.

[MR08] investigates the use of instance-based matchers and combinations of instance-based and other COMA++ matchers in application to matching web directories. Web directories are ontology-like hierarchical structures containing annotated web links which are assigned to different categories. The authors experiment with web directories from Google[46], Yahoo[47], Dmoz[48] and Web.de[49] (all in German language). The authors

---
[46] http://directory.google.de/Top/World/Deutsch/

compare the performance of the match algorithms to the manually created reference mappings between the web directories. The authors however do not specify the criteria for creating such reference mappings with respect to the semantics of the individual correspondences.

Similarly to the work presented in this thesis, the correspondences in the mappings represent a generic similarity measure without semantic differentiation. Thus, [MR08] and the work presented in this thesis potentially share some of the drawbacks caused by the low semantic expressiveness of the COMA++ correspondences.

In contrast to our approach which uses two tools, COMA++ and iFuice, the matching approach presented in [MR08] is completely done in COMA++. Such approach allows more versatile combination of instance-based and other matchers. However, for our particular application -- creation of an integrated website -- COMA++ amended with instance matchers would not be sufficient alone. iFuice would still be needed since it has rich possibilities for script-based manipulation of the mappings which COMA++ doesn't provide.

One aspect of the instance-based matching which is investigated in [MR08] is the use of instances directly associated to a category in comparison to use of instances associated both directly and indirectly, i.e. directly associated to a subcategory of a category. The authors find out that the use of indirectly associated instances may be beneficial for the quality of the mapping. This corresponds to the approach which we take in this work: we implicitly convert all indirectly associated into directly associated instances, which is stipulated by the fact that some of our important source ontologies explicitly store indirect links as direct. [MR08] analyses average recall, precision and f-measure with respect to the manual reference mappings in 6 matching tasks (each of the mentioned four ontologies matcher pair-wise). The authors indicate that the input ontologies which were used in [MR08] exhibit various degrees of pair-wise heterogeneity, from quite homogeneous (Dmoz vs. Google) to very heterogeneous. The authors achieve average f-measure of 0.79 with their best matching algorithm comprised of 6 single matchers. In our work, the maximal achieved f-measure was ~0.7, however using different input data.

Although the results of [MR08] and our results are not directly comparable, one interesting common result is that in both works the combination of metadata-based and instance-based matchers has brought an increase of f-measure between 15% and 35% compared to both metadata-only and instance-only approaches (excluding the instance-based mapping in our work which uses EAN code – this mapping has relatively high quality due to unambiguousness of EAN, therefore the combination with metadata-based matchers brings only ~7% improvement).

[EM07] also provides a comparative study on how the use of instance-based matchers improves the quality of the ontology mapping. According to their results,

---

[47] http://de.dir.yahoo.com/
[48] http://www.dmoz.org/World/Deutsch/
[49] http://dir.web.de/

utilizing the proposed algorithms, in particular the content-based matchers, improves the average precision by 10% and the recall by 13%.

Glue

The system Glue developed at the University of Washington is described in [DMDH04] and [DMDH03]. Glue uses machine learning to match ontologies. To match the ontology concepts based on the instances, Glue first performs the classification of the instances utilizing several machine learning approaches. The joint probability distributions of concepts in the ontologies are calculated. Then the system estimates the similarities of the concepts as function of their joint distributions. Finally, a so-called relaxation labeling technique is applied to choose the best correspondence candidates based on the computed similarity between concepts.

FCA-Merge

The system FCA-Merge is described in [SM01]. The system is based on the formal concept analysis techniques described in [GW99]. The system focuses on merging two input ontologies into one output ontology based on the analysis of the instance data. The ontology merging is done in three steps: instance extraction, application of the FCA-Merge core algorithm to create the concept lattice, creation of the resulting ontology. The result of the process is a merged ontology rather than a mapping between ontologies. The last step of the merging process requires human intervention.

IF-Map

IF-Map [KS02][KS03] is the system inspired by the Barwise-Serligman theory of information flow [BS97]. The system matches local ontologies using reference ontology, assuming that the local ontologies are usually populated, whereas the reference ontology is usually unpopulated. The system works by the classifying the instances on the input local ontologies with respect to their concepts and determining the local logic of both local and reference ontologies. Then the system infers the logical morphism which can transform one local logic into another. The core IF-Map algorithm is implemented in Prolog.

S-Match

The S-Match approach (also known as Semantic matching) is presented in the series of works [GSY04][GYG05][GSY05][GYS07]. The authors discuss application of their approach to relational and object-oriented schemas, concept hierarchies and ontologies. The authors focus on matching of tree-like structures. For non-tree-like structures the authors rely on the known techniques such as one described in [BMPQ04] to convert such structures into tree-like structures.

In contrast to many other schema and ontology matching platforms, such as Cupid [MBR01], Rondo [MRB03], COMA[DR02] and COMA++ [ADMR05], the semantic matching approach uses not "weighted" correspondences but "typed" correspondences. The following types of correspondences are used: *equivalence, more general, less general, disjointness, unknown*. The types of correspondences in the above list are ranked according to their *binding strength*, with strongest being equivalence and the weakest *unknown*. During the matching, the S-Match algorithm tries to find the strongest existing correspondences between the nodes in the ontologies which are being matched. An additional filtering step can be applied to prune correspondences which can be inferred from the stronger correspondences. This is similar to the intuition we have used for creating our manual ontology mapping between Amazon and Softunity ontologies.

Another important feature of the approach is that S-Match does not use the information stored in the ontology nodes and their labels for matching immediately. At first, this information is subjected to preprocessing. During preprocessing S-Match matches this information to concepts in an extensive global ontology such as WordNet. This is done both for individual nodes and for complete paths from the root to a given node. After preprocessing, S-Match uses a combination of numerous matchers to establish correspondences between the calculated concepts from the global ontology. These matchers include lexical matchers such as EditDistance, N-Gram and Affix but also special matchers which operate on the information specific to WordNet. After the correspondence candidates are determined using the matchers, the matching problem is transformed into the propositional satisfiability problem and solved using so-called SAT solver[50].

The authors state that their approach is schema-based and that instances are not considered during the matching [GYS07]. An exception constitutes the matching of ontologies, where instances are also used for matching as long as they are present in the ontology. Since no difference is made between the processing of the concept data and the processing of the instance data, such approach may exhibit performance problems in case when the amount of instance data is very large, which is a quite common case. Apart from this, the authors place a special value on the efficiency of their matching algorithm and propose a number of optimization techniques.

The authors evaluate their matching approach by comparing its results to the results obtained by Cupid [MBR01], Rondo [MRB03] and COMA[DR02]. The evaluation was performed on matching tasks from different application domains, such as company profiles, purchase orders schemas and university course catalogs. The results show that S-Match can achieve better results in matching company profiles and university course catalogues than the other systems while lying slightly behind COMA in matching purchase order schemas. Additional experiments on matching web directories (Google vs. Yahoo vs. Looksmart) were performed to explore the efficiency of the matching of larger ontologies (about 1000 nodes) and highlight the effects of the optimization techniques.

---

[50] D. Le Berre. A satisfiability library for Java. http://www.sat4j.org/.

T-Tree

T-Tree is a system described in [Euze94]. The T-Tree system is capable of inferring correspondences (so-called "bridges") between the ontology classes based only on the instance data. It is assumed that the correspondences between the instances are known in advance. The algorithm for inferring the bridges is iterative and is guaranteed to be extension-minimal. Being extension-minimal means that in cases when some less general bridges which can be inferred from the more general bridges exist, only the more general bridges are returned. The authors point out that the bridges found by the algorithm are not guaranteed to be semantically sound, which is in fact a common shortcoming of all instance-based methods including ours. This is consistent with our observations that certain distribution of instances may be a result of coincidence. In our experiments an example of this is the correspondence between "Films->Genre->Animation Films" and "Films->By Production Land->Japan".

QOM

QOM is described in [ES04a] and [ES04b]. As the abbreviation QOM standing for Quick Ontology Mapping suggests, the project deals with efficiency of the ontology matching, as opposed to most other ontology matching projects which focus on the quality of the resulting mapping. QOM expects input ontologies to be in the RDFS format. QOM uses special heuristics to find the most promising candidates for matching. Multiple similarity functions for the ontology concepts are supported, among them also instance-based similarity. The resulting similarity for a correspondence is a weighted sum of normalized values of the individual similarity functions. The calculation of the instance-based similarity of the two concepts is based on multidimensional scaling [CC94]. In contrast to our approach, this approach takes into account individual similarity values between the instances to calculate the similarity of the respective concepts.

Thor, Hartung et al.

The work [THG+09] focuses on mappings between evolving ontologies. The authors argue that stability of the correspondences is an important aspect which needs to be considered in the situation when the mapped ontologies evolve over time. The authors take the ontologies from the life science domain as example for such actively evolving ontologies and propose three metrics which reflect the stability of the correspondences within the mapping. The metrics take into account the historical development of the mapping and the changes in similarity of the corresponding concepts over time. Since the e-commerce ontologies which we employ in this part of the thesis are also evolving over time, using stability metrics for the correspondences utilized by EC-Fuice would be an interesting extension of our architecture.

OLA

OLA (OWL-Lite Alignment) [ELTV04] is a system designed for alignment of ontologies expressed in OWL-Lite language. OLA targets to cover all possible types of matching: terminological, structural, extensional (i.e. instance-based), semantic. The algorithm which computes the similarity is iterative and uses fix-point computations. The algorithm starts from the lexical similarity measure and gradually brings in contributions from other similarity functions. Although the internal representation of the ontologies in OLA allows relations of several types within ontologies, the correspondences based on calculated similarity between the concepts of the different ontologies are not typed.

SCM

SCM stands for Semantic Category Matching and is described in [HYNT04]. SCM performs matching of the ontologies based on the statistical analysis of the instance data. SCM computes a feature vector for all concepts in the input ontologies based on keywords found in the instances. Then it calculates the similarity of the feature vectors. To calculate the vector similarity, a common coordinate system is created based in all keywords which are found in the input ontologies. The correspondence candidates found using the feature vector based similarity are then refined by a structural matcher. The structural matcher resolves the structure violation problems which we discussed in Section 11.2.4.

14. SUMMARY

In this part of the thesis we have investigated how the navigation utilizing web recommendations can be implemented on the e-commerce websites based on integrated data sources. The integrated e-commerce websites are an interesting use case for web recommendations. One of the reasons for this interest is that many modern, large and economically successful e-commerce websites follow the integrated approach. Another reason is that especially in the integrated environment, due to the lack of the pre-defined semantic connections between the data, the web recommendations step forward as means of enabling user navigation. In this chapter we have presented the architecture for the websites based on integrated data sources named EC-Fuice. We have also presented the prototypical implementation of our architecture which serves as a proof-of-concept and investigated the challenges of creating navigation on an integrated website.

The following issues were addressed in this part of the thesis:

- Combination of several state-of-the-art tools and techniques in the fields of databases, data integration, ontology matching and web engineering into one generic architecture for creating integrated websites.

- Comparative experiments with several techniques for instance matching (also known as record linkage or duplicate detection). Investigation on using the ontology matching to facilitate the instance matching.

- Comparative experiments with several techniques for ontology matching. Investigations on the instance-based ontology matching and the possibilities for combining instance-based ontology matching with other techniques for ontology matching.

- Investigation of the possibilities to improve user navigation in the integrated data environment with different types of web recommendations.

- Review of the related work in the fields of data integration and ontology matching and discussion of the contact points between the research described here and other related projects.

The main contributions of the research described in this part of the thesis are the EC-Fuice architecture, the novel method for matching e-commerce ontologies based on combination of instance information and metadata information, the experimental results of ontology and instance matching performed by different matching algorithms and the classification of the types of recommendations which can be used on an integrated e-commerce website.

PART IV. SUMMARY

In this thesis we have investigated approaches for implementing web recommendations in on e-commerce websites. Recommendations are very important for such websites because of the ongoing growth of the amount of information and the increasing competition between sellers. The immense numbers of different products on modern e-commerce websites and vast amount of information about these products become an obstacle for the customers looking for the products that match their interests.

Web recommendations have already become indispensable on large e-commerce websites, however is probable that the peak of their popularity is yet to come, possibly in connection with distributed advertising systems such as Google AdSense[51], with which the web recommendations share a number of common characteristics.

Until present time, no single approach to generating web recommendation could claim supremacy over all others. Moreover, many researchers point out that the most promising architecture needs to combine several approached in one hybrid approach ([Bal97], [SKR02], [Burk07] and others). In Part II of this thesis we have proposed a novel architecture for combining recommendations generated by different approaches and a technique which allows optimizing the presented recommendation basing on the user feedback. We have performed comparative investigation of the different technical and algorithmic possibilities for selecting and optimizing our recommendations. In particular, we investigate several approaches to solving the problem of balancing between exploration and exploitation, i.e. balancing between using web recommendations and learning their quality. Our experiments illustrate the increase of the user acceptance of recommendations as a result of our optimization. The experimental results which we present are based on data obtained both on real-life prototypes and in a simulated environment. We have also described a way to incorporate versatile domain knowledge into our recommendation system to provide the different recommendation approaches with a unified source of relevant information. The domain knowledge in our architecture can be both extracted automatically from the available data and supplied by the human experts. We pay special attention to the storage structures in which this knowledge is stored in our system and investigate the comparative performance of the different storage structures.

In the Part III of the thesis we have investigated the generating of web recommendations for e-commerce websites which are based on data coming from multiple data sources. Integration of data from different data sources is a common characteristic found in many modern large e-commerce websites, such as Amazon and eBay. We have built a prototype of such integrated website named EC-Fuice and discussed some of the data integration challenges which arise in this prototype. In particular we pay significant attention to the problem of matching product ontologies. We combine matching based on the information contained within the ontology structure with matching based on the information provided by the product instances to improve the quality the mapping. An important issue which has to be addressed in the context of e-commerce ontologies is the evolution of ontologies and respectively the evolution of the corresponding ontology mapping. EC-Fuice uses the instance and ontology mappings to provide recommendations

---

[51] http://www.google.com/adsense/

to the web users. We have explored different types of recommendations which can be used on integrated websites and have shown that recommendations are an important means of enabling user navigation in the integrated data.

The main scientific contributions of this thesis are the following:

- An architecture of a novel semantically enriched recommendation system which is capable of combining several techniques for generation of web recommendations.
- A recommendation optimization algorithm which is able to learn the best recommendations online based on the behavior of web users.
- The evaluation of the proposed recommendation system on two real-life websites and in a simulated environment.
- An architecture of an e-commerce website built using data integration and recommendations and a proof-of-concept prototype website built according to this architecture.
- An algorithm for matching ontologies by combining instance data with lexical, syntactical, structural and other information contained in the ontology; a comparative evaluation of this algorithm.

The practical orientation of our work determines the areas of further research.

So, the recommendation system architecture presented in Part II of the thesis has influenced the design of a commercial recommendation system deployed on several top e-commerce websites in Germany. Our research on dynamically integrated websites is finding its continuation in the ongoing research on so-called "mashups", i.e. dynamically integrated websites which are becoming popular as a part of Web 2.0 paradigm.

Another possibility of further development of our recommendation approach along the Web 2.0 paradigm is the consideration of the social aspect of recommendations. For example, the websites where users share and recommend bookmarks to each other such as http://del.icio.us have become very popular in the last years. Investigation of the applicability of our optimization approaches and data integration approaches to such websites is an interesting topic for further research.

The problem of creating mappings between ontologies belongs to an active area research. The combined instance-based and metadata-based approach which we described in this thesis can be further improved to achieve better matching quality on real-life ontologies. An interesting data integration problem statement arose within the EC-Fuice framework, namely the need for combination of the offline, physical data integration (data warehouse) with ""live" data integrated online (live recommendations using iFuice mappings). This need emerges also in the context of other types of data integration projects which are commonly found in the industry. We plan further investigation of the possible solutions for this problem and of the applicability of these solutions to the problems found in the industrial environment.

REFERENCES

[ABM+04] Abiteboul, S., Benjelloun, O., Manolescu, I., Milo, T., Weber, R.: Active XML: A Data-Centric Perspective on Web Services. Web Dynamics 2004: 275-300

[ADMR05] Aumueller, D., Do, H.H., Massmann, S., Rahm, E. Schema and ontology matching with COMA++. SIGMOD Conference 2005-06

[AG03] Acharyya, S., Ghosh, J.: Context-Sensitive Modeling of Web-Surfing Behavior using Concept Trees. Proc. WebKDD, 2003

[AKA91] Aha, D., Kibler, D., Albert, M.: Instance-based learning algorithms. Machine Learning, 6:37--66. 1991

[AKS96] Arens, Y., Knoblock, C., Shen, W.-M.: Query Reformulation for Dynamic Information Integration. J. Intell. Inf. Syst. 6(2/3): 99-130 (1996)

[AM03] Anand, S., Mobasher, B.: Intelligent Techniques for Web Personalization. ITWP 2003: 1-36

[AM05] Mobasher, B., Anand, S.: Intelligent Techniques for Web Personalization, IJCAI 2003 Workshop, ITWP 2003, Acapulco, Mexico, August 11, 2003, Revised Selected Papers Springer 2005

[AM07] Anand, S., Mobasher, B.: Introduction to intelligent techniques for Web personalization. ACM Trans. Internet Techn. 7(4): (2007)

[AT01] Adomavicius, G., Tuzhilin, A.: Multidimensional Recommender Systems: A Data Warehousing Approach. WELCOM 2001: 180-192

[AT01a] Adomavicius, G., Tuzhilin, A.: Extending recommender systems: A multidimensional approach. In Proceedings of the International Joint Conference on Artificial Intelligence (IJCAI-01), Workshop on Intelligent Techniques for Web Personalization (ITWP2001), Seattle, Washington, August 4 -- 6.

[AT05] Adomavicius, G., Tuzhilin, A.: Toward the Next Generation of Recommender Systems: A Survey of the State-of-the-Art and Possible Extensions. IEEE Trans. Knowl. Data Eng. 17(6): 734-749. 2005.

[Bal97] Balabanovic, M.: An Adaptive Web Page Recommendation Service. CACM, 1997

[BB04] Beneventano, D., Bergamaschi, S.: The MOMIS Methodology for Integrating Heterogeneous Data Sources, IFIP World Computer Congress. Toulouse France, 22-27 August 2004

[BBB+02] Beneventano, D., Bergamaschi, S., Bianco, D., Guerra, F., Vincini, M.: "SI-Web: A Web based interface for the MOMIS project", Proceedings of the Convegno Nazionale Sistemi di Basi di Dati Evolute (SEBD2002), Isola d'Elba, 19-21 June, 2002

[BBB+04] Benassi, R., Beneventano, D., Bergamaschi, S., Guerra, F., Vincini, M.: "Synthesizing an Integrated Ontology with MOMIS", International Conference on Knowledge Engineering and Decision Support (ICKEDS). Porto, Portugal, 21-23 July 2004

[BBB+06] Beneventano, D., Bergamaschi, S., Bruschi, S., Guerra, F., Orsini, M., Vincini, M.: Instances Navigation for Querying Integrated Data from Web-Sites. WEBIST (1) 2006: 46-53

[BDKM00] Barish, G., DiPasquo, D., Knoblock, C., Minton, S.:Dataflow Plan Execution for Software Agents, Proceedings of the Fourth International Conference on Autonomous Agents, ACM Press, Barcelona, Spain, Carles Sierra and Maria Gini and Jeffrey S. Rosenschein, 138--139, 2000

[Bell57] Bellman, R. : Dynamic Programming. Princeton University Press. 1957

[BGV02] Bergamaschi, S., Guerra, F., Vincini, M.: A Data Integration Framework for e-Commerce Product Classification. International Semantic Web Conference 2002: 379-393

[BH04] Basilico, J., Hofmann, T.: Unifying collaborative and content-based filtering. Proc. 21th ICML Conference. Banff, Canada, 2004

[BL99] Borges, J., Levene, M.: Data Mining of User Navigation Patterns. WEBKDD 1999: 92-111

[BMC+06] Buriano, L., Marchetti, M., Carmagnola, F., Cena, F., Gena, G., Torre, I.: The Role of Ontologies in Context-Aware Recommender Systems. MDM 2006: 80

[BMPQ04] Bernstein, P., Melnik, S., Petropoulos, M., Quix, C.: Industrial-strength schema matching. SIGMOD Record 33(4), 38–43. 2004

[BR04] Bhushan, N. , Rai, K. , editors.: Strategix Decision Making: Applying the Analytic Hierarchy Process. Springer, 2004.

[Brian59] de la Briandais, R.: File Searching Using Variable Length Keys, Proceedings of the Western Joint Computer Conference: 295–298. 1959.

[BS00] Berendt, B., Spiliopoulou, M.: Analysis of Navigation Behaviour in Web Sites Integrating Multiple Information Systems. VLDB J. 9(1): 56-75 (2000)

[BS03] Baron, S. , Spiliopoulou, M.: Monitoring the Evolution of Web Usage Patterns. Proc. ECML/PKDD, 2003

[BS97] Balabanovic, M., Shoham, Y.: Content-Based, Collaborative Recommendation. Commun. ACM 40(3): 66-72. 1997

[BS97] Barwise J., Seligman, J. :Information Flow: the Logic of distributed systems. Cambridge Tracts in Theoretical Computer Science 44. Cambridge University Press, 1997.

[Burk02] Burke, R.: Hybrid Recommender Systems: Survey and Experiments. User Modeling and User-Adapted Interaction, 2002

[Burk06] Burke, R. Hybrid Recommender Systems: A Comparative Study. CTI Technical Report 06-012. 2006. (Available at http://www.cs.depaul.edu/research/technical.asp.)

[Burk07] Burke, R.: Hybrid Web Recommender Systems. The Adaptive Web 2007: 377-408

[CAC01] Castano, S., De Antonellis, V. , De Capitani di Vimercati, S. : Global Viewing of Heterogeneous Data Sources. IEEE Trans. Knowl. Data Eng. 13(2): 277-297 (2001)

[CAFP98] Castano, S., De Antonellis, V. , Fugini, M.G. , Pernici, B.: Conceptual Schema Analysis - Techniques and Applications. ACM Trans. on Database Systems 23(3), 286-333, 1998

[CC94] Cox, T., Cox, M.: Multidimensional Scaling. Chapman and Hall (1994)

[CFP+02] Colombo, E., Francalanci, C., Pernici, B., Plebani, P., Mecella, M., De Antonellis, V., Melchiori, M.: Cooperative Information Systems in Virtual Districts: the VISPO Approach. IEEE Data Eng. Bull. 25(4): 36-40 (2002)

[CGGM03] Chaudhuri, S., Ganjam, K., Ganti, V., and Motwani, R. 2003. Robust and efficient fuzzy match for online data cleaning. In Proceedings of the 2003 ACM SIGMOD international Conference on Management of Data (San Diego, California, June 09 - 12, 2003). SIGMOD2003. ACM Press, New York, NY, 313-324.

[CGGM05] Chaudhuri, S., Ganjam, K., Ganti, V., Motwani, R.: Fuzzy Lookup and Fuzzy Grouping in SQL Server Integration Services 2005. Microsoft Corporation. MSDN Library September 2005. http://msdn2.microsoft.com/en-us/library/ms345128.aspx

[CGH+94] Chawathe, S. , Garcia-Molina, H. , Hammer, J. , Ireland, K. , Papakonstantinou, Y., Ullman, J. , Widom,. J. : The TSIMMIS Project: Integration of Heterogeneous Information Sources. In Proceedings of IPSJ Conference, pp. 7-18, Tokyo, Japan, October 1994.

[CGM99] Claypool, M., Gokhale, A., Miranda, T.: Combining Content-Based and Collaborative Filters in an Online Newspaper. In: Proc. ACM SIGIR Workshop on Recommender Systems, 1999

[CK68] Cleverdon, C., Kean, M.: Factors Determining the Performance of Indexing Systems.Aslib Cranfield Research Project, Cranfield, England.1968.

[CM05] Chen, A., McLeod, D.: Semantic-Based Similarity Decisions for Ontologies. ICEIS (3) 2005: 443-446

[CTS99a] Cooley, R., Tan, P., Srivastava, J.: Discovery of Interesting Usage Patterns from Web Data. WEBKDD 1999: 163-182

[CTS99b] Cooley, R., Tan, P., Srivastava, J.: WebSIFT: The Web site information filter system. In Workshop on Web Usage Analysis and User Profiling (WebKDD99), San Diego, August 1999.

[DCES04] Das, S., Chong, E., Eadon., G, Srinivasan, J.: Supporting Ontology-Based Semantic matching in RDBMS. VLDB 2004: 1054-1065

[DEFS99] Decker, S., Erdmann, M., Fensel, D., Studer, R.: Ontobroker: Ontology Based Access to Distributed and Semi-Structured Information. DS-8 1999: 351-369

[DMDH03] Doan, A., Madhavan, J., Dhamankar, R., Domingos, P., Halevy, A.: Learning to match ontologies on the Semantic Web. VLDB J. 12(4): 303-319 (2003)

[DMDH04] Doan, A., Madhavan, J., Dhamankar, R., Domingos, P., Halevy, A.: Ontology Matching: A Machine Learning Approach. Handbook on Ontologies 2004: 385-404

[Do06] Do, H.H.: Schema Matching and Mapping-based Data Integration, Dissertation, Department of Computer Science, Universität Leipzig, Germany, 2006

[DR02] Do, H.H., Rahm, E.: COMA - A System for Flexible Combination of Schema Matching Approaches. VLDB 2002: 610-621

[ELTV04] Euzenat, J., Loup, D., Touzani, M., Valtchev, P.: Ontology alignment with OLA, in: Proc. 3rd ISWC2004 workshop on Evaluation of Ontology-based tools (EON), Hiroshima (JP), p. 59-68, 2004

[EM07] Engmann, D; Maßmann, S: Instance Matching with COMA++. BTW Workshops 2007: 28-37

[ES04a] Ehrig, M., Staab, S.: QOM - Quick Ontology Mapping. International Semantic Web Conference 2004: 683-697

[ES04b] Ehrig, M., Y. Sure: Ontology Alignment - Karlsruhe. Proc. 3rd Intl. Workshop Evaluation of Ontology-based Tools (EON), 2004

[Euze94] Euzenat, J.: Brief overview of T-tree: the Tropes taxonomy building tool. In Proc. th ASIS SIG/CR workshop on classification research, Columbus (OH US), pages 69–87, 1994.

[FGJ+06] Felfernig A., Gordea S., Jannach D., Teppan E., Zanker M.: A Short Survey of Recommendation Technologies in Travel and Tourism. In: ÖGAI Journal, 4/2006, Volume 25, pp. 17-22. 2006

[Flyn06] Flynn, L.J.: Like This? You'll Hate That. (Not All Web Recommendations Are Welcome.). New York Times 2006.

[GAP07] Goy, A., Ardissono, L., Petrone, G.: Personalization in E-Commerce Applications. The Adaptive Web 2007: 485-520

[GR04] Golovin, N., Rahm, E.: Reinforcement Learning Architecture for Web Recommendations. Proc. ITCC2004, IEEE, 2004

[GR05] Golovin, N., Rahm, E.: Automatic Optimization of Web Recommendations Using Feedback and Ontology Graphs. ICWE 2005: 375-386, 2005.

[GSY04] Giunchiglia, F., Shvaiko, P, Yatskevich, M.: S-Match: an Algorithm and an Implementation of Semantic Matching. ESWS 2004: 61-75

[GYG05] Giunchiglia, F., Yatskevich, M., Giunchiglia, E.: Efficient Semantic Matching. ESWC 2005: 272-289

[GSY05] Giunchiglia, F., Shvaiko, P. Yatskevich, M.: Semantic Schema Matching. OTM Conferences (1) 2005: 347-365

[GYS07] Giunchiglia, F., Yatskevich, M., Shvaiko, P.: Semantic Matching: Algorithms and Implementation. J. Data Semantics 9: 1-38 (2007)

[Gupt00] Gupta., A.: Some Data Integration and Database Issues in E-Commerce. Invited talk, EDBT2000, Konstanz. http://www.edbt2000.uni-konstanz.de/invited/talks.html

[GW99] Ganter, B., Wille, R.: Formal Concept Analysis: mathematical foundations. Springer.1999.

[HKTR04] Herlocker, J., Konstan, J., Terveen, L., Riedl, J.: Evaluating collaborative filtering recommender systems. ACM Trans. Inf. Syst. 22(1): 5-53 (2004)

[HMAC02] Hayes, C., Massa, P., Avesani, P., Cunningham, P.: An on-line evaluation framework for recommender systems. In Workshop on Personalization and recommendation in E-Commerce, Malaga, 2002. Springer.

[Howa60] Howard, R.: Dynamic Programming and Markov Processes, The M.I.T. Press, 1960

[HRO06] Halevy, A., Rajaraman, A., Ordille, J: Data Integration: The Teenage Years. VLDB 2006: 9-16

[HS04] Haase, P., Sure, Y.: State of the art on ontology evolution, 2004. Available at www.aifb.uni-karlsruhe.de/WBS/ysu/publications/SEKT-D3.1.1.b.pdf

[HSH03] ten Hagen, S., van Someren, M., Hollink, V.: Exploration/exploitation in adaptive recommender systems. Proc. European Symposium on Intelligent Technologies, Hybrid Systems and their Implementation in Smart Adaptive Systems, Oulu, Finland. 2003

[HYNT04] Hoshiai, T., Yamane, Y., Nakamura, D., Tsuda, H.: A Semantic Category Matching Approach to Ontology Alignment. Proc. 3rd Intl. Workshop Evaluation of Ontology-based Tools (EON), 2004

[ILW+00] Ives, Z., Levy, A., Weld, S., Florescu, D., Friedman, M.: Adaptive Query Processing for Internet Applications. IEEE Data Engineering Bulletin, Vol. 23 No. 2, June 2000

[JDW01] Jin, Y., Decker, S., Wiederhold, G.: OntoWebber: Model-Driven Ontology-Based Web Site Management. SWWS 2001: 529-547

[JFM97] Joachims, T., Freitag, D., Mitchell, T.: Web Watcher: A Tour Guide for the World Wide Web. IJCAI (1) 1997: 770-777. 1997

[JKR02] Jameson, A. , Konstan, J. , Riedl, J.: AI Techniques for Personalized Recommendation. Tutorial presented at AAAI, 2002

[JM03] Jin, X., Mobasher, M. : Using Semantic Similarity to Enhance Item-Based Collaborative Filtering. In Proceedings of The 2nd IASTED International Conference on Information and Knowledge Sharing, Scottsdale, Arizona, November 2003.

[KIBG08] Koutrika, G., Ikeda, R., Bercovitz, B., Garcia-Molina, H.: Flexible recommendations over rich data. RecSys 2008: 203-210

[KK05] Kazienko, P., Kolodziejski, P.: WindOwls-Adaptive System for the Integration of Recommendation Methods in E-Commerce. AWIC 2005: 218-224

[KK06] Kazienko, P., Kolodziejski, P.: Personalized Integration of Recommendation Methods for E-commerce. IJCSA 3(3): 12-26 (2006)

[KLM96] Kaelbling, L., Littman, M., Moore, P.: Reinforcement Learning: A Survey. J. Artif. Intell. Res. (JAIR) 4: 237-285 (1996)

[KMA+01] Knoblock, C., Minton, S., Ambite, J.L., Ashish, N., Muslea, I., Philpot, A., Tejada, S.: The Ariadne Approach to Web-Based Information Integration. Int. J. Cooperative Inf. Syst. 10(1-2): 145-169. 2001

[Kost96] Koster, M.: A Method for Web Robots Control. http://www.robotstxt.org/norobots-rfc.txt. 1996.

[KR05] Kirsten, T., Rahm, E.: BioFuice: Mapping-based data integration in bioinformatics, Proc. of 3rd Int. Workshop on Data Integration in the Life Sciences (DILS), 2005

[KR99] Konstan, J., Riedl, J.: Research resources for recommender systems. In CHI'99 Workshop Interacting with Recommender Systems, 1999.

[KS02] Kalfoglou, Y., Schorlemmer, W.M.: Information-Flow-Based Ontology Mapping. CoopIS/DOA/ODBASE 2002: 1132-1151

[KS03] Kalfoglou, Y., Schorlemmer, W.M.: IF-Map: An Ontology-Mapping Method Based on Information-Flow Theory. J. Data Semantics 1: 98-127. 2003

[KS05] Kalfoglou, Y.;Schorlemmer, W.M.: Ontology Mapping: The State of the Art. Semantic Interoperability and Integration, 2005

[KW04] KnowledgeWeb. D2.2.3: State of the Art on Ontology Alignment. EU-IST Network of Excellence IST-2004-507482 KWEB. http://knowledgeweb.semanticweb.org/.

[KW04a] KnowledgeWeb. D1.2.2.2.1: Case-based recommendation of matching tools and techniques. EU-IST Network of Excellence IST-2004-507482 KWEB. http://knowledgeweb.semanticweb.org/

[Lawr03] Lawrence. , S. :Implicit feedback: Good may be better than best. Invited Talk. Workshop on Implicit Measures of User Interests and Preferences, SIGIR2003. http://research.microsoft.com/~sdumais/SIGIR2003/FinalTalks/Lawrence-implicit-feedback-good-may-be-better-than-best.ppt. August , 2003. access time: 07.11.2007.

[Lenz02] Lenzerini, M.: Data Integration: A Theoretical Perspective. PODS 2002: 233-246

[Lev66] Levenshtein, V. Binary codes capable of correcting deletions, insertions, and reversals, Doklady Akademii Nauk SSSR, 163(4):845-848, 1965 (Russian). English translation in Soviet Physics Doklady, 10(8):707-710, 1966.

[Lieb95] Lieberman, H.: Letizia: An Agent That Assists Web Browsing. In Proc.of the 14th International Joint Conference on Articial Intelligence (IJCAI). 1995

[LRO96] Levy, A., Rajaraman, A., Ordille, J.: Querying Heterogeneous Information Sources Using Source Descriptions VLDB 1996: 251-262

[LSY03] Linden, G. , Smith, B. , York, J.: Amazon.com Recommendations: Item-to-Item Collaborative Filtering. IEEE Internet Computing. Jan. 2003

[Mahe96] Mahadevan, S.: Average Reward Reinforcement Learning: Foundations, Algorithms, and Empirical Results, Machine Learning , Special Issue on Reinforcement Learning (edited by Leslie Kaebling), vol. 22, pp. 159-196, 1996.

[MAK+04] Michalowski, M., Ambite, J., Knoblock, C., Minton, S., Thakkar, S., Tuchinda, R.: Retrieving and Semantically Integrating Heterogeneous Data from the Web, IEEE Intelligent Systems., Vol. 19, No. 3, pp. 72-79, 2004.

[MASR02] Middleton, S., Alani, H., Shadbolt, N., De Roure, D.: Exploiting Synergy Between Ontologies and Recommender Systems. Semantic Web Workshop 2002

[MB87] MacGregor, R. Bates, R.: The LOOM knowledge representation language. Technical Report ISI/RS-87-188, USC/ISI, 1987. Also appears in Proceedings of the Knowledge-Based Systems Workshop held in St. Louis, Missouri, April 21, 1987.

[MBNL99] Madria, S., Bhowmick, S., Ng, W., Lim, E.: Research Issues in Web Data Mining. DaWaK 1999: 303-312

[MD00] Melnik, S., Decker, S.: A Layered Approach to Information Modeling and Interoperability on the Web. ECDL 2000 Workshop on the Semantic Web. 21 September 2000, Lisbon Portugal.

[MGR02] Melnik, S., Garcia-Molina, H, Rahm, E.: Similarity Flooding - A Versatile Graph Matching Algorithm. Proc. Intl. Conf. Data Engineering (ICDE), 2002

[MJZ03] Mobasher, B., Jin, X., Zhou, Y.: Semantically Enhanced Collaborative Filtering on the Web. EWMF 2003: 57-76

[MJZ04] Mobasher, B., Jin, X., Zhou. Y.: Semantically Enhanced Collaborative Filtering on the Web. Proc. European Web Mining Forum, LNAI, Springer 2004

[MR07] Mahmood, T., Ricci, F.: Learning and adaptivity in interactive recommender systems. ICEC 2007: 75-84

[MR07a] Mahmood, T., Ricci, F.: Towards Learning User-Adaptive State Models in a Conversational Recommender System. LWA 2007: 373-378

[MR08] Mahmood, T., Ricci, F.: Adapting the interaction state model in conversational recommender systems. In Proceedings of the ICEC '08, vol. 342. ACM, New York.

[MR09] Mahmood, T., Ricci, F.: Improving recommender systems with adaptive conversational strategies. In Proceedings of the 20th ACM Conference on Hypertext and Hypermedia HT '09. ACM, New York, NY, 73-82.

[MRB03] Melnik, S., Rahm, E., Bernstein, P.: Rondo: A programming platform for generic model management. In: Proceedings of SIGMOD, pp. 193–204. 2003

[MRS01] Middleton, S., De Roure, D., Shadbolt, N.: Capturing knowledge of user preferences: ontologies in recommender systems. K-CAP 2001: 100-107

[MRV09] Mahmood, T., Ricci, F., Venturini, A.: Learning Adaptive Recommendation Strategies for Online Travel Planning. In Information and Communication Technologies in Tourism 2009, Pages: 149-160, Springer.

[MRVH08] Mahmood, T., Ricci, F., Venturini, A., Höpken, W.: Adaptive Recommender Systems for Travel Planning. In Information and Communication Technologies in Tourism 2008, proceedings of ENTER 2008 International Conference, Innsbruck, Springer

[MS99] Manning, C., Schütze, H.: Foundations of Statistical Natural Language Processing, MIT Press: 1999.

[MSR03] Middleton, S., Shadbolt, N., De Roure, D.: Capturing interest through inference and visualization: ontological user profiling in recommender systems. K-CAP 2003: 62-69

[MSR04] Middleton, S., Shadbolt, N., De Roure, D.: Ontological user profiling in recommender systems. ACM Trans. Inf. Syst. 22(1): 54-88 (2004)

[MSS+01] Mädche, A., Staab, S., Stojanovic, N., Studer, R., Sure. Y.: SEAL - A Framework for Developing SEmantic portALs. In: BNCOD 2001 - 18th British National Conference on Databases. Oxford, UK, 9th - 11th July 2001, LNCS, Springer Verlag, 2001.

[MR08] Massmann, S., Rahm, E.: Evaluating Instance-based Matching of Web Directories. Proceedings of the 11th International Workshop on Web and Databases (WebDB 2008), Vancouver, Canada, 2008.

[MWK00] Mitra, P., Wiederhold, G., Kersten, M.: A Graph-Oriented Model for Articulation of Ontology Interdependencies. EDBT 2000: 86-100

[NM03] Nakagawa, M., Mobasher, B.: A Hybrid Web Personalization Model Based on Site Connectivity. Proc. 5th WEBKDD workshop, Washington, DC, USA, Aug. 2003

[Noy04] Noy, N.: Semantic Integration: A Survey Of Ontology-Based Approaches. SIGMOD Record 33(4): 65-70. 2004

[NS05] Noy, N., Stuckenschmidt, H.: Ontology Alignment: An annotated Bibliography. Semantic Interoperability and Integration 2005

[NUU95] Nuutila, E.: Efficient Transitive Closure Computation in Large Digraphs. Acta Polytechnica Scandinavica, Mathematics and Computing in Engineering Series No. 74, Helsinki 1995, 124 pages. Published by the Finnish Academy of Technology. ISBN 951-666-451-2, ISSN 1237-2404, UDC 681.3.

[OF01] Omelayenko, B., Fensel, D.: An Analysis of B2B Catalogue Integration Problems. ICEIS (2) 2001: 945-952

[OF01a] Omelayenko, B., Fensel, D.: An Analysis of Integration Problems of XML-Based Catalogs for B2B Electronic Commerce. DS-9 2001: 221-235

[OF01b] Omelayenko, B., Fensel, D.: A Two-Layered Integration Approach for Product Information in B2B E-commerce. EC-Web 2001: 226-239

[PP04] Preda, M., Popescu, D.: Using Reinforcement Learning to Generate Adaptive Web Recommendations, Advances in Intelligent Systems – Theory and Applications AISTA'2004, November 15-18, Luxembourg, 2004

[PP04] Preda, M., Popescu, D.:Using Reinforcement Learning to Generate Adaptive Web Recommendations, Advances in Intelligent Systems – Theory and Applications AISTA'2004, November 15-18, Luxembourg, 2004

[PP05] Preda, M., Popescu, D.: Personalized Web Recommendations: Supporting Epistemic Information about End-Users. Web Intelligence 2005: 692-695

[PPPS03] Pierrakos, D., Paliouras, G., Papatheodorou, C., Spyropoulos, C.: "Web Usage Mining as a tool for personalization: a survey". User Modeling and User-Adapted Interaction, v. 13, n. 4, pp. 311-372, 2003

[Prud06] Prudsys AG: "Individuelle Produktempfehlungen bei quelle.de", August 2006, http://www.prudsys.de, access date: 2007-11-12.

[PSF02] Perugini, S., Goncalves, M., Fox, E.: A Connection-Centric Survey of Recommender Systems Research CoRR cs.IR/0205059. 2002

[PSF04] Perugini, S., Goncalves, M., Fox, E.: Recommender Systems Research: A Connection-Centric Survey. J. Intell. Inf. Syst. 23(2): 107-143. 2004

[PZ03] P. Paulson, A. Tzanavari: Combining Collaborative and Content-Based Filtering Using Conceptual Graphs. Lecture Notes in Computer Science 2873 Springer 2003

[Quin93] Quinlan, J.R.: C4.5: Programs for Machine Learning. Morgan Kauffman, 1993

[RB01] Rahm, E., Bernstein, P.: A survey of approaches to automatic schema matching. VLDB J. 10(4): 334-350 (2001)

[RB06] Rahm, E., Bernstein, P.: An online bibliography on schema evolution. SIGMOD Record 35(4): 30-31 (2006)

[RCT04] E. Reategui, J. Campbell, R. Torres, R. Using Item Descriptors in Recommender Systems, AAAI Workshop on Semantic Web Personalization, San Jose, USA, 2004

[Rijs79] Van Rijsbergen, C.: Information Retrieval. 2nd Edition, Butterworths, London, 1979.

[RN94] Rummery, G., Niranjan, M.: On-line qlearning using connectionist systems. Technical Report CUED/F-INFENG/TR 166, Cambridge University. 1994.

[RS03] Rahm, E., Stöhr, T.: Data-Warehouse-Einsatz zur Web-Zugriffsanalyse. Web & Datenbanken 2003: 335-362

[RT05] Rahm, E., Thor, A.: Citation analysis of database publications, SIGMOD Record 34(4), 2005.

[RTA+05] Rahm, E., Thor, A., Aumueller, D., Do, H. H., Golovin, N., Kirsten, T. : iFuice - Information Fusion utilizing Instance Correspondences and Peer Mappings. 8th International Workshop on the Web and Databases (WebDB). 2005-06

[RTA07] Rahm, E., Thor, A., Aumueller, D.: Dynamic Fusion of Web Data. XSym 2007: 14-16

[SB98] Sutton, R., Barto, A.: Reinforcement Learning: An Introduction. MIT Press,1998.

[SBH02] Shani, G., Brafman, R., Heckerman, D.: An MDP-based recommender system. In Proceedings of the Seventeenth Conference on Uncertainty in Artificial Intelligence, pages 453-460, 2002.

[Schw93] Schwartz, A.: A reinforcement learning method for maximizing undiscounted rewards. Proceeding of the Tenth Annual Conference on Machine Learning, pages 298--305, 1993.

[SF98] Spiliopoulou, M., Faulstich, L.: WUM - A Tool for WWW Ulitization Analysis. WebDB 1998: 184-103

[SHB05] Shani, G., Heckerman, D., Brafman, R.: An MDP-based recommender system. Journal of Machine Learning Research 6: 1265-1295, 2005.

[Shop07] Shop.org. The State of Retailing Online. Study. http://www.shop.org

[SKKR00] Sarwar, B., Karypis, G., Konstan, J., Riedl, J.: Analysis of Recommendation Algorithms for E-Commerce. Proc. ACM E-Commerce, 2000.

[SKR01] Schafer, J., Konstan, J., Riedl, J.: E-Commerce Recommendation Applications. Data Min. Knowl. Discov. 5(1/2): 115-153 (2001)

[SKR02] Schafer, J., Konstan, J., Riedl, J.: Meta-recommendation systems: user-controlled integration of diverse recommendations. CIKM 2002: 43-51

[SM01] Stumme, G., Maedche, A.: FCA-MERGE: Bottom-Up Merging of Ontologies. IJCAI 2001: 225-234

[SP01] Spiliopoulou, M., Pohle, C.: Data Mining for Measuring and Improving the Success of Web Sites. Data Min. Knowl. Discov. 5(1/2): 85-114. 2001.

[SRQ00] Stöhr, T., Rahm, E., Quitzsch, S.: OLAP-Auswertung von Web-Zugriffen. GI-Workshop Internet-Datenbanken 2000: 95-104

[SS01] Sinha, R., Swearingen, K.: Comparing recommendaions made by online systems and friends. In: Proceedings of Delos-NSF Workshop on Personalisation and Recommender Systems in Digital Libraries. 2001.

[SSR98] Santamaria, J., Sutton, R., Ram, A.: Experiments with reinforcement learning in problems with continuous state and action spaces. Adaptive Behavior, 6(2), 1998.

[Sutt96] Sutton, R. :Reinforcement learning and information access, in AAAI Stanford Spring Symposium on Machine Learning and Information Access, March 1996.

[Swet63] Swets, J.: Information retrieval systems. Science 141, 245–250, 1963.

[TAK03] Thakkar, S., Ambite, J., Knoblock, C.: A view integration approach to dynamic composition of web services. In Proceedings of 2003 ICAPS Workshop on Planning for Web Services, Trento, Italy, 2003

[TAR07] Thor, A., Aumueller, D., Rahm, E.: Data Integration Support for Mashups. Sixth International Workshop on Information Integration on the Web, IIWeb, 2007. Vancouver, Canada. 2007-07

[TAXT03] The Active XML Team. Active XML Primer. Technical report, Gemo, INRIA-Futurs, Orsay. July 2003.

[TB07] Thess, M., Bolotnicov, M.: XELOPES Library Documentation Version 1.2.3, Prudsys AG, June 2007, http://www.xelopes.de, access date: 2007-07-09.

[TGR05] Thor, A., Golovin, N., Rahm, E.: Adaptive website recommendations with AWESOME. VLDB J. 14(4): 357-372, 2005.

[THG+09] Thor, A.,Hartung, M., Groß, A., Kirsten, T., Rahm, E.: An Evolution-based Approach for Assessing Ontology Mappings - A Case Study in the Life Sciences. Proc. of BTW2009.

[TK07] Taghipour, N., Kardan, A.: Enhancing a Web Recommender System based on Q Learning. LWA 2007: 21-28

[TKG07] Taghipour, N., Kardan, A., Ghidary, S.: Usage-based web recommendations: a reinforcement learning approach. RecSys 2007: 113-120

[TKR07] Thor, A., Kirsten, T., Rahm, E.: Instance-based matching of hierarchical ontologies. BTW 2007: 436-448

[TM07] Tintarev, N., Masthoff, J.: A Survey of Explanations in Recommender Systems. ICDE Workshops 2007: 801-810. 2007

[TR04] Thor, A., Rahm, E.: AWESOME - A Data Warehouse-based System for Adaptive Website Recommendations. Proc. 30th Intl. Conf. on Very Large Databases (VLDB), Toronto, Aug. 2004

[TR07] Thor, A., Rahm, E.: MOMA - A Mapping-based Object Matching System. Proc. of the 3rd Biennial Conference on Innovative Data Systems Research 2007

[VMP03] Velegrakis, Y., Miller, R., Popa, L.: Mapping adaptation under evolving schemas. In VLDB 2003, Proceedings of 29th International Conference on Very Large Data Bases, September 9-12, 2003, Berlin, Germany, 2003.

[VMP04] Velegrakis, Y., Miller, R., Popa, L.: : Preserving mapping consistency under schema changes. VLDB J. 13(3): 274-293, 2004.

[VMPM04]Velegrakis, Y., Miller, R., Popa, L., Mylopoulos, J.: ToMAS: A System for Adapting Mappings while Schemas Evolve. ICDE 2004: 862 [Wang06] Wang, T.: Action Selection in Bayesian Reinforcement Learning. AAAI 2006

[Watk89] Watkins, C.: Learning from delayed rewards. PhD thesis, University of Cambridge, Cambridge, England. 1989.

[Yao95] Yao, Y. Y.: Measuring retrieval effectiveness based on user preference of documents. J. ASIS. 46, 133–14, 1995.

[YP05] Yang, Y., Padmanabhan, B. : Evaluation of online personalization systems: a survey of evaluation schema and a knowledge-basedapproach, Journal of electronic commerce, 2005.

APPENDIX 1. SCREENSHOTS OF WEB RECOMMENDATIONS

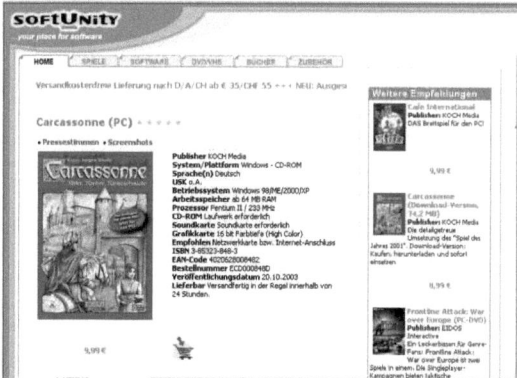

Figure A1.1. Screenshot of the product detail page of the website http://www.softunity.com (EC). The recommendations are shown on the right side. Up to five recommendations are shown for each products, if available. Depending on the screen resolution of the client browser, three, four or five recommendations are visible without scrolling.

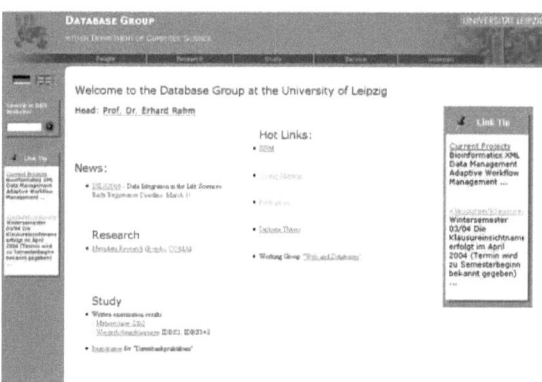

Figure A1.2. Screenshot of the website http://dbs.uni-leipzig.de (EDU). The recommendations are shown on the right. Up to two recommendations are shown, if available.

APPENDIX 2. EXAMPLES OF RECOMMENDATION OPTIMIZATION

A2.1 Examples of weight learning for the algorithm REW_ONLY_0

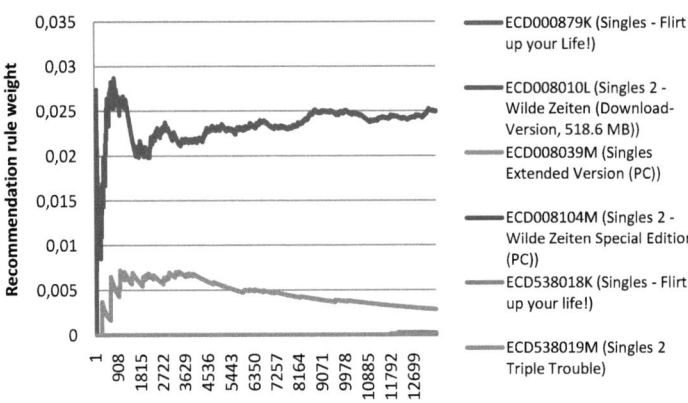

Figure A2.1. Learning weights for the product "Singles 2 – Wilde Zeiten(Hammerpreis)".

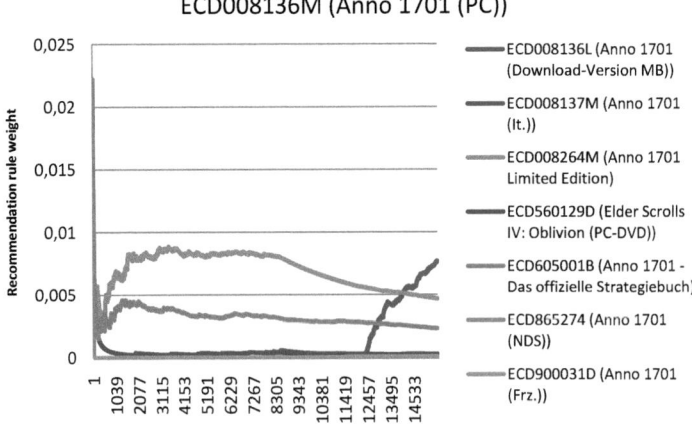

Figure A2.2. Learning weights for the product "Anno 1701(PC)".

A2.2 Example of weight learning for the algorithm REW_DEC_0

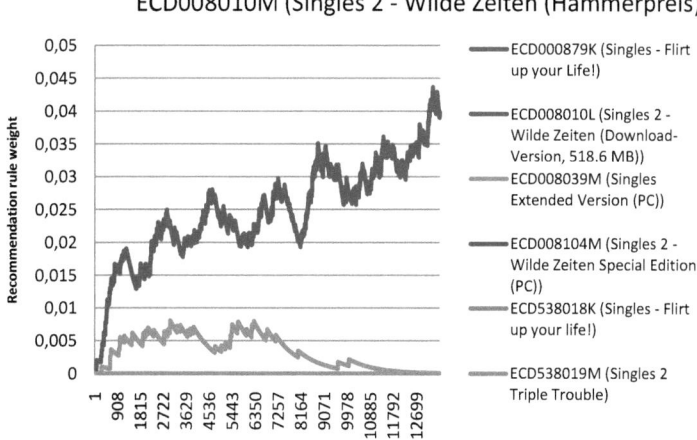

Figure A2.3. Learning weights for the product "Singles 2 – Wilde Zeiten(Hammerpreis)".

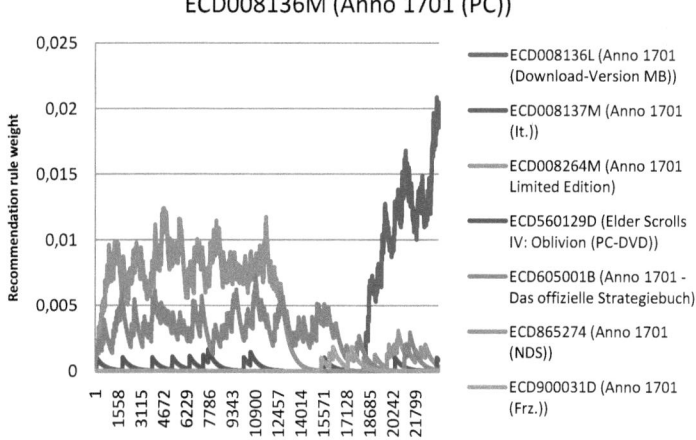

Figure A2.4. Learning weights for the product "Anno 1701(PC)".

A2.3. Examples of weight learning for algorithm REW_PEN_0

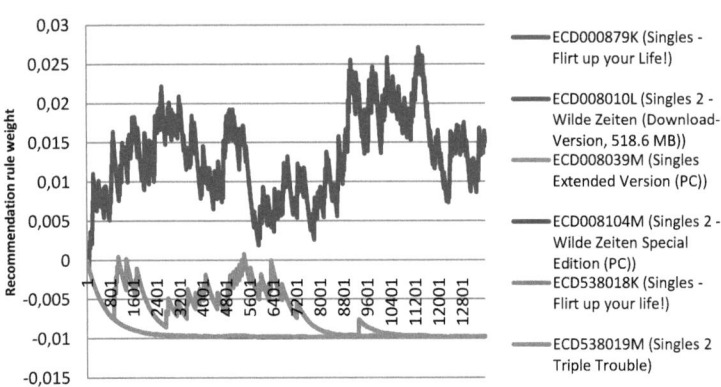

Figure A2.5. Learning weights for the product "Singles 2 – Wilde Zeiten(Hammerpreis)".

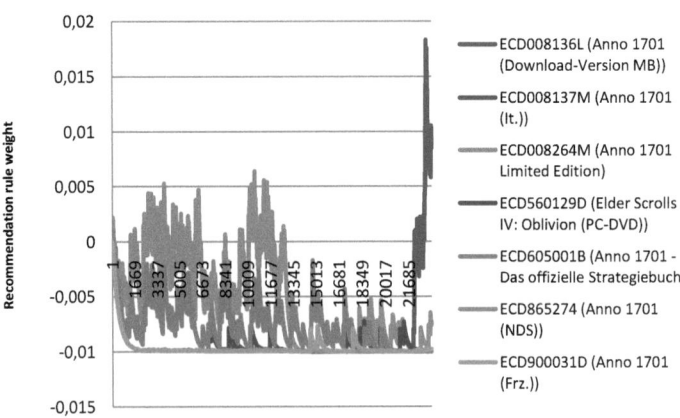

Figure A2.6. Learning weights for the product "Anno 1701(PC)".

APPENDIX 3. EC-FUICE DATA PREPARATION SCRIPT

```
// Get Softunity ontology
$suonto:=queryInstances(Ontology@Softunity,\"ALL\");
// Get Ebay ontology
$ebonto:=queryInstances(Ontology@Ebay,\"ALL\");
// Get Amazon ontology, except for the manually pruned nodes and their
children
$amonto:=queryInstances(Ontology@Amazon,\"ALL EXCEPT
14238651,554846,547084,
547086,528052,528030,547088,554416,1099832,525470,13325641,547644,1039674
,14238441,
738564,656070,1099834,3118641,13503881,13533241,13532261,13531771,1353275
1,1027142,
1027152,1027162,1027180,1027190,1027208,1027218,1027228);
//load pre-caclulated onto mapping Amazon->Ebay
$amebontom:=map($amonto,Ebay.ontoAmazon2EbayMerged);
//create inverse onto mapping
$ebamontom:=inverse($amebontom);
//load pre-caclulated onto mapping Amazon->Softunity
$amsuontom:=map($amonto,Softunity.ontoAmazon2SoftunityMerged);
//create inverse onto mapping
$suamontom:=inverse($amsuontomm);
//compose onto mapping Softunity->Ebay from mappings Softunity->Amazon
and Amazon->Ebay
$suebontom:=compose($suamontomm,$amebontom);
//create inverse onto mapping
$ebsuontomm:=inverse($suebontomm);
//get mapping from Ontology to products for Softunity, the product ids
are loaded into object cache
$suontoprod:=map($suonto,Softunity.OntoProd);
//get all Softunity products from object cache
$suprod:=queryInstances(Product@Softunity,\"1=1\");
// get all attributes for Siftunity products into attribute cache
getInstances($suprod);
//create mapping from Sofunity products to Ebay products
$suebprod:=map($suprod,Ebay.Softunity2Ebay);
// Load ontology to product mapping from Amazon. Products are loaded by
querying all ontology categories to get
// the products which belong to these categories
$amontoprod:=map($amonto,Amazon.OntoProdBulk);
//get the list of products
$amprod:=range($amontoprod);
//get all atributes for products
getInstances($amprod);
$amebprod:=map($amprod,Ebay.Amazon2Ebay);
// for ebay products, we do not use all but only those which have
correspondences either on Amazon or on Softunity
$ebprod:=union(range($amebprod),range($suebprod));
//Ebay has too large number of products for all attributes to be loaded
in one operation.
// We are using loop to load the product attributes in portions
```

Appendix 3. EC-Fuice data preparation script

```
$i:=0;
while $i<=9 do
      $ebprodtemp:=queryInstances($ebprod,"[id] like '%"+$i+"'");
      getInstances($ebprodtemp);
      $i:=$i + 1;
end;
```

I want morebooks!

Buy your books fast and straightforward online - at one of the world's fastest growing online book stores! Environmentally sound due to Print-on-Demand technologies.

Buy your books online at

www.get-morebooks.com

Kaufen Sie Ihre Bücher schnell und unkompliziert online – auf einer der am schnellsten wachsenden Buchhandelsplattformen weltweit!
Dank Print-On-Demand umwelt- und ressourcenschonend produziert.

Bücher schneller online kaufen

www.morebooks.de

OmniScriptum Marketing DEU GmbH
Heinrich-Böcking-Str. 6-8
D - 66121 Saarbrücken
Telefax: +49 681 93 81 567-9

info@omniscriptum.com
www.omniscriptum.com

Printed by Books on Demand GmbH, Norderstedt / Germany